DANCER INTE

A true exposé of a ballerina's fall from grace.

Susan Priver

Tampico
PRESS BOOKS

Dancer Interrupted is a work of nonfiction.
Text copyright © 2020 by Susan Priver

Tampico Press Books
Pasadena, California
Tampicopressbooks.com

Priver, Susan
Dancer Interrupted, by Susan Priver
Summary: Actress Susan Priver remembers her life as a young ballerina handpicked to attend George Balanchine's School of American Ballet at age 14 and the nervous breakdown that followed.
Subjects: 1. Memoir. 2. Ballet. 3. Acting. 4. Coming of age. 5. Theater. 6. Eating disorders. 7. Depression.

ISBN-13: 978-0-9899194-2-5

Caption opening page: *New York City dance studio, 1981.*

Cover photography by Guy Webster

Designed by Manuela Gomez Rhine

EDITOR'S NOTE

It was perhaps 2006 when I took my first yoga class taught by Susan Priver. I recall the room being full—maybe 40 or more students—and her complete mastery of the large group. She had presence and was skilled at making the class both challenging and fun. Several of the regulars in her class that day had been practicing with her for years.

I became one of those regulars and over the last 12 years we became friendly when not doing vinyasas. I'm a journalist by trade—a writer and editor—so that gives me a degree of what some would call curiosity. I'm generally interested in people and their lives and how they got to be where they are.

I was driving south from San Francisco one day on Interstate 5 with my wife and we were talking about Susan's classes and what made them so special to us. Suddenly curiosity jumped in and I decided to look her up on Google. I was surprised that she was born in Los Angeles but had been a dancer working in ballet companies in New York, Cleveland and Europe. I thought it an interesting way to live.

One day, a year or so ago, Susan was between teaching her two morning classes and seemed a bit distraught. I asked what was up and she told me she was writing a memoir and had just found out that she had been dropped by her literary agent. She didn't know how good her manuscript was or what to do next.

I was on a brief respite from work and had some extra time so I told her I would look at her book. My long career at the *Los Angeles Times* had included some senior editor positions and a brief stint as book editor.

Being a book editor doesn't necessarily give one expertise in writing books but it does give one a sense of story, of place, of what is interesting to many.

And Susan's life, as I found by helping her connect the dots of her fascinating journey, is very interesting.

I hope you find it so.

Jon Thurber

FOREWORD

Playing Blanche Du Bois in A Streetcar Named Desire. *Photo by Michael Lamont*

When I was twenty-three, I dated a man from the Actors Studio before I went off to Cleveland for my last professional job as a ballet dancer. My going-away present was a stack of plays by Tennessee Williams. My friend said, "I think you'll like these. Read them in your spare time." And I did.

Although I never thought of myself as someone using words as a vehicle of expression, I read voraciously each play I was given. My friend, the actor Robert Viharo, knew something about me that I didn't quite know myself.

Something about the longing of the human spirit. Something that Tennessee brought to poetic life in almost everything he wrote. They say that ballet is poetry in motion. In my early dance life, I knew intrinsically that I couldn't live without it. The great dancer Anna Pavlova said, *Once you've tasted the fruits of the theater, you can never go back.* And when I fell from grace, as many artists eventually do, my search, my entire journey, has been to find some way back.

More than thirty years later, through the prompting of certain people and through events that I had little control over, I have become a theater

4

actress. My search for the same things Tennessee wrote about has led me to delve deeply into his characters over time. Something I wrote in my journal in 1987: *How will I ever get poetry back in my life?*

Perhaps that is why I wrote this memoir.

It is the summer of 2019 and I have just concluded a six-week run playing one of the greatest and most challenging roles ever written for a woman: Blanche Du Bois, the central character in Tennessee William's *A Streetcar Named Desire*. Everything I've written about in these pages played into my research to find a way to get under the skin of this multi-dimensional character, so beautifully realized by Tennessee, one of the greatest writers of the twentieth century. Perhaps this tale of my personal unraveling filled Blanche's shoes in a poetic way. My great hope is that Tennessee looked down on the production, witnessed my portrayal and, with his soulful smile and enticing chuckle, might have said, *You've finally brought poetry to your life.*

Chapter 1

TIARA

Dance Studio, New York City, 1981.

Cleveland, Ohio, 1983

My private three-by-two-foot space backstage at the Cleveland Opera House was neat and orderly. Every item I used to apply my makeup, or do my hair had its place. Hair spray in far-right corner, deodorant in far left; make-up base, two tones of eyeliner, lipstick, make-up sponges and eyeliner brushes were assembled neatly in an ornamental box. Rubber bands, hairpins and hairbrush in their own separate decorative container, near my false eyelashes. No pictures of friends or family, which some of the other dancers had, just a few tools for the quiet ritual of preparation for the only thing that had meaning in my young life: to dance on stage.

Peering into my mirror, I was there. I was present. I couldn't even hear the back-stage gossip. Dabbing my dampened thin brush into that familiar pod of black eyeliner, I guided the soft pointed brush along the inner crease of my eyelid and traced it way past the line of my own eye. I'd been taught this specialized craft by one of the more experienced dancers

6

at my first professional job: *The Nutcracker* with The Eglevsky Ballet, in New York City. "You have the perfect eye-socket shape for stage," Elisa had said. "Your eyes will look huge out there, if you learn how to do this right."

The constant background chatter didn't distract me from applying the glue to the rim of my false eyelashes. I delicately placed that first one on the very edge of my own natural lash line and held it down for a few seconds.

One, two, three, four, five...done.

Struggling to get my jeweled-tiara straight, my heart fluttered when I saw it glistening in the fully lit mirror before me. Did I truly deserve to be wearing this odd ornament? Somehow it was a symbol of all that I didn't possess, all that I had overcome. Yet, I was safe, employed in the only thing I knew how to do, the only thing that protected me from the real world. I had arrived.

My friend Donna sat quietly a few feet from me, expertly placing her own crown onto her head with fingers accustomed to this craft. She made it look so fucking easy. My fingers fumbled, even if I was an expert at stage make-up. I looked at her in the mirror, still struggling with the crown on my head, and we exchanged knowing smiles, both so happy to be here, immersed in part of our pre-performance ritual.

A few weeks earlier, the corps de ballet, which included Donna and I, received an official letter from Dennis Nahat, The Cleveland Ballet's Artistic Director, informing us that all corps members must lose a minimum of five pounds. The soloists and principals were definitely meatier than the rest of us in the corps, so we felt uniformly insulted and collectively hungry. We bitched about it amongst ourselves, and soon the sounds of vomiting became part of our cloistered, anorexic, backstage world.

I checked myself in the mirror one more time. My collarbones protruded and the bones in my chest were now visible above my beautiful black-sequined costume. There was no womanly flesh pushing out of it. No more décolleté, thank God. A few weeks before the weight-loss letter came, I actually had something there. For me, it took starving to not have breasts.

Tutu snapped in back, tiara on straight, and pointe shoe ribbons tucked in securely. Almost ready. Weighing in at 115 pounds and close to five-foot-eight, my partner Eddie would have no trouble lifting me on to his skinny shoulder for that one assemblé lift at the end of the second movement. I bent down to check my pointe shoe ribbons one more time, for safety. Donna floated up next to me, and I glared at her perfectly placed tiara. I straightened up and admired her serene beauty in the same black sequined tutu, the same absurd crown. She peered at my head like there was something wrong with it. Was my tiara crooked?

"Let me get that," she said. And suddenly there she was, spraying those pesky flyaway hairs down.

"*Merde*," I said, in the fog of hairspray that enveloped us both. (*Merde* means shit in French, and ironically, good luck in backstage-dancer-language.)

"*Merde*," Donna replied, placing that pink Aqua Net hair spray canister back on her dressing table. We wrapped our long arms around each other; our plastic jewels, sequins, and stiff black tulle, crackling.

My pointe shoes were broken in a bit, so I could get through one performance of George Balanchine's *Theme and Variations*. Too hard, I wouldn't be able to point my feet, too soft I wouldn't get through the entire performance, an exact science I had learned over the years, dealing with my mortal feet. Not born with a naturally beautiful arch, an absolute necessity for a professional ballet dancer, I spent hours at home as a child with both feet jammed under the low pedal of our baby-grand piano, molding and sculpting those imperfect feet into the pliable and strong instruments that would ultimately be just good enough.

But they weren't ever going to be the way I ached for them to be, like Lisa Lockwood's, my good friend from ballet school who now danced for American Ballet Theater in New York, where all my dreams could have come true...*if only I had those perfect feet, that tiny body, and that perfect classical technique.*

A couple of months earlier, Donna and I were both dancing as otherworldly sylphs in Michael Fokine's lyrical, and dream-like *Les Sylphides*, a ballet I'd danced in the year before on a severely raked stage (meaning it sloped toward the audience) in an ancient castle garden in Hannover, Germany, draped in a long white tutu that hung down past my knees, similar to our Cleveland Ballet costumes. Now, my comrade and I both had the honor to wear a short, jeweled tutu and that well-earned tiara, finally showing off our meticulous technique and the beautiful line we'd both taken years to create, finally true ballerinas.

I was new in the company as was Donna. We were still on trial, so to speak, and truly cared about what Dennis thought. Our lives were on the line. At twenty-three, we were both a bit old to be in the corps de ballet, but what did it matter? We were dancing and getting paid to connect to our souls. Certainly, we both ached to be soloists, wanting to express our own individuality, our own peculiarities.

No connections, no nepotism, just pure force of will and the inevitable sweat, toil, and tears had brought us here. The act of dancing on stage is truly a calling. Money is never a true concern, except to pay rent, and have enough for sustenance. There had been boatloads of rejections already. In the five years of being a professional, auditions had become a flurry of, *what's wrong with me...why won't anyone hire me?* Even though I'd already danced for three companies, I hadn't found a permanent home.

8

Until now.

And now, here we both were in freezing cold Cleveland, Ohio, where the homeless people we passed on our brisk jaunts together to the theater for company class or rehearsal, were sometimes dying in front of us. Their tears and snot would freeze right before our eyes; such a great dichotomy of our spirited and seemingly purposeful lives, passing by those who had given up. "Gotta keep dancing so I don't end up like that," went my chattering brain, taking in the sad reality of a life not lived on stage.

As elegant and sophisticated as Donna and I appeared in our tutus and tiaras, our real lives were often different. Earlier in the season we were dining with some of the stagehands at a run-down Cleveland bungalow that looked like it had never been cleaned or painted. Neither of us had the right words to say, *No thank you*, when the frogs legs were pulled from the dilapidated oven. And this would be our Thanksgiving meal. The stagehands that lived in this crumbling house were friendly enough but Donna and I barely said a word to either of these two twenty-five-year-old tough guys, our social skills completely undeveloped. As we picked at our frog legs that freezing cold Thanksgiving, we both wondered where our lives were headed. Neither of us had been home for Thanksgiving in years as we were always employed, performing in *The Nutcracker* somewhere around the country.

When I did manage to go home to my parents' house in the San Fernando Valley, my father would hand me a stack of empty grocery bags and say, *I saved these; you might be needing them one day.* I think he was scared for me. He worried about the uncertainty of my dancing life and what might happen if it didn't all work out. He knew it was the only thing I cared about, obsessed over.

Perhaps I shouldn't have shared with him my encounter with a particular bag lady that I'd often pass when entering the subway station at Seventy-Second Street and Broadway, when I lived in New York in my early dancing years. Somehow she always had some words for me: *I used to be exactly like you,* she'd say as I dropped my tokens in the subway turnstile. *And look at me now.*

She made an impression I never forgot: Her desperate smile, her sunburned and aging skin, her elephantine legs, the smell of urine surrounding her, and the sign she always had beside her that said, *Help me get to California to cure my cancer.*

Walking onto the stage alone to mark the steps, and to make sure every muscle in my body was warm, I peered into that sea of empty red seats– such a majestic universe out there. Down in the orchestra pit, a few of the violinists were warming up, and plucking at their instruments. It was such a familiar and glorious sound. A cool draft of air whooshed across my face, and the vast expanse of the stage was all mine for a moment. I moseyed to

9

the wings to put rosin on my pointe shoes, and when I came back on stage, there was that wonderful cool air gliding across my face, yet again. Absolute joy.

The heavy dark red velvet curtain swayed slightly. Behind it, ten members of the corps de ballet stood stoically in fifth position, both feet turned out and pressed against each other. I didn't move a muscle. I didn't anticipate what might come next, immersed in this brilliant stillness. Dancers learn early on the absolute joy of living in the moment and often develop a sense of inner calm, inner satisfaction. We are all called to this spiritual endeavor, like nuns, priests, or monks, somehow.

Would we be able to impress our artistic director? Balanchine's *Theme and Variations* was a technically challenging ballet that required a lot of stamina. Would that beet juice I drank a couple of hours earlier sustain me? The chicken salad and coleslaw I ate at 3 p.m. was digested and my stomach was empty. One never eats before a performance, although some of the bulimics might have tried.

Feeling particularly secure in my own dancer skin, Dennis seemed to like my style, even if it was challenging for me to stay in line and dance exactly like everyone else. He looked at me so lovingly during rehearsals and company class. We were simpatico artists, even if he sometimes screamed at me for nothing in particular. I waited desperately for that curtain to open, waiting to be free.

The electronic sound of the heavy velvet drapes being pulled made my body vibrate with happy adrenaline. The warm footlights beamed on my face. The conductor raised his baton. The first notes of Tchaikovsky's brilliant score began and I extended my highly arched foot in that first tendu in perfect time with Donna, and the corps de ballet.

My wide smile came from pure joy, a connection to something bigger than myself. Every time I danced on stage, some heavy and unexplained burden was relieved, and living in the real world just wasn't as strange or difficult afterwards. I couldn't fathom how I'd ever exist without this particular bond that made me feel okay in the world.

When the corps de ballet began moving together like an amoeba of ethereal creatures, I knew my place. I had no need to be separate. Mental and physical pain completely extinguished. No words will ever be able to describe what it's like to dance on stage. There is no thought, only instinct and the music. Nothing else exists in those glorious moments of connecting deeply to what we really don't see but, what we surely all feel.

Bowing gracefully with the rest of my comrades at the end of the final movement, tears came to my eyes. Sweat and tears were so similar. No one would ever notice. I had arrived. I was finally wearing that coveted tiara, and knew somehow I'd never be that happy ever again.

Chapter 2

MIRROR

Los Angeles, 1984

Who was this person staring at me in the mirror? Was this who my parents wanted me to become? Was I fulfilling their pleas to have a normal daughter?

I glared at the red marks on my face, taking a short break from squeezing my tiny blackheads. There was no make-up on my newly scarred face. Instead of applying the mascara or eyeliner that had been a daily ritual of my stage life, I just stared at those flaming welts.

I had once, not too long before, used the mirror to discern the line of my body in the fully- mirrored-classrooms that were part of my daily life. It can be a disturbing thing to grow up in front of your own reflection, constantly scrutinizing your own body and technical progress, as though your very presence is something to be judged. But that was a fact of the last fifteen years of my monastic life, my calling as a ballet dancer.

Catching my image for another disturbing flash, the odd face staring back was unrecognizable. Something in the eyes was gone. My face had grown a bit puffy and had those red marks all over it. There was no one in that mirror in my parent's bathroom. No one looked back at me.

"What are you doing in there?" mom yelled anxiously outside the bathroom door.

"Oh, just finishing my shower" I muttered, nervous she'd find me picking at my face. As though I didn't hear her, I went back to obsessively squeezing my pale and damaged flesh. There was some kind of relief in seeing the white puss pop out of my microscopic pores, or to hope for it, anyway. The wood floor outside the door creaked. Mom left me alone a little longer to damage myself. Those scars that I was creating would now be visible to her. Finally, I would be loved for existing with all the flaws that were part of any young person who was no longer a ballerina—who no longer wore a tiara for a living.

Four months earlier there were no pimples or discernable marks on my pale skin as I walked up the creaky stairs to Dennis Nahat's office in

11

anticipation of good news: I would be promoted to soloist in the next year if I kept up the good work! Being invited to a private meeting with the artistic director of the Cleveland Ballet was like going to see the Wizard of Oz. I was incredibly aware of his esteemed career with American Ballet Theater. I'd seen him dance there before being hired for this company and loved his performance style. It was full of whimsy and passion. I had an odd platonic crush on him—admired and feared him at the same time. He held my life in his hands.

Running his hand sensuously through his black wavy hair, he peered at me with his dark and soulful eyes. "Sit down, sit down," he said in his haunting voice, indicating the rickety chair facing him. I'd never seen him at a desk before. There was something odd about him not extending an arm or a leg in the expressive way he always did when he worked with us, his dancing children. He was all business and looked at me in a manner I'd never seen from him before.

Then he began.

"You're such a passionate dancer and I see your absolute commitment, your striking performance ability," he said. "But I'm going to have to let you go."

What did he just say? Rewind.

"You're such a passionate dancer and…"

A broken record went off and infiltrated my foggy and nutritionally starved brain.

"I'm going to have to let you go."

Did he say what I think he just said? It's not possible. I better rewind here again.

"You're such a passionate dancer and I see your absolute commitment, and your striking performance…"

Time always stood still for me on stage, but does time stand still in tragic times too? On stage, I never wanted those incredible moments of connecting to something bigger than myself to end. But time stood still in a completely different way, when I actually heard Dennis's voice.

"I'm going to have to let you go."

I did hear it. I felt like I might throw up, and I was never bulimic. It felt as if I'd been given a huge shot of Novocain, as the numbness washed over my entire body.

"I'll write a letter of recommendation for you to a couple of Broadway producers I know. You're very suited for the stage. I think you'd be happier on Broadway. I've danced there myself. It's a blast," it sounded like he said.

Did he just say a blast? That is not a ballet dancer word. That's such a Los Angeles surfer word!

Maybe Dennis knew the legendary dancer/choreographer Bob Fosse, since his adorable daughter Nicole (her mother was Gwen Verdon) currently had an apprentice position with the company.

Was I stuck to this chair? I couldn't move, and my disorientation with the real world was rearing its ugly head. I felt frozen in time. Maybe I needed a sandwich. He leaned in towards me, as though he was going to bite my head off, but instead asked, "Have you ever considered becoming an actress?"

Did he just ask me if I wanted to be an actress?

"You're not really meant for the corps de ballet," it sounded like he said. He pulled his elegant body back into his swiveling and squeaky leather chair.

Did he just say I don't stay in line and dance like everyone else? Wait...Maybe he's promoting me to soloist! No, he said something about "letting me go!" not about being a soloist next year.

I thought he liked me. He always acted like he did, even if his partner Ernie, our ballet master, hated me. And that was just personal. Ernie had a mad crush on the handsome, talented, and heterosexual new corps member Jose, who just happened to be paying a little too much attention to me—*so perhaps he was a little jealous.*

Still glued to the rickety chair I stared at Dennis as though I was hearing him with a rational mind. In my thawing brain, I had a flashback to the one time I auditioned for the great Bob Fosse (yes, Nicole's father) and made it to the very last cut of the Broadway musical, *Dancing.*

The audition was held in one of those large but intimate Broadway theaters. There must have been five hundred dancers lined up in the winter cold, outside the theater. Everyone seemed excited and positive, as though this was going to be his or her one big break. This was completely new for me. I'd never seen so many dancers at an audition. My heart raced and the butterflies in my stomach fluttered, knowing I'd soon be moving across that stage, doing what I loved to do without a damn mirror in front of me. Outside the theater, I was handed number tag 276. Standing in the cold was worth the opportunity to dance for the great Bob Fosse.

By the time I got into the theater, the number of dancers had dwindled. Perhaps some had already been dismissed, or maybe they couldn't handle an open audition for one of the greats of Broadway? What did I know? This was a first for me. I wasn't yet jaded at nineteen and hadn't been hurt by rejection of this kind.

I looked around and noticed that some of the girls were putting on character shoes with actual heels. Some of those girls I was competing with actually had breasts. It seemed these young women wanted to look sexy for Mr. Fosse. Nobody acted like a ballerina. Girls and boys chatted and hugged, re-acquainting themselves from previous shows or classes. I knew absolutely no one in this arm of theater. This was the world of professional gypsies, Broadway dancers better known as hoofers.

I wore black tights instead of the typical pink ones that were required at ballet auditions and borrowed a pair of jazz shoes from my friend Naomi. They were black to match my seamed black tights. I went to the audition on a dare from an acquaintance who thought Fosse might like me. He apparently liked tall ballet dancers. Maybe I had a shot.

And then it began.

The dance captain started demonstrating the intricate and sensual choreography, and I stood in rapt attention, mimicking her every move. Once we absorbed those Fosse steps, we were split into groups of twenty and dismissed into the nearby rehearsal rooms so we would have time to work on our own. I grabbed my dance bag, trekked over to a studio and began working on the brilliant yet surprisingly simple choreography.

Feeling as confident as I'd ever been, I couldn't wait to show off my strong connection to his sensual choreography. I felt my heart would jump out of my body with excitement and anticipation. Would I be able to pull this new thing off? Ballet dancers don't show off their sexuality. Fosse dancers do. That jutted out hip; those jazz hands; that *watch me I'm here*, razzle-dazzle kind of style. Fosse dancers perform; ballet dancers live in their own ethereal world and stay in line with everyone else.

Two or three hours into the audition process I was surprisingly still in the running. Mr. Fosse hadn't yelled out, *Number 276, thank you for coming*. I was with a bunch of forty or so hoofers and we were asked to perform the three-minute *Tea for Two* combination across that expansive stage, yet again. Ten more number-tagged dancers were excused very kindly, almost personally, and number 276 was still in the running.

"Alright, everybody…bring out your music. Henry will accompany you," a voice beaming gruffly from the middle row of the theater. I finally spotted Mr. Fosse, the shy and elusive genius, seated in the middle of the theater, dressed in all black, his signature look.

Every one of those number-tagged dancers bent down to their dance bags and drew out some kind of papers. No questions asked. *Was that sheet music? Oh my God! These people sing too!* Staring out into the abyss, empty-handed, I heard a warm and resonant female voice.

"Do you have a song to sing," said the great Gwen Verdon. I stood there like a deer in the headlights, staring at the fair-skinned, redheaded queen of Broadway.

"I didn't know I had to bring one," I managed in my thin and stammering voice.

"You can just wing it," she said, sitting next to Mr. Fosse. "Ballet dancer, right?"

"Right," I whispered, wondering what the hell I would do.

Watching the other dancers bring their sheet music, one by one, to the pianist, I stood frozen in my tracks, waiting and wondering what the hell I was going to do. Hearing each one of them sing told me that I'd really

14

made a bad decision showing up there. I had no idea how to sing; my first experience as an imposter.

I almost fainted when I heard my number called.

"Number 276 come on out!"

Walking onto that empty stage as though I might know what I was doing, the stage lights beamed in my face. The king and queen of Broadway sat there respectfully as I shook in fear.

Here it goes. "I'll sing *Happy Birthday*," I whispered to the pianist, assuming it was something he could play. He chuckled at my odd request.

Cringe-worthy would be a good description of my attempt at singing. It's not like I expected to be good. I was a devoted ballet dancer with little need for a singing voice. Just speaking in front of more than two people was an absolute assault to my shy and undistinguished voice.

Gwen Verdon yelled out from the suddenly cold theater, "You're a beautiful dancer, darling. Next time bring in a better song, and work on it. *Happy Birthday* is not a great song for an audition."

"Oh, all right...thank you," I said, my voice still shaking. I gathered my things, knowing that I was only there on a fluke. I took one last look at both of these extraordinary people that gave me a chance, letting me fake my way through that whole audition. There were so many great hoofers that could sing. What did they need me for? I'd done pretty well on a dare. Ballet was what I understood.

"I'm going to have to let you go."

It came back to me, as I snapped into some version of reality. I was still glued to my rickety chair and didn't think I'd be able to get up. "What am I going to do?" I whispered to Dennis, trying to hold back my tears.

"You'll dance," he said, as though that's what would really happen. Where was I going to go? Where could I get a job? No one else liked tall ballet dancers! I couldn't move back to New York. It had been four years since that audition for Fosse, and I hadn't taken Gwen Verdon's advice about the singing. They'd never remember me, anyway. *I'll write a letter of recommendation to a couple of Broadway producers I know*, was what I thought Dennis had said a minute ago.

"Many are called, but few are chosen," were the words mom had often repeated to me as a teenager on the cusp of becoming a professional dancer. Dennis' line reverberated in my numb ears. *You'll dance*. I turned around and trekked back down those creaky wooden stairs. I passed a long mirror on my way back to the dressing room and stared for a moment. It seemed like there wasn't anyone there; like there wasn't even an image in front of me.

Maybe mom was right. I had been called, but not chosen.

There were a few more performances of the season to finish with before I headed out of Cleveland. I had to keep my head on straight to keep performing, and eventually pack up my minimal belongings. We were finishing another long run of *The Nutcracker*, and the snow that would be shaken down on us from above, during the Snowflake scene was becoming increasingly dirty after being re-used for every performance, so the stage was becoming terribly slippery. It was all I could do to keep from sliding and knocking over another dancer.

Slowly disappearing with my new reality, my presence on stage was diminishing; my light was dimming. A sort of depression was slipping in. It wasn't as though I'd never experienced bad depression before, but this one was cutting deep.

I had always felt more alive on stage than anywhere else, and now I felt completely disconnected from my once musical ear. I was crawling back into a little shell, to protect my shattered spirit. It wasn't just sadness. I was disappearing. Sadly, dancing on stage was the only way I was capable of expressing my true self, and suddenly I didn't seem to have one.

Even though I only had a couple more weeks to complete my contract, it seemed that Ernie held some gleeful delight in my new predicament. He'd stand right in front of me during barre work in company class, and say, "pull up from your pubic bone." I'd shake when he came near me. It was clear that he enjoyed my discomfort, and I had no defense system that might have saved me from this humiliation.

Donna, my one good friend, and even my two roommates seemed distant. And it wasn't their fault. I was the one drifting away. They all had the same comment on my sudden demise. "Susie, you're going to get an even better job, and be thankful you don't have to live in this armpit that is Cleveland, anymore. You're free."

It felt as though I'd been thrown into a bottomless sea without a life vest. The deepest part of me that was full of love, and joy, and, yes, some existential pain was now stripped from my soul, as though I didn't exist.

Chapter 3

OBSESSION

Perhaps it was dancing with scarves, Isadora Duncan style at the private school I was attending, or the attention I'd get while dancing by myself at the Bar Mitzvahs and weddings my family attended, but, by the age of seven, I loved being the center of attention. Moving to music in wide-open spaces released an unbridled joy in me. And somehow, as long as I didn't have to speak, there was some need to be noticed for my existence. Maybe that's true for most children, but by the time I hit eight, the most thrilling part of my day was spent in a room with old wooden floors and black-painted iron barres along the walls that also held the floor-to-ceiling mirrors, a must for all ballet studios. The grueling preparatory barre work– the constant scrutinizing, the sculpting of my musculature, would one day fulfill my fantasy of becoming a ballerina.

It seemed there must have been a magic wand that made mortal women become so ethereal. I was determined that would be me one day. After seeing the 50-year-old Margot Fonteyn dance with the great, and much younger, Rudolph Nureyev, on the Ed Sullivan Show, I begged my parents to find the right teachers for me, so I could fulfill my fantasy. I wouldn't accept no for an answer in my desire to train, classically.

And with a childish but obsessive determination, my wish was granted. A respected ballet teacher, and ex-principal dancer from the famed Ballet Russe de Monte Carlo, was found. Natalie Claire, my new teacher, saw a glimmer of talent in me. Perhaps it was my strong desire, or my innate musicality, but my devoted teacher showered attention on me, almost from my first day in class. I knew in the deepest part of my heart that this was the only thing I was meant to do, and somehow, she did too. I didn't need to worry about school or education, and soon talked my parent's into sending me to public school. "Private school isn't worth your money," I'd told them. "I am going to dance."

My joyous dancing existence was soon interrupted by real life.

My idyllic life taking daily classes came to a sudden end when I came down with a severe case of strep throat and soon after, contracted a blood disease called Idiopathic Purpura, caused by that bacterial infection. My mother had discovered tiny red spots, called petechiai on different parts of my body, and small bruises that never seemed to go away. Her registered nurse's brain immediately clicked in that all was not right with her joyful, dancing child.

After consulting my pediatrician, we made our first of many trips to a lab in West Hollywood, to have blood work done, and then to UCLA for a spinal tap. The kind doctor at UCLA stuck a huge syringe into my spine. My terribly worried mom held my hand, but I didn't utter a peep.

The diagnosis of Idiopathic Purpura in a child is not fatal, but my mother acted as though it were. And this was the beginning of a loving and clingy relationship that resembled a sort of co-dependence. She doted on me, as though I might actually die. My platelet count was dangerously low, so there was some need for concern–only if I fell on my head and hemorrhaged. The pediatrician suggested, "no dancing, and no recess, just in case you take a little fall."

Devastating news for me. I needed to move to be happy; I needed to perform for my parents to make them happy. But mom took over and listened to the doctor. And I found a way to be her patient–making beaded necklaces, playing piano, reading. I got to stay home from school whenever I wanted and got a pass on most of my chores. "Careful, you might slip…let me do that for you," she'd say. I got most of the attention, which made my then fourteen-year-old brother, Mark, jealous. The special attention made me feel loved.

After a year, my childhood Idiopathic Purpura miraculously went away. With my platelet count back to normal, my parents allowed me back into my cherished 4 p.m. ballet class–back on track to what I loved to do.

In junior high, a new kind of tension started mounting between my mother and me. My strong need to feel independent bothered her. I wanted to be in the dance studio, or with my friends, and that didn't sit well with her. She seemed to always criticize my friends, and even criticized my wonderful dance teacher Natalie in a way that made me think she was jealous. Being healthy changed the entire dynamic of our relationship. She didn't want to let me go. She still wanted to be my caretaker. She seemed happier when I was ill.

After a year of being confined and coddled, I would finally be on pointe–what I'd been dreaming of ever since I started dancing. My once fantasy was coming true, and the physical pain I'd soon encounter was a reminder of what it took to become something more than mortal. There would be bloody blisters, toenails falling off, and my new pointe shoes stained with blood every day. There was the grinding hard work, restructuring of my musculature for the required "turn out" and "line" that all ballet dancers must develop. The work fed me in a way, and the physical exhaustion allowed me a kind of peace. And, freed from mom's domination, my obsession was consuming. I was on my way.

18

Two years after I'd recovered from my blood disease, I was still in junior high, and now attended Natalie's advanced class. One night as class ended and as I started to leave, Natalie called me to the side.

"Susie," she said, "I'd like to talk to you." She took off her big sunglasses and looked deep into my eyes with great sincerity. The other young dancers filed out of the ballet studio, rushing to the dressing room to change out of their sweaty leotards and tights, giggling about all things teenager. Nobody seemed to notice that I'd been called to this private little meeting. Michael, our brilliant accompanist, and Natalie's partner, gave her a *let's get going* look, and started packing up his sheet music from the old black upright piano. Natalie brushed away some platinum blonde hair that was stuck in her glossy hot pink lipstick, and said, "You've improved so much in the last year, and I think it might be time for you to get to New York."

Looking up at her naively, I stopped fidgeting, and said, "New York?"

"Yes, Balanchine's school."

Oh my God, she didn't really say that, did she?

The butterflies in my stomach danced with excitement. That's where all the really good dancers went. They never came back to L.A. They became professional.

"Maria thinks you're ready to audition for the School of American Ballet."

I recalled the tall and beautiful, dark-haired former prima ballerina that had graciously sat in on a couple of advanced classes I had attended a few days earlier.

"You mean Maria Tallchief?" I exclaimed, thrilled that she even noticed me.

"She thinks that Mr. B will love you," Natalie whispered. "She used to be married to him."

My dream was coming true. I could be just like Heather Watts, who was now a soloist at New York City Ballet. This could be my ticket out of the cultural desert of the San Fernando Valley. I could finally escape all those football and basketball games my family loved watching while I locked myself in my room, drenched with the great music of Debussy, Chopin, Stravinsky.

The New York City Ballet just happened to be in town, performing at the Greek Theater. Perhaps that's why Maria was visiting Natalie's studio. On Maria's suggestion, she persuaded Natalie to take me to a company class so I could actually meet Mr. B before my audition. Natalie drove me in her 1960 turquoise Thunderbird to the Los Feliz venue and escorted me onto the huge stage where the great maestro would eventually appear. At least fifty company dancers were warming up and chatting, getting ready for class.

My heart dropped when he came onto the stage. There he was, one of

19

the greatest artists of the twentieth century and I was going to take class with him. The idle chatter stopped the moment he approached the ballet barre. He greeted everyone with, "Good morning. Let's get to work." He gave me a quick glance. I thought I would die from nerves right there. But as soon as the pianist started the first few bars of music for plies, I was home. When he came over to fix my foot in an arabesque, I felt his energy and excitement at a new prospect.

Now in his sixties, he was a slight man with a balding head but absolutely the most elegant man I had ever encountered, a real enigmatic Russian. Throughout the class, he used his expansive port de bras to give direction. The expression through his hands was extraordinary to me; they spoke their own language. I was also mesmerized by the way he looked at the female dancers with great love and admiration. I understood even then he appreciated them for what they would give to his art. When he looked at me I knew I was in the gaze of greatness.

Who ever I was in love with at school was now a second thought. All of my love would go to Balanchine and what he desired to create his chorography. The possibility of becoming one of his muses gave me a reason to live, even if he was a man I would never get to know. The mystery of him made it even more exciting. Not literally sexual but perhaps sensual in a way I wasn't even yet aware of in my barely adolescent mind and body. Because I knew that he liked to see bones, I decided I would starve myself for him.

The big audition came a few weeks later, on a beautiful spring day. Mom drove me to Vine Street in Hollywood, near Capezio's, the famous dance shoe store I often frequented. She parked her big white Mercedes not too far from the creaky old dance studio. I opened the heavy door almost immediately, anxious to get inside. I couldn't wait to move.

"Good luck," she said, as I grabbed my dance bag. "I know you'll do well."

I believed for a moment that she really meant it. But I wasn't sure. Just her very presence made me, somehow, insecure.

"See you in a while," I said, shutting her car door. I turned towards the ballet studio, the butterflies in my stomach dancing with glee.

Thank God she didn't ask to come in with me. I knew she'd probably humiliate me in front of all the other stage moms in attendance. Most of those women would be gushing over their daughters as if they were something very special. Mom was too unpredictable, especially now that I wasn't sick anymore.

Confidently climbing up the wooden and dusty stairs, I breathed in that familiar smell of mold and old sweat. It felt completely right. It felt almost Russian. I was finally there. Lots of chatter permeated the green-carpeted lobby, and suddenly, there was Natalie heading towards me, clutching a little piece of white paper in her long pink-painted fingernails.

20

"Susie, here's your number tag," she said, pinning it on to my green leotard with a small gold safety pin. Number 143. "Go have fun, and don't hide in the back. Remember, keep your shoulders down."

Wandering towards an empty spot at the barre, I saw the other young dancers warming up and chatting. I didn't recognize anyone. Starting my own warm-up, I couldn't wait for the pianist to play that first bar of music for the pliés. I peered at Natalie through the open doorframe. She gave me a reassuring smile. She was so different than mom. She was supportive in a way mom could never be. She understood my drive. She knew I loved to dance. Even if it had been over twenty years since she'd been a professional ballerina, she understood. She was my ballet mom.

The Russian man, seated at the baby-grand piano at the front of the dance studio, placed his fingers on the yellowing keys, and my world began. The plié music started, and finally I was transported to a place where I truly existed. I didn't have to talk or explain myself. Finally, I could express through my arms and upper body what it felt like to just be alive. This was my language. This was absolute purity of thought and feeling. The sweat immediately started pouring down my face, and I knew that they were watching, the people who might give me a chance. Even though I'd worked hard on my technique and knew how to make my feet look better than they really were, had the muscular control to balance, and land delicately out of jumps, my instincts took over. My still tiny body could speak the music. If I had any gift, it was this. I would make Natalie proud.

Getting to New York took over my consciousness, especially while sitting in class at school. Daydreaming of choreography and anything related to ballet consumed my mind. Every day when I'd come home, I'd run to the mailbox, hoping to find a letter of acceptance.

It was a long and anxious month before I received my letter admitting me to the School of American Ballet. I did have a crush on bad boy Sean Fitzgerald from school, but my innocent flirtation was nothing compared to my fixation over Balanchine's renowned school. I was working my way out of normal. I was becoming a ballerina.

Chapter 4

SUMMER

My plan was to dance until I died. And hopefully, that would be on stage doing what else, but, *The Dying Swan*. I'd seen a film of the extraordinary Russian ballerina Maya Plisetskaya doing that very ballet when I was thirteen, and made my plans to die that way. I figured I'd be somewhere in my forties, just like Maya was in that glorious old black and white film. I didn't think life was worth living past an age when I could no longer dance. Somehow, I was aware of how little our lives meant in the scheme of things. I truly wanted my finale to be dramatic, to mean something.

In my young mind, there was nothing like the Russians when it came to true drama and passion in art, especially ballet. I knew just from watching that film how much Maya had suffered. Dostoyevsky, Tolstoy, Chekov, Prokofiev, Shostakovich, Stravinsky, Tchaikovsky, Mussorgsky, Rimsky–Korsakov. They were my heroes. Even Michael, the brilliant but often inebriated pianist from my little studio in Toluca Lake, was Russian.

How could a girl from the San Fernando Valley, where everything appeared comfortable, and painfully superficial, want to embrace the Russian soul?

I'd clearly never experienced the political and social repression that they had. I'd certainly never experienced the famine of the Russian Revolution, even though I was constantly on some kind of diet and constantly hungry. But somehow, I related to their particular human frailty, to their hanging on for dear life. Somehow, I loved the existential Russian drama that was so much bigger than the Southern California mystique and the sun and surfers that I grew up around.

So, it was only right, that I felt comfortable walking down the long, marble entryway of the Julliard building at Lincoln Center. Balanchine's School of American Ballet was home to a number of Russians. My dream was starting to come true at the institution that the great star Maria Tallchief had expected me to attend.

There was always some anxiety in the air when I walked the long halls with the other actors, dancers and musicians, on their way to some serious study. We all had to check in with security at the end of that long corridor. It was all so terribly official.

"How's your morning going young ladies," the jovial African-American man, wearing a spotless brown and beige uniform with golden buttons, asked. He tipped his little cap to the three anorexic-looking teenagers, myself included.

"We're fine," we giggled and floated to the elevator with those other budding artists pursuing their creative talents.

"You have a good day, you three," he said. "And have a wonderful class."

"Oh, we will," we said, again in unison. "We have Danilova this morning." And the elevator door closed on the three young Balanchine disciples.

The other young and nubile dancers were mostly quiet on those rides up the elevator of the Julliard building. Everyone was incredibly serious about this great honor to be one of the chosen few.

Oh my God, there's Rudolph Nureyev! He's getting off on the same floor as me! He's wearing a fur hat and coat in the middle of a sweltering summer! What an amazing looking man, especially with all that fur. He had an absolute air of grace and royalty. Everyone was invisible around him. He was as astonishing up-close, as he was on stage, even if the prime days of his ballet career were pretty much over.

Getting off on the third floor, we got ready for class with the legendary Alexandria Danilova. One of the great stars of The Ballet Russes (the legendary Paris-based company that performed from 1909 to 1929) in her day, now she would enter the classroom in almost full stage make-up, wearing strings of pearls, and a carefully selected set of a matching leotard and flowered chiffon skirt. Her thick Russian accent, and grand-dame appeal was almost absurd in this modern, and sterile environment. Passion poured out of her. I admired her old-world authenticity, and even though her performing days were over, she seemed to be thriving at seventy. "You must give from heart," she'd say, while demonstrating her soulful, and lyrical *port de bras*.

I was drawn to her, and I think she liked me, too. She always looked at me with great sincerity, under those fluttering false eyelashes. She liked the dramatic dancers, the ones with feeling and musicality, myself included. Of course, she drilled us on our technique but knew that the ability to perform would be our ticket to get closer to Balanchine. She knew what he liked, and this aspect of ballet was what she understood deeply. Of Balanchine's five wives she had been number two.

When I went home after my first six-week scholarship at the School of American Ballet, the deal was sealed. I was one of Danilova's favorites so she made sure I was asked back for the next summer, and the next after that. I wouldn't have to audition again. The pressure was on; my work ethic would have to become even more stringent. I'd have to give up a few more things, including time with friends, and diet more stringently, if I were to be taken seriously. I knew I'd eventually be asked to stay for the winter sessions, and eventually become part of New York City Ballet. Most of the teachers there liked my style, my individuality and my way of expressing the music. I was not a pure classical dancer. I held things too long; I moved large and wide; my wrists flapped like most of my young peers, and most of Balanchine's favorites. My heels never hit the ground and staying in line with other dancers was never a necessity. I ate up space with my bony, muscular body. I was a Balanchine dancer.

That same summer of 1976, I was offered a summer scholarship at the Pennsylvania Ballet, having auditioned during the school year in Los Angeles, so I took the train to from New York to Philadelphia a day after my School of American Ballet scholarship concluded. I was certainly on a roll, but my obsession with staying bone thin was starting to affect me. My energy was waning from dancing on about eight hundred calories a day. Lupe Serrano, the ballet mistress at Pennsylvania Ballet, took notice. She'd encourage me to work hard, but to eat some protein because she thought I had a good chance of joining the company and was looking too thin. Suddenly, I had another mentor besides Danilova.

Lupe was strong and vibrant and non-theatrical. She had been a healthy dancer, especially in her years away from Balanchine. It was only Balanchine who liked his dancers to look almost skeletal. And it was truly only Balanchine who I wanted to dance for. So even though I was offered a winter scholarship to the Pennsylvania Ballet, I turned it down. I also turned down the opportunity to dance for John Clifford's Los Angeles Ballet as a professional company member.

How could I stay in Los Angeles and achieve my fantasy? That would be impossible around my parents who would find a way to stifle my dream with their negative messages that I wasn't good enough. My dream of becoming a dancer could only happen in New York. Besides, the aroma of the New York City subway represented freedom for me. Strangely, I loved the odor of urine, trash, and burning rubber. Anything was better than being in the car on an L.A. freeway with my mother.

I flew back to L.A. to collect some things for the winter in New York, and to spend a bit of time with my family and friends. Once home, I auditioned for the San Francisco Ballet School, just in case I didn't get the call to become a Balanchine muse. But, after a week at home, they called. I was finally asked to "stay for the winter." So, if I held up for a full winter or two at the school, I would have a chance to become part of New York City Ballet. Only if I kept up the good work, didn't freak out, and didn't gain an ounce, even though I wasn't yet fully developed, and hadn't yet reached my full height.

At sixteen, my whole life was ahead of me. I was in a place that I could actually make it all work. But, something was happening to me internally that was incredibly new. It started happening when I was in Pennsylvania, a couple of weeks before, when Lupe was encouraging me to eat more–or enough to get through a whole class. Suddenly, I didn't love moving anymore. I was experiencing my first depression. In this strange physical manifestation my mouth would get dry, making it hard to swallow, and surprisingly, to speak. I was strangely over-taken with anxiety and sadness, even though with my newly received Ford Foundation Scholarship I certainly had a lot to be grateful and happy about.

"This is normal," mom said as we wandered through the Woodland Hills mall to pick up some winter clothes for my year ahead. "You're just going through some changes. You'll be fine."

"I think I want to stay home and just finish high school, and maybe get ready for college," I said, completely disregarding the fact that the only thing I wanted during those three summers at the School of American Ballet, was to be asked to stay for the winter. I should have felt honored and thrilled about my scholarship. Instead, I was struggling with this new feeling that was completely overtaking me: crippling anxiety and depression.

"You're too thin," mom said, as we scanned the racks of clothing in the junior section at Bullock's department store. "I think there might be something going on with your brain chemistry for you to be this sad," she said, pulling out a gorgeous angora sweater. "There's nothing to be sad about. You have everything that you've ever wanted."

I took the few items we chose together into the dressing room and tried them all on. Mom preened over me and reminded me how happy she was for me, adoring my new winter wardrobe, the kind of clothes that she wouldn't get to wear in sunny Los Angeles. She paid for my new fluffy winter sweaters, a couple pairs of warm pants, and my first ever winter coat. Then we wandered out of the mall and back to her car, my overwhelming sadness piercing our time together.

Within a few days of our shopping spree, I was sitting in my grandfather's medical office to get some blood work done, and to have my first gynecological exam. Mom made the appointment, of course. I wouldn't have gone, otherwise. Her nurse's brain clicked in about the fact that although I was almost seventeen, I hadn't yet gotten my period, and maybe my screwed up hormones were what was causing my sudden depression and anxiety.

Grandpa was a highly revered OB-GYN. Many years earlier, he'd delivered the children of several celebrities, including Jane Fonda. He actually delivered both my brother Mark and me at Cedars Sinai Hospital, in the days when it was okay to have a family member as a patient. How my mom let her father-in-law deliver both her children is beyond me. How she got me to see my own grandfather for an exam at sixteen was pretty much beyond me, too.

The female doctor at the office gave me the invasive exam, thank God. Grandpa, a dead ringer for the love child of Carol Channing, and Groucho Marx, and blessed with a voice that sounded like Walter Matthau, was the one though that gave my mother and me the disturbing news. We were seated in the office at his Wilshire Boulevard practice, chatting with his longtime nurse, Reggie. He opened the door with some files in his hand and delivered the news in a deep and kind voice.

"You don't have enough progesterone to create a menstrual-cycle," he said. "You have an infantile womb and might not be able to have children, if you don't eventually develop."

Who cares if I have an infantile womb! I'm a ballerina!

Mom gave me a recriminating look and I turned my gaze to the light green wall, wondering how I ended up in my grandfather's medical office to hear this not terribly interesting news.

"I knew it," mom cried. "Look what you've done. You've ruined yourself! You'll never have children!"

My grandfather's voice brought me back to some kind of attention. He seemed so terribly reasonable compared to my mother. "Susie, I suggest you go on the pill to bring on your period, at least for a while. You might gain a little weight."

There's no way I'm gaining any weight. These people are crazy!

I wasn't going to show my grandfather my anxiety at even the possibility of gaining any weight, or ever getting my period. It was so strange to be talking to my grandfather about this, anyway. I quietly acknowledged that gaining weight would be a good idea.

Looking around the office, I prayed no one heard mom's ridiculous overreaction. As a reluctant stage mom, but a stage mom nonetheless, she'd been tolerant of my need to be ridiculously thin. Now she was on a rampage to publicly display her feelings about what I'd done.

"But mom, I don't want children, so what's the big deal?" I admitted, trying to act like I knew everything.

"See Morrie," mom said to my grandfather. "I can't control her."

My grandfather just stared at us like we were aliens. Reggie gave me a look of compassion, unlike mom, who was incapable of containing her angst, or her own growing neurosis. "You're going to miss out on one of the greatest joys of life," mom pleaded, shaking her head as though I was the instigator of everything terrible in her life. She stood up and looked through her purse for her car keys.

My grandfather remained stoically silent but Reggie piped up. "Jean, she's a dancer, and that's what she has to do. At sixteen, nobody is thinking about children."

I felt suddenly respected for that which I was, and said, "Balanchine says any woman can have children, but there are few that can become ballerinas."

"I don't care what that Balanchine says," mom fumed yet again. It was as though she had no idea what had been going on in front of her for the past three years. "He's made you ruin yourself just for that ridiculous art."

"I thought you were proud of me. You're always boasting about me to your friends," I said, thinking that was actually true.

"I've never supported you being this thin," she said, talking past me to my grandfather. "This is all her doing." It was as though she was standing up for herself and her perfect mothering. But mostly she was losing control.

"She's going to be fine, Jean," Reggie said. " Susie, you're a beautiful dancer, according to your mom, so stick with what you love. Most people never find what they love."

"Alright, let's go. I just don't know what I'm going to do with her." Mom's voice trailed off as we exited the office. We rode the elevator quietly down to the ground level and got into her big white Mercedes Benz. Then she complained some more about me during the drive into the San Fernando Valley. I was quiet, as usual. There was nothing I could say. I truly needed to live in New York. I couldn't stand being in the car with her anymore.

Chapter 5

WINTER

On the flight from LAX to JFK Airport, I fidgeted in my seat. The rain and loud thunder poured onto the huge American Airlines 747. The atypical Los Angeles weather certainly didn't feel like an omen of good things to come. This was to be my saving grace, to get out of L.A. and away from both the heat and blinding sunshine, and the grating voice of my mother. Dancing in the most famous school in the country would save me. Dancing always had. But, those grey skies and the steady rain felt like a stark reminder that I wasn't on good footing.

I kept fidgeting as I looked out the airplane window.
I wasn't comfortable in my skinny dancer's body anymore. I couldn't shake the devastating depression that had overtaken me in the three weeks I spent at home, preparing for the year ahead. And, I had rejected my grandfather's recommendation of going on the pill to possibly improve my diagnosed condition of a shrunken pituitary gland, and not enough hormones to create a menstrual cycle.

There was no way I was going to gain any weight.
And then I was there. I was back in New York.
Jacques De Amboise' wife showed me up to my new quarters on the fourth floor of their charming brownstone on Seventy-fourth Street near Broadway.

I'd be sharing the upstairs attic space with three other young dancers from the school, who were apparently also new to the winter curriculum. I was first to arrive. My head almost touched the ceiling as I slowly unpacked. My new sterile-looking quarters housed two twin beds, covered with new pink bedspreads. The white and gold wooden armoire looked eerily similar to the one I had as a child.

The attic space had newly painted white walls, exposed light bulbs, and a really ugly blue and gold linoleum floor that lined the kitchen, hallway, bathroom, and the two bedrooms that would house the four of us. Our upstairs floor felt cold and separate from the rest of the warm and colorful townhouse. The school administration had arranged these living quarters for us. Jacques was still one of the male stars at the New York

City Ballet, so it was a pretty prestigious place to stay, even if it looked like a bunker in Eastern Europe.

The other girls finally arrived one by one. I still felt uncomfortable in my own skin and my anxiety made it hard for me to sleep. That first night, I stared enviously at my roommate, Julie, sleeping soundly, seemingly without a care in the world. I remembered her from the summer session that had concluded only weeks before, and even though we didn't know each other, I thought she was extremely talented. I had no idea that we were going to be living together. Who planned all of this?

The three other sixteen-year old blossoming ballerinas all seemed happy and positive, and I really liked Julie, the super-gifted one sharing my bedroom. She could jump and turn like no one else, had beautiful technique, and was particularly expressive.

The next morning we walked together those eight short blocks to our first day of the winter session at the School of American Ballet. Everyone else seemed to be bubbling over with the joy of being alive, and it was hard for me to keep up with the conversation. It was a sparkling and beautiful day, but I was still flooded with sadness and anxiety. I just stared at the delis, bakeries, shoe stores, liquor stores, and the people who seemed to have purpose in their lives, to have somewhere to go. Everyone in New York City, that fall of 1976, looked like they had somewhere to go, at least, to me. I felt nothing but uncertainty about where I was going.

The long marble-floored corridor in the glistening Julliard building seemed forbidding as the four of us entered my old home, but it was no longer my home. There was a different security guard this time, and he wasn't jolly. My depression was coloring everything.

We got into our 9 a.m. class right on time to choose our spots along the long mirrored walls, with the familiar wood ballet barres that I'd held onto many times before. All the girls in my class were wearing the required black leotard and pink tights. We pretty much looked the same, all sixteen to eighteen years old, with tightly pinned buns, skinny legs and skinny arms. In the summer sessions, we could wear any colors, so Rit dye transformed most of my neutral-hued dance attire over the last three summers, except for the required pink tights, of course. Now, I looked like everyone else.

When it was time to move to the center of the room for the first slow adagio, I went into the back row hoping not to be seen, which was strange, because the adagio always highlighted my lyrical quality, something I knew was my gift. I'd been invited on scholarship to this school because I had made myself visible that summer session only a few weeks before, whether dancing across the room, or in the adagios. Danilova had told me, "Stand in front as often as possible, so everyone can see you. Don't hide in back, my darling. Be proud."

My new internal dialogue reflected mom's constant refrain, *Many are called, but few are chosen*. She had repeated this cliché to me all the fucking time and I wasn't able to get her negative thoughts out of my head. I just wanted to hide.

A few weeks into the winter session, I'd made one friend–Naomi Goldberg, from Teaneck, New Jersey. She had a certain strength that I admired–she seemed secure. Her beautiful long arms and legs, and stunning dark-haired and exotic looks weren't typical at Balanchine's school where everybody was really white. Her out-going and whimsical personality wasn't either. "Susie, come stand in front with me," she said, taking my hand and moving us both to the front of the class on one of the cold winter mornings that were becoming increasingly bleak.

That morning, the white walls and grey linoleum floors of our mirrored studio felt particularly oppressive. The pianist was pounding out the music for our step across the floor, and I danced beside her, but I wasn't really there, not in the passionate way I was when I wasn't depressed. I could feel the floor vibrate under my feet as the other beautiful young dancers pranced across it. In the last month, since my depression had taken hold, my body felt like it didn't belong to me anymore. I was a dancer disconnected from her body.

I did try to keep up, tried to dance, to listen to Naomi, but before I knew it, I was sprawled on the floor. I fell out of a jump and had twisted my ankle. Completely humiliated, I sat there, stunned, watching my foot blow up like a balloon. "Come on Susie, let's go put some ice on that," Naomi said, helping me up from the floor. Not another person, including our teacher, noticed that I'd fallen. Class went on as though I wasn't even there. If it had been a stampede of rhinos, I would have been dead. Even Naomi wouldn't have been able to save me.

Limping towards the safety of the benches in the huge, locker-lined dressing room, Naomi held me up and comforted me. There were a few New York City Ballet dancers there, changing out of their sweaty leotards, tights, and legwarmers, chatting about how hard class was with Mr. B. I tried to be quiet, not wanting any of those real professionals to hear my whining. "I have to get out of here," I stammered to Naomi. And suddenly she disappeared.

Returning in a matter of seconds, she placed an icepack on my swollen foot, and looked at me with her sincere golden eyes. She held that excruciating cold bag down, and I wanted to pull my injured foot away, but didn't. "Thank you," I said, wondering where she miraculously found that icepack so fast.

"No big deal. Falling is always a really good sign," she said. "It means you're really trying."

"Something weird is happening to me," I whispered, still embarrassed that any of the professionals nearby would hear me. They'd know I was weak. They'd know I wouldn't be able survive this.

"You're going to be okay," Naomi said, maternally. "I did the same thing a while ago."

"I'm so embarrassed."

"Don't be," she said. "It's normal. You're so musical. Do you know that?"

"Yeah, that was a real musical fall," I said, managing a little laugh.

"Why are you so hard on yourself?" she asked, pressing the ice harder on my excruciating foot.

Why, in the midst of all of this competition, would a lovely and talented girl be so kind to me? None of my roommates rushed to help me. They kept going, just like every other skinny, bun-head. They had to. Only the strong survive.

"I've got to get back in class," she said, checking the swelling in my foot.

"Go ahead, I'll be fine, I think."

"You need to stay here, Susie. Balanchine loves you. That's why we're all here."

A few weeks earlier, when I first arrived back in New York City, and was already feeling out of place, I was invited to Lincoln Kirstein's elegant Chelsea apartment with a few of the other new dancers from the school and company. I couldn't even fathom what an honor it was to be there. Not all of my classmates were there, only a handful. Why would this legendary and towering cultural figure invite me to his apartment? He was like Diaghilev from the Ballet Russes! He was a true impresario and had been since 1934, when he founded the School of American Ballet with George Balanchine.

Peering at the beautiful art in his opulent apartment, I was taken by a row of small paintings: The *Seven Deadly Sins*, lining the long eggplant-colored hallway. I laughed silently at the one called *Gluttony*.

"Do you like that one?" the question came from a tall and completely bald man wearing an elegant black suit and wire-framed glasses.

Looking up at his imposing presence, and feeling completely unsure of myself, I whispered, "Yes, I do. They're all beautiful." Lincoln Kirstein, the man who held my future in his hands, looked at me as though he knew me. But I was sure he had no idea who I was.

"I personally like this one," he said.

"You mean *Greed*," I whispered back.

"Yes, it's very dark and fitting, isn't it?"

"Yes, they all are. I mean...fitting."

When I turned to comment on the painting titled *Envy*, he was already on his way to acquaint himself with the other young dancers who were lining up for the elegant buffet. I eyed one of them scrutinizing the crudité, probably calculating the calorie content of the dip.

Four weeks later I would fall, sprain my ankle, and crumble under the pressure. That very day that I injured myself, I found myself seated in the main office of the School of American Ballet and looked down at my shaking hands. I remembered the flight from L.A. in the pouring rain when I felt like I wasn't on good footing, and now here I was with a sprained ankle. There was nothing else I could do but go home and figure out why I had lost my confidence, or maybe figure out a way to get it back. I looked up for a moment, and there she was, the head secretary of the school. She had on her huge black frame glasses, and was looking at some paperwork on most likely me. She stared right through me when she looked up, as though I wasn't there. Her tight suit accentuated her curvy figure, and her perfect short bob hairstyle was very unusual there. The young dancers and the professionals all had long hair that was often pinned into a bun or a French twist. Somehow, she didn't belong there. There was no light in her eyes, and no sense that ballet held any meaning in her life.

"You can stay at the school and observe class while your ankle heals and we can finally get you enrolled in the Professional Children's School," she said in her tinny-sounding voice. "You'll get your high school diploma from there." My only thoughts were, *call mom and get a reservation to fly home tomorrow. I know she'll be happy to have me home. It will be okay to prove her right about not being good enough. She will love me all over again and will be happy to take care of me.*

"I think I should just go home and finish high school, "I said in a raspy whisper.

"But darling, if you leave, you probably won't be asked back, and your scholarship is for the whole year. We could have awarded that scholarship to someone else. Your leaving so abruptly will not be looked upon very highly, especially by Mr. Kirstein," she said, without a glimmer of a smile.

"I don't think I can handle being here and not being able to dance," I said, disregarding my scholarship, disregarding my personal invitation with the select few to Mr. Kirstein's townhouse, and our shared conversation about *The Seven Deadly Sins.*

"We're willing to wait your injury out if you can just be patient, and see the company doctor," she said.

"I need to go home," was the only response I could muster. I looked around her very organized office and peered at a framed black-and-white photograph of Danilova in her early days. She was so beautiful, in that balletic way. Not like a movie star, not like the pretty surfer girls I grew up around, but in that dramatic Russian way. I was never going to be like that. This was the end for me. I would die unnoticed.

"You're making a big mistake."

"I know," I said, getting up from my chair, limping out of her office in a daze.

I would never enter that concrete modern building again. I had given up. I didn't say goodbye to Danilova. I didn't even say goodbye to Naomi. And I certainly didn't say goodbye to the distinguished provider of that hard-won scholarship, Lincoln Kirstein.

Chapter 6

MANHATTAN

Cleveland, Ohio, 1984

I stared out of the foggy car window as we drove away from Cleveland and from the only thing that made my life worth living. The leaves on those glorious trees alongside the highway to New York City were an incredible shade of electric green, and a vibrant orange. The sight of them reminded me how much I loved living in any part of the country that actually had seasons. Mostly, I ached with shame, reminding myself again and again that my parents were right. I was never good enough. Now, I'd have to face real life. And I had no skills to speak of, besides dancing.

My apathy was well beyond words, so I just pondered the meaning of life, watching the beautiful trees go by. I couldn't go back to L.A., where the smog and the heat would just be another blow to my senses. I couldn't go back under my parent's roof to find my place in life. I needed to dance to make sense of the world and to feel like I had a purpose. I needed those endorphins that kept me from falling into the depths of life's dark corners.

We were five young ballet dancers, all now unemployed, chugging along the open highway in an old, beat-up Oldsmobile. We'd all been let go, so we could either move on to a different company, or maybe a new life. I never asked anyone else in the car if they got a letter of recommendation, as I did, for a Broadway show. I was just too humiliated about being fired and thought of that letter as more of an insult than an actual recommendation. I threw it away, in fact.

The four guys seemed okay with the whole thing, and the magic mushrooms that they all indulged in for the more than 400-mile ride made the trip away from their last job bearable. They joyously sang stupid songs, as though they didn't have a care in the world, and I just stared out the car window, fearing what was to become of me.

"Who wants to live in fucking Cleveland, anyway?" the adorable Jose said, waking me from my dismal thoughts.

"There's nowhere to party there anyway," Joe Mikael chuckled, batting his long eyelashes. The remnants of his full drag makeup hadn't yet been cleaned entirely from his angelic face. He was such a dichotomy with his sensitive light-blue eyes, translucent skin, and ever-expressive potty mouth. His caked-up make-up must have been from the night before, in one of the clubs near the State Theater, where we all had our last performance.

This little crew of misfits had been in New York for most of our dance lives, anyway. It was the only city we could get back into professional-level classes and find auditions for a New York company or a regional one.

I felt lost without dance, the only job I knew how to do, and equally petrified at the thought of having to audition for anything ever again. I knew I'd have to get back in class every day, if I were ever to be employable again. It was a daunting thought. How could I access myself in the mirror accurately with Dennis' words going through my head? "Have you ever thought of being an actress?" What a fucking insult! He may as well have said, "Have you ever thought of working at Macys!"

We were getting close, and what I saw through those smudged car windows made my undernourished ballerina body shudder. Thousands of clearly visible head stones in the cemeteries framed both sides of the highway. I'd always noticed them when coming in from JFK Airport on earlier trips, but they now seemed more prevalent, like this would be my end. I would die unnoticed and be buried on the side of the road, like the rest of these decaying people.

New York City could be magical for the right person at the right time. It always pulsated with a life force like no other city. But now suddenly, everything looked darker. Even those small towns along the highway as we approached Manhattan seemed haunted and so terribly sad. My mind raced with the desperation and anxiety of adapting yet again to a new environment, especially one without work.

"Here we are," said Richard, our driver, as he double-parked in front of my new home. I bid my unemployed friends goodbye, dislodged myself from the clunky old Oldsmobile and grabbed my two bags with all I owned. I peered at the numbers on the outside of the five-story, railroad apartment building.

Walking up the dirty stairs to the foyer of my new residence on Sixteenth Street between Seventh and Eighth Avenue, the awful fluorescent light and chemical smell brought back recent memories of my New York dancer's life. Ringing that awful sounding flat buzzer, BZZZT, my old friend Patrick answered through the intercom with a delighted cheer. "Hey! Vernon and I have been waiting all day for you."

Just his sense of cheer was encouraging enough to get my frayed nerves up those three flights of dusty stairs. Huffing and puffing by the time I got to his apartment, Patrick held the door open, and dragged my bags inside. "My knee's been bothering me," he complained. "Otherwise, I would have taken these up for you."

Laughing at his dancer's litany of injuries, it was as though no time had passed between us, even though I'd been away for almost three years. Patrick's long and lanky frame looked exactly as it had when I had crashed there briefly before my trip abroad. His beautiful and kind blue eyes were still framed by gorgeous, golden blonde hair. His adorable over-bite and mischievous smile always inspired me to be okay with whatever life offered. He opened his arms for a big hug, and we fake cried together, not letting each other go. He smelled so good in his freshly laundered sweats. I wanted to stay entwined with him until I finally felt better, like myself. I was lucky to have a friend like him who could relate to an unemployed dancer on the edge of insanity.

Patrick had branched out. After a few years of dancing, and professional hairstyling, he was now studying psychology. And because he was now single, he was more than happy to share his apartment with me--- and his joy about life in the big city.

He helped me drag one of my bags down the long cream-colored hallway with the smooth hardwood floors. An absolutely beautiful tiger-striped grey and black cat appeared from nowhere and sat down next to me as I unpacked. He stared at me with his huge green eyes, acting as though I was an intruder.

"I guess this must be Vernon."

"Say hi to Aunt Susie, Vernon."

"Meow."

"I think I'm really going to just lose it this time," I complained as Vernon stared at me with great concentration.

"Susu, do I need to call the men in the white coats for you?" Patrick asked, hoping he'd get a laugh from me.

Avoiding his comment, I opened one of my bags, brimming with leotards, tights, cut-up sweatshirts, and ratty leg warmers. There were safety pins and torn bits in every piece of dance attire I owned–the style for professional dancers of the early 1980s. Vernon jumped on top of my clothes and started rolling around inside my bag.

"I guess this means it's okay for me to stay in his apartment?" I said, trying to make light of everything.

Patrick looked at me with that familiar twinkle in his eye. "You can't be as bad as Gelsey Kirkland, can you?"

"Do you have to remind me how mediocre I am?" I asked of the prima ballerina who had been my idol since I was a young teenager.

"You mean in your insanity or your dancing," he chuckled. "Most dancers are a little crazy, you know."

Patrick opened the empty drawers to the armoire that I had given to him when I left New York to find that dance job in Europe. It was one of the items that I'd managed to move before my ex-landlord changed the locks on my doors. I hadn't paid my last month's rent and figured my security deposit would cover it. I was wrong. I ran my hand along the smooth old oak and stared at the beautiful curlicue engravings of the only piece of furniture I'd ever purchased by myself.

"You have the whole room to yourself now," he assured me. "We're going to have some fun. Come on, Susu. Cheer up. Everything will work itself out."

I walked down the long slippery hallway to the living room and draped myself on his red velvet 1940s fainting couch. Peering around at the expertly framed movie posters, also from the 1940s–suddenly, four beautiful eyes stared down at me – two blue and sincere, two green and menacing.

"Vernon's just checking you out," he said. "He did that with Robert at first, too."

"Sorry I never got to meet him. So glad you finally fell in love."
"Love sucks," he said. "But, I'm not going to whine all day about it like Miss Bun-Head here."

"Thanks for keeping my armoire and not throwing it in the garbage can like Dennis Nahat just did to me." I headed back to my new room and listlessly started piling my rolled-up leotards and tights inside my armoire. "Susu, dancers get fired from dance companies all the time. That's life."

"Yeah, but at least they know they'll get hired by someone else, somewhere else."

Helping me unpack my toiletries, he studied the labels and contents like a scientist. "I'm going to have to donate some time to your hair this week," he said. "How about a new color? That mousy brown could use a little brightening."

Leaning over to pet Vernon, I moaned, "I'll never get another job. Dennis is the only one that got me, and the only one besides Balanchine who likes tall dancers."

"You are obsessive, you know that, "he said. "And, you're not that tall."

I took a couple more layers of sweaters off, while both of them stared at me. "Do you think you might have an eating disorder?" Patrick asked, innocently. "You used to be a little meatier, I think."

"Yeah, right," I said. "That's never going to happen."
"What happened to your boobs?" he asked.

I laughed, then got up and went back down the hallway for a quick check in the fridge, Vernon, gliding beside me. "So, you think my hair looks bad?" I said, trying to change the subject. I opened his vintage 1960s-era fridge hoping he'd have something that I could eat. Now that I wasn't dancing for a company, I'd have to be even more strident with my calorie restriction. More weight would mean one more problem to deal with.

"I just said it could use a little brightening," he reassured me.

I rummaged around his fridge for a minute, studying the contents and labels, just as Patrick had with my toiletries. "Do you have any carrots? I asked. "I'm starving."

Even though it was pretty clear that I was one unstable girl, Patrick hired me to work in the coatroom that he owned and ran at The Greene Street Bar, in SoHo. He had an eye out for survival, hence the income from the coatroom. I started work the next day, basically hanging fancy coats for fancy people. No education required. He trusted me and considered me still sane.

Coming in from the cold winter air, I basked for a few seconds in the opulent beauty of the upscale restaurant and then pasted on a fake little smile. I felt so out of place and disconnected, but I needed a job. "I got fired, I got fired, I got fired," my brain chattered of my exit from the Cleveland Ballet as I greeted the sophisticated night manager.

I tried to be cordial and put on a happy face, but I felt like a liar every moment I was there. Dressed in the absolute best thing I owned, a Norma Kamali snap-front, red corduroy top and matching ruffled short skirt, I stood in the little doorway of the coatroom and smiled at the passersby. I reached out my weak arms, grasping their elegant coats and luscious furs from Barneys, Saks Fifth Avenue, or Lord & Taylor, places I knew about but never entered. Exotic perfumes and colognes wafted into my little coatroom and I wondered if I'd ever get to smell like that.

"You don't really work here, do you?' A dark-suited and sophisticated fiftyish man asked on my third night of work. He handed me his fancy wool coat that looked like it cost at least a thousand dollars. "You must be an actress or a dancer or something."

Not knowing how to reply or take the compliment, my voice came out like a garbled whisper. "I do really work here for the time being," I said, taking a whiff of his fabulous cologne.

"May I have your number?" he asked confidently, while I whisked his gorgeous coat onto a heavy wood hanger. I tried to look like I knew what I was doing, even though the small task of hanging a nice-smelling coat was strangely taxing. *Why is he asking for my number? What the hell do I say? No...can't you see how much older you are than I am, and can't you see I'm probably going to be a hot mess and no fun at all?*

I wrote out Patrick's number, not believing that he might actually call. "Thank you," he said like a true gentleman, and turned away into the great big restaurant.

He'd probably share a nice time with normal people who were happily content. Maybe he'd pay for everyone's dinner.

Watching the fair-skinned, fair-haired, and diminutive man walk away, I wondered why I gave him my number. He appeared successful, at something. I doubted that he knew any real ballet dancers, or people who struggled financially, or existentially.

A couple of days later, the phone rang as Patrick washed the red, mud-like henna out of my hair. "You are no longer going to be the sad, brown-haired, skinny girl," he told me. Water drained down my neck and into my clothes. "I'll get it," he said, leaving me drenched, but with new auburn-tinted hair. "It might be Robert…I mean I hope it is. It probably won't be. Stay there."

Watching him glide down the long hallway, I reached for a towel. Patrick's voice resonated all the way to the bathroom. "She's a little tied up now, but it's your dad," he whispered loudly, in my direction. I wrapped my dripping wet, auburn hair into a fraying towel.

I walked anxiously toward Patrick and grabbed the phone from his hand. I loved the sound of my dad's deep reassuring voice, a beautiful and commanding voice that served him well as a trial lawyer. It had such security in it. I prayed that this time he would be nice. Patrick gave me a look that said *take care of yourself*, knowing how tough my father could be.

I put the receiver to my ear. "Hi dad, how are you?"

"Mom told me you got fired. Is that right?"

"Yeah, but I wasn't the only one."

"What are you going to do about money?" His voice vibrated through my ear.

"Patrick got me a job, and I've got some unemployment checks coming, eventually." I unraveled the towel and ran my free hand through my damp hair. "I want to come home for a while…maybe. I think I need some help."

"What kind of help?"

"Oh, maybe a psychiatrist, or something."

"There are psychiatrists out there, if you insist you need one. Didn't you already have one a few years ago when you had that first…or was it the second breakdown? Go back to him."

I lay down on the hallway wood floor and curled up into a fetal position. Patrick came by and whispered, so dad wouldn't hear. "Don't take anything he says seriously. Toughen up, Susu."

There was a psychiatrist that I'd seen a few years earlier in New York. I was going through a similar trying time, when my contract with the Eglevsky Ballet ended. Depression and anxiety had overwhelmed me then, too, so, friends referred me to a doctor whose practice consisted of counseling primarily performers. I certainly wasn't alone in my burgeoning neurosis.

"You need to clean your apartment. You need to swim every day. You need some endorphins in your brain. Your depression is partly from not moving." I listened to that knowing doctor four years earlier, when I was only nineteen. "You're not your mother. You're a dancer and that's what you need to do."

I snapped back to the reality of the moment and heard my father's diatribe.

"I told you you'd get fired, didn't I?"

"You were joking, I thought."

"Who knows why I said it...don't take everything so seriously."

"I'm not the only one that got fired," I said. "They had to let a few of us go, because they lost some funding for the year." My voice diminished by the moment in this *defend myself* conversation. I motioned Patrick for an extra towel.

"So then stay in New York, and get another job, and a psychiatrist. You can't come home!"

"I don't know what else to do," I said.

"Your mom is going to coddle you and treat you like a child, you know."

"No, she's not," I insisted. "Dennis gave me a letter of recommendation for a Broadway show."

Patrick rolled his eyes at my desperate attempts to make my father believe I wasn't a complete loser and handed me another towel.

"Then make use of it. I don't think it's a good idea for you to come home. Use that letter."

"I threw it away," I said. "I can't sing, remember?"

"Believe me, coming back home won't be good for you," he said, actually starting to sound compassionate.

"Right," I said, aching for some kind of parental love.

"You're an adult now," he added. "You don't want to become a child again, do you? Why don't you take some singing lessons?" he suggested, not comprehending what a complete mess I was.

"I can't sing."

"You can learn," he said, trying to make me believe it. "I have to go."

"Bye dad, talk to you soon."

I got up from my fetal position and stood, but my strong legs felt suddenly weak, not like a dancer's legs. Dragging the henna-stained towels back to the bathroom to be hung, I peered in the mirror at my new color of hair–auburn that was like the dancer Leslie Browne's in the movie, *The Turning Point.*

"Hey Patrick, come here. What do you think?"

He walked up behind me with his sweet smile. His beautiful blue eyes were so bright, and so terribly forgiving. "You're like Rita Hayworth, without the boobs and hips and ass and..."

"Talent," I moaned. "At least she could sing, and act, and she lived in

Hollywood, poor thing." I turned around and wept onto his terry-cloth robe.

"Let's blow-dry your hair. Then we're going to take a walk and smell the roses, if we can find any."

His spirited demeanor reminded me that I wasn't completely alone. Patrick's voice and presence had always been healing in the past. Now it sounded more like an echo, as I reverted deeper into my own pained little world.

Chapter 7

LIMOUSINE

Frantically getting ready for the date I had with that elegant gentleman I met at my job hanging coats, the one who thought I did something besides work in that tiny wood-paneled room, I threw on my dress-up clothes, some heavy stockings, and my western boots, ran a brush through my now henna-colored hair, and dabbed on a little mascara. A few days earlier in the coatroom, I gave the stranger my number, figuring he'd never call. Well, he did. He wanted to see *Cats*, and having nothing better to do, I said yes, not really knowing how to say no.

I saw the limo pull up in front of our stoop from the window, arriving exactly on time. I bid Vernon goodbye, and whispered, "I'm going to see a show about your kind." I grabbed my bag, and ran down the five flights of dirty stairs, to the front door of the building. The limo driver tipped his hat, and he kindly opened the back door to the shiny, black town car.

"Hello," said the fair-haired, fair-skinned fifty-something-year-old man I barely knew. He held his hand out to me to help me settle into the luxurious seat next to him. "I'm so happy to have you here with me." From the driver's seat, the chauffeur peered through the closed window separating the three of us, mouthing something to his boss with a little mischievous smile.

And off to a Broadway theater we went. I was still in a state of duress. Even the luxurious limo couldn't keep me from falling away from reality, and the looped message in my head: I got fired, I got fired, I got fired. "Would you like a drink?" he asked opening the shellacked oak bar. He poured what looked like whiskey into a crystal glass and plopped a couple of ice cubes into the honey-colored liquid.

"No, that's okay," I said. I peered at his perfectly coiffed haircut, manicured nails, navy-blue pinstriped suit, and wondered what this seemingly kind and clearly wealthy man's intentions were. He smiled and sipped his drink. He reached over for my hand.

I gently pulled it away.

"You're very beautiful, you know. Why are you so sad?"

Clearly, my inner life was darkening my veneer that said I'm okay. I looked at him and then looked away, almost too embarrassed to reveal who

I was and what I once did. Why would he care? I forced out a self-conscious whisper. "I was a dancer, and I don't know if I'll ever dance again." *Okay, that's it. That's all I have to say tonight. Now he knows I'm not a complete mute.*

The Broadway musical *Cats* starred the remarkable Betty Buckley playing an old dying cat and featured a lot of great dancers. But the production didn't hit me because I was too busy being distracted about my next step in life and how disconnected I felt in Maggie Black's professional ballet class earlier in the day. I agonized about my image; how much I hated it now, even if I was thinner than I'd ever been. What was I going to talk about at the supper that was planned for afterwards? I had so little to say about anything that existed in anyone else's reality. I wondered how I was going to get out of seeing him again.

We arrived at Café Une Deux Trois, one of the hip and fancy places in the Broadway Theatre District. I was escorted from the limo as though I was somebody. We glided by glamorous people, busy laughing and enjoying themselves, seeming to not have a care in the world.

We slid into the cozy leather booth at the back of the restaurant, and he looked at me with his sincere, hazel eyes. It was as though he understood what was going on in my fucked-up, ballerina bun-head. The lighting was very mysterious, almost like a film noir movie. It was the perfect place for some kind of romance. My mood was more in the help me area, although there was no way that he would be the one to do that.

"What do you think you'd like to do with your life?" he asked as the waiter in a black tuxedo poured Champagne into each of our flute glasses.

"I'm not really sure, but my friend thinks I should become an actress." He picked up his glass, clinked mine that was still sitting on the table.

"Who's your friend?"

"Oh…um…Harvey Keitel," I whispered, wrapping my fingers as delicately as I could around my own glass. "He's a film actor." I took a little sip of the very dry Champagne. "Oh, and the artistic director of the company I just danced with seemed to think so, too."

"You're friends with Harvey Keitel?"

"Yes. I mean sort of. He used to go out with a friend of mine, a dancer named Yvonne."

"I guess she likes older men?"

"I guess so."

"Would you like for me to pay for you to study acting?"

"Why would you do that?" I said. "You don't even know me." I glanced around the restaurant looking at all the sleek people who seemed happily engaged in the moment. They didn't seem to need any help.

"Because I like you, and think you deserve a chance in this life."

"I'm not sure I'm staying in New York," I said.

He reached out and put his manicured hand on mine again.

"Everything could be right here at your feet."

"That's okay. I don't think I'm worth your investment." I gently took my hand away, yet again.

"So, do you like older men? Like your friend…Yvonne, is it?"

As we got up to leave, I shuffled not so delicately behind him, inhaling the scents of heavy perfumes, and briefly glancing back at the glamorous and exotic models. They all wore fancy jewels, and furs, and slicked-back hair. These clearly pampered women seemed to have a purpose beside the distinguished-looking older men they accompanied. They probably snorted a lot of coke–the drug of choice in the 1980s–in the jeweled, black and gold bathrooms. I looked nothing like these elegant and sophisticated women, wearing long strapless dresses with super strappy high heels. They looked like they fit comfortably in this place that I would never be invited back to again.

On our way to the front door, I spotted a celebrity that I knew from one of my favorite TV specials as a child, *Cinderella*. There she was, in a slinky white sequined gown, the star, Lesley Anne Warren. She was not only still beautiful; she was sophisticated and looked like she belonged with the crowd of people around her. She was from my world, from where I grew up and had been one of my inspirations as a child. She'd been a dancer. Strangely enough, I knew her, peripherally. She'd been married to my mother's hairdresser in the 1970s, Jon Peters, who had become a big movie producer (and later produced *A Star is Born* after marrying Barbra Streisand). I'd had a little girl crush on him when I was ten and had drawn hearts all around his picture on his advertising pamphlet after he trimmed my long, sandy brown hair.

He had recommended to my mother that I book a session with Guy Webster, a big celebrity photographer of the time, so I could model or something. Lesley would take ballet class with Stanley Holden, the same teacher I would study with on my occasional trips back to Los Angeles.

And there she was, six degrees of separation. Lesley still the star and me starting to lose my mind.

The chauffer awaited us at the front entrance, next to the town car. He held the door open one more time and gave me a kind smile. What was next? Would my suitor try something? He probably could have had one of those sleek women in the restaurant that might have appreciated him, but for this date he got me—a leaf blowing in the wind.

We drove back in almost utter silence to Sixteenth Street between Seventh and Eighth Avenue, where nobody ever arrived or departed in a limo.

"Can I see you again?" he pleaded as I reached for the door handle. His efficient chauffeur opened the door for me and gave me another sincere smile. I looked back at my date who seemed untarnished by my clear rejection of his offerings. "I'll pay for you to study acting," he reiterated as I stepped out of the car. "It seems that's what you're wanting to do?"

"I think I'm just going to go home and figure it out. "I said, leaning towards him, but safely out of reach. "Thanks so much for the beautiful evening."

"I'll call you in L.A.," he yelled from the open window, as I headed for the steps to the front door of the building. "I live there half of the year. I have a house in the Hollywood Hills," he boasted, perhaps thinking that fact would change my mind about seeing him again.

"Okay," I said, assuming he'd never call. I wrote out my parent's number and handed it to him.

"Thank you," he replied. The buzzing sound of the rising electric car window filled the moment.

The emptiness of that evening was a reflection of my disconnected life. I felt tossed every which way by almost every occurrence, and with my fragile sense of self, was particularly vulnerable to the whims of anyone who approached me.

I struggled every day in Maggie Black's fabulous ballet class, frequented by numerous professionals, mostly from American Ballet Theater. I couldn't feel the floor under my feet anymore, couldn't look in the mirror, and my natural instincts to dance were diminishing by the day. The feeling was similar to what I'd experienced at the School of American Ballet, at seventeen, when I was making a grand exit from my body, fell and sprained my ankle during class.

It was happening all over again. But this time, because I was older, the existential pain cut even deeper. I'd lost my confidence again and had allowed the dismissal from the Cleveland Ballet to ruin my sense of self. I had no tools to discriminate without my identity of dancer, and felt that I was open prey in the jungle of New York City.

Still not knowing how to say no, I said yes, yet again to another guy I met at my job in the coatroom in SoHo. This time it was a scrappy thirty-year-old with a not so elegant coat that I had checked a week earlier. He said he was going to take me out on a private plane to New Jersey for dinner. He seemed as harmless as the wealthy man I'd gone out with the night before. I decided to go because it was hard for me to be alone, even if I had nothing to talk about except my existential angst, and how bad I felt about my morning ballet class, and my waning technique. I was definitely not good dating material.

He picked me up in a loud rumbling van in front of Patrick's apartment. I'd seen vans of this kind in New York City, but they usually had a locksmith, plumbing, or bug control sign painted on the side. This one was just plain white, and covered with dents and scratches. My hand fumbled on the van's freezing cold door handle. I got in tentatively and

45

wondered what the hell I was doing with this guy who was going to take me to New Jersey. He certainly didn't look like a guy who had a private plane!

"You look really pretty," he said as I hopped up onto the high, uneven seat next to him. The springs nearly burst through the plastic covering. A Virgin Mary dangled from the rear-view mirror. This was the complete opposite of the luxurious town car from the evening before.

"Thanks," I said, staring at the dangling figurine. I looked down at my western boots and studied the salt stains that were slowly disintegrating my only pair of winter shoes. He pressed his foot deeply on the gas pedal as though he was in some kind of a hurry. I could feel my heart start to race, nervous about being in a van of any kind. Why did I agree to this? I looked around and spotted a dark gray blanket in the back that looked big enough to have bodies beneath it. "What's under the blanket back there?" I asked, my throat tightening.

"Oh, I go through some really rough neighborhoods when I deliver the stereos I've been selling," he said, as though I had no reason to be curious.

"But what's under the blankets?" I asked, trying to not appear paranoid.

We had traveled just a few blocks when he pulled over. The engine still running, he leaned over and nonchalantly lifted the blankets up a bit. "What are you so nervous about? Check it out; just a few stereos and a couple of baseball bats," he said. "You're not afraid I'm going hit you on the head with a bat, are you?" he chuckled.

"No. I'll get out here," I said, glancing at a huge machete lying right next to the baseball bats. "I'm not feeling very well," I stammered. My fumbling hand unhinged the door and I jumped from the ridiculously high seat out onto the icy street. I caught myself from falling on my face and as he drove off I heard him yell out the window that I was going to miss a great time.

I straightened up and peered onto Eighth Avenue, ready for my ten-block trek home, to Patrick's apartment, relieved that I survived, but severely depressed. I took a step and slipped on the ice under my worn boot. I picked up that cold foot to check it out. There was a nice big hole in the sole of my only boots.

Climbing up the three flights of dirty stairs to the sad and empty apartment, I dragged myself in, only to be greeted by Vernon. Patrick's joyful presence was missing. I didn't have the energy to call any of my New York dancer friends. I felt so terribly alone in my disintegrating boots, and one cold foot; safe from the possible serial killer but lost in the apartment, my essence, slowly disappearing.

I wandered into the kitchen and made a cup of tea. Vernon jumped on to the kitchen table, to once again, observe me. It felt like he was staring straight through me. Was that an evil eye? I looked into his beautiful green eyes, with that gorgeous black line around them, like the sleek liquid eyeliner I once used on stage. Decision made. I picked up the phone and dialed information.

"American Airlines, please…departing flights." I hung up and stared at the telephone number for the airline. Dad begged me not to come home. I picked up the phone receiver and dialed. "Hello, do you have any direct New York to L.A. flights tomorrow, or the next day? Kennedy or La Guardia is fine. Thank you. Just one."

I was going home.

Chapter 8

HOME

Bob and Jean Priver, Los Angeles.

I should have known that my arrival home wasn't going to be well received. Dad had been pretty firm about that on the phone a few weeks earlier. And yet, there he was, waiting impatiently in the arrival area of LAX, wearing his oil-stained work-outside-in-the-garage clothes, with cigarette smoke wafting from the hand he used to hold his carved ivory cigarette holder. I imagined that he would come to the airport dressed in one of his beautiful suits he wore to his law office. I imagined there would be some compassion in his expression and in the tone of his voice. I was wrong.

"Grab your bags; let's get to the car," he said gruffly, as I reached for my heavy luggage coming around the baggage carousel. He grabbed one from me, but I could feel his agitation at having to drive all the way to LAX, as we walked quickly to his vintage Porsche. The cigarette holder dangled from his mouth as he loaded my bags into the trunk.

On the 405 Freeway I stared out the front window, contemplating my next move. I loved the change of seasons on the East Coast, and here I was, back in the L.A. heat and smog. That drive home to the San Fernando Valley seemed endless as dad barely said a word.

We approached our respectably small house on Placidia Avenue. Built in 1936, it was just down the street from comedian Bob Hope's enclave, which took up an entire city block. Halloween was always a treat for the neighborhood kids. We'd always get a huge chocolate bar of some kind, graciously handed to us by the Hope family butler. Dad opened the wrought iron gate and got back in the car and as we drove up the long driveway, fear engulfed me.

Mom had finished her shift at Children's Hospital and was sitting on the couch in the den waiting for us, when we walked in the house. Getting up to greet us, she looked tired, and a bit haggard. Her grey hair was untouched, and her face was free of make-up, but she seemed happy to see me. "We're going to take care of you," she said softly with some true compassion. I fell into her arms, and the tears that I'd been holding back since I was fired from my dream job in Cleveland, fell onto her white nurses' uniform. She was going to make it okay for me to recover. She'd done it before and was particularly good at it.

I gave up a part of my childhood to become a dancer, and I missed out on knowing who I was without the mirrors, the stage, and the deep connection to music that made everything else bearable. Now, mom, who'd begged me in the last few years to go to college, would save me from this devastating fall from grace. Just her hug made me believe I was loved. Now, I could let go and completely fall apart. She would be there to save me. I knew she loved me–especially when I couldn't take care of myself.

Not long after arriving at my parent's house, my private hospital in Los Angeles, I was watching the news with dad, and there on the screen was a photo of the man who had taken me out on that uncomfortably quiet date in New York City to see *Cats*. He had called me once, a few days after I had come home and became firmly entrenched on the couch in the den. I had told him, "I'm kind of busy." Ha!

Horrified, I watched a shot of his body on a stretcher, being carried out of his fancy Laurel Canyon home. It turned out that he was a big player in the clothing industry and he had been murdered in what was presumed to be some sort of a mafia hit. My eyes widened as I watched the screen.

"Can you believe he took me to see *Cats*," I said as my father sipped his gin martini. "He told me he'd pay for me to study acting. He seemed like such a nice man."

"You know how to pick um," dad quietly remarked.

I hadn't left my parent's couch in a couple of months and I could feel the fat literally attaching itself to my once-skinny dancer's body. I could feel pinpricks on my thighs, arms, and belly. I was sprouting real breasts, and they felt atrocious on my once nearly flat chest. But these were even bigger than the full A cups I possessed while dancing for the Cleveland Ballet. Was this what it was like to be a woman? Many women in L.A. paid good money for boobs and I was getting them free of charge and hating every minute of it. My thighs burned from rubbing against each other on those infrequent times I got off the couch to look in the refrigerator or go to the bathroom. My skin felt like clay that had been slapped on by a mad sculptor who was creating a circus freak. After years of starving myself, I was horrified by the roll that was forming on each side of my waist. I felt the weight especially when I bent over to pick up one of the many crossword puzzles that I was madly working on, trying to distract myself from my depression.

Mom was now getting her wish. I finally looked like a woman. Perhaps not the woman she imagined I would become, but a version of her. She liked me being needy, the weak one, the underdog. It made her feel useful. My years of traveling had empowered me, had allowed me to be separate and to do what I knew I was meant to do. But in my fall from grace, I needed her. And in a strangely disturbing way she liked that. She was at fifty-three still incredibly attractive. She had been a knockout when she was young but was never really confident about her looks. Not only was she tall and statuesque, she had a beautiful smile, high cheekbones, and wide-spaced eyes that were framed by beautifully shaped eyebrows. She resembled Shirley MacLaine with a little Jack Palance thrown in. Her nose had been broken at school when she was very young, and after a botched surgery as a teenager, her bridge ended up being flat, kind of like Jack Palance's. Sadly, she lost her sense of smell in that botched nose job.

She had a thing about mirrors when I was growing up. If I brushed my hair for too long, or looked too long at a new cool outfit, she would dismiss it as vanity, and to her, vanity was a sin. At least, that's what all the nuns told her when she was growing up. The ironic part was that I spent an hour-and-a-half a day or more in front of very large mirrors, scrutinizing my progress as a ballet dancer. She was left-handed but was forced by the Catholic nuns in her school to write with her right hand. The left hand was the hand of the devil, she was told time and again. She ended up ambidextrous in spite of those Catholic nuns, but still, disdainful of mirrors.

She was the baby in the family, having grown up in the small town of Steelton, Pennsylvania, with three brothers, and eight sisters, who all lived above the restaurant-bar that her mother—my grandmother Kate—owned and ran. Her father died from tuberculosis when she was seven so she never really experienced having a male parent. Her strict, Catholic, blue-collar upbringing, and large family was the complete opposite of my father's.

He was an only child who grew up well educated in a Jewish family in Los Angeles. They met when my father was stationed in Baltimore, after having fought in the Korean War. Mom just happened to be a stripling nurse in Baltimore. Mom was drawn to his beautiful blue eyes, quick wit, and his masculine, tough guy sensibility. They were both twenty-five and I suppose it was just time, at least for mom, to tie the knot before it was too late to have children. So, they married in a Catholic Church in Baltimore before mom's huge Catholic family, and my father's tiny Jewish one.

It was probably a hard adjustment to leave everything she knew behind for a lonely life with dad in beautiful, sunny, Los Angeles, with his small and insular family. I imagine she felt like an outsider, not having grown up with some of the privileges my father had known. She loved kids and wanted a big family to make up for the one she was missing. Dad didn't seem to like children very much. When I was a little girl, I remember him saying more than once, "You wouldn't be here if it weren't for your mother. I didn't want any children. She would have had three more if I let her." Two was going to be the limit, and my brother and I made two.

Her lean and statuesque frame was often draped in fashionable clothes, when she wasn't in her nurse uniform or at-home-cleaning clothes. Add a little make-up and she could look dazzling. Now that we were about the same size, she was happy that I could wear her clothes, whether I liked them or not. Except that I wasn't going anywhere outside of the house. My mind and body had grown accustomed to the required skeletal look of a ballerina, and the thought of wearing the same size as mom was, frankly, horrifying.

Three-and-a-half months into my tenure on their couch, I had showered maybe ten times. I battled with my mother on the day she managed to force me up and into the bathroom for shower number eleven. When I came out of the bathroom, she was holding up one of her not so favorite cleaning outfits. "This will fit," she said, displaying a dress size 10 that can only be described as puke green. The below the knee culottes outfit, with a front zipper had an elastic waistband covered by a little belt. Mom knew that waistband would contour to my ever-expanding body, and she still wanted me to look just like her, even if it was on a cleaning day.

"I'm not wearing that ugly thing you picked up at the Salvation Army," I cried, as though I was still wearing my tiara from Cleveland. It was an insult to my higher taste in fashion, but I also knew that I desperately needed mom's help in any decision-making. So, I grabbed it from her, walked into my bedroom, put it on, and then went back to the couch so I could get back to a crossword puzzle. *Okay, I'll act normal now. I have her damn dress on.*

Days later, I was still on the couch, my head with its tangled birds nest hair

51

was covered with the blanket that mom had crocheted, but it didn't cut the sound of my father's pained voice. "She's got to leave! This is not a fucking hotel!" After nearly four months, dad had clearly grown tired of watching his only daughter do absolutely nothing. "I don't care what she's been through, or what she's feeling. She's not doing it here," he said, lighting another cigarette. I turned my head to the other side of the couch, still swathed in the blue and green blanket.

"Where is she going to go?" mom cried. She peeked her head out the den door as my father headed to the garage to load his shotgun shells for his serious trap and skeet-shooting hobby. "She has no one but us!"

"Maybe one of her ex-boyfriends wouldn't mind putting up with her for a few weeks," he yelled back toward the open door.

"She's not ready yet," my mother said, closing the den door. "You will be, eventually," she muttered quietly, pulling the blanket away from my matted hair. "We're going to take care of you. Don't worry about what your father says."

My disintegration may have fed into something terribly painful for my father. Fourteen years earlier, a few hours after my afternoon ballet class with Natalie, and our family meal, dad received a call. He didn't tell us who it was, but asked us all to forget about the dishes, and to get into mom's car. We did as we were asked. We kept asking where we were going so late–it was after 9 p.m. and my brother and I had school the next day.

Dad stared fixedly out the car window and didn't say a word. And then we arrived at my grandparent's home in Beverly Hills.

We piled out of the car, entered their spacious home quietly, and followed my grandfather down the long hallway. It was so terribly silent, and then he suddenly buckled over, holding on to the bar in the den.

"She called my office and said she was going to let the maid go early," he murmured, "And then she took a whole bottle of sleeping pills. I don't know why."

My mother had carted off my fourteen-year-old brother into another room, so he didn't hear the details that I also wasn't supposed to hear. My grandmother had committed suicide. I stood near my father hearing my grandfather's pained voice. It was the first time I'd seen my father cry. It was the only time I saw my grandfather cry. "She was supposed to leave for Houston tomorrow…the pain clinic," my grandfather said.

Before my grandmother became confined at fifty-eight in a hospital bed at home because of painful sciatica in her back, she had been a champion of my dancing and would often call me Nijinsky when I danced around their huge living room, brimming with ecstatic joy. She would teach French to my brother and I, take us to the La Brea Tar Pits, the historic Farmers Market, and to museums. I loved her in the way a child can love a grandmother. She was a huge presence in our lives. And then she wasn't. The doctors had told her she shouldn't move. We'd visit her weekly, hoping she'd get better. She hoped so too. But she didn't.

When we piled back in the car it was silent. This was my first experience of devastating loss, of our impending mortality. In the wake of her death, I had danced for my parents, hoping that they would find joy in my performances, and it would bring them out of their sadness. It didn't.

Now, I could sense that my father was watching my decline and fearing the worst; that I would somehow end up like my beloved grandmother Josephine who died because she couldn't move.

Another uneventful week later, I was still hidden away from the world on a scorching summer Saturday, sweating profusely from the Mexican food I had just devoured. Mom was home for the day and she just watched me continue to ruin my once ethereal look.

"I should have kept dancing," I moaned, as she sat down next to me. "I wouldn't be stuck here on this couch with nowhere to go."

"You can still dance. Get dressed. I'll drive you to Stanley Holden's class," she said, bolting off the couch. "You're taking a shower right now. I don't care if you just ate an entire platter of Mexican food."

She was starting to get sick of her position as caretaker, enabling her once ballerina daughter in her own destruction. She grabbed her car keys from her purse to emphasize her resolve to get me out of the house. But the sound of her jangling keys sent a wave of fear through me. Being seen by anyone I might know at Stanley Holden's ballet class was a humiliation I knew I could never endure.

"I can't go. Look how fat I am," I wailed, still stuck under the blue and green blanket. "You'll never understand what I'm feeling."

"I don't care if you don't want to dance anymore, but you've got to take a shower!" she pleaded. "You've got to start caring for yourself."

"I will tomorrow, I promise."

"You can't do this to yourself," she cried, pulling at my arms, trying to get me to the shower. "Just go for yourself, because you love to dance."

Her pain was etched deeply across her face, as though there was no help for me anywhere. I pulled hard against her grip, burrowing deeper into the couch, making it impossible for her to move me. I was still physically strong, and thirty years younger.

She opened the den door. "You need some fresh air and sunshine. Why don't you apply to college with dance as a major?"

"Are you fucking kidding me?" I said, as I got up to slam the door shut. "Real dancers don't go to college to dance."

"So real dancers just give up if they can't get exactly what they want?"

She threw down her purse and watched me mope back to the couch and grab the television remote. I started flipping the channels and stopped at the Olympics.

It was, after all, the summer of 1984 and life in Los Angeles was going on in a vibrant and charged way, not too far from my disintegration on my parent's couch. Amazing athletes from around the world were winning medals and displaying amazing feats of skill, and here I was on my parent's couch in the San Fernando Valley unable or unwilling to get off. I really didn't care who won or lost. Nothing mattered to me. I turned it off.

Thirty years earlier, my mother was practicing her brand-new nursing-skills in a mental hospital in Baltimore. I was not a great reminder of her early days there. Nobody got any better in mental institutions. A lobotomy was certainly out of the question, although my father probably considered it, just to get me out of the house and away from my overbearing mother. But something had really changed. There's no way she was going to send me to an institution. I wasn't that crazy, and I hadn't tried to hurt myself, even though my disintegration could have been considered a form of suicide. I was her daughter. I couldn't be *that* bad.

Chapter 9

HARVEY

On a quiet afternoon about five months into my debilitating retreat, I found myself staring blankly at the pine walls in the den in my parents' house. Not only was I psychically disappearing, my will to live was becoming terribly weak. Certain commercials about illness on television created a hypochondria in me. Was I coming down with a terminal illness?

Suddenly the phone rang, disturbing my miserable isolation. I burrowed deeper into the couch and prayed silently that it wasn't for me. Thankfully, one of my parents picked up the phone.

"Hello, yeah she's here," dad whispered. "It's Harvey," he said as he headed towards me, unraveling the phone's long plastic cord. "Do you want to talk to him?"

My heart began beating wildly. Harvey Keitel! Shit! "What should I do?" I whispered to my dad, suddenly paranoid about being discovered as a sloth-in-the-making.

"I don't really give a shit what you do," he joked with his usual sarcasm, "but it would be nice if you could find a way to move out of my house. Maybe he'll come and get you out of here." He made it seem like it was any old phone call, even though he knew it was Harvey Keitel, the actor, the movie star.

Gingerly taking the phone, I sat myself up, and said, "Can I have some privacy, please?" I hadn't held a phone in five months, so it felt even more uncomfortable when my mother came out of the kitchen with a dishrag in her hand, urging me on. "That's so nice someone is calling you," she said. "You need to talk to whoever it is. We're not listening."

I wanted to die of embarrassment right there; Harvey, probably hearing the humiliating exchange, holding the line.

"Hello?" I said, and a flood of memories came back.

I first met Harvey three years earlier in 1981. I was living in New York City with my dancer friend Yvonne and her mother on Central Park West. Yvonne and I were on one of our many breaks from The Eglevsky Ballet, and were taking a long walk like the rest of New York City on a beautiful spring day. The cool, crisp air made the city seem so alive and vibrant, and the communal joy felt palpable.

Yvonne was five-feet tall, waif-like, and twenty-one. She was seeing Harvey at the time, who was probably also dating a few other adolescent-looking women. Suddenly, there he was in front of us at the corner of Columbus and Seventy-second Street.

"Hey Harvey!" Yvonne blurted out. She introduced us in a sweet and unassuming way.

"You must be a ballerina too," Harvey said, showing me way too much attention, considering one of his girlfriends was standing right there. "You're tall, aren't you," he said as the comparatively tiny Yvonne looked on.

"Hi," I said, though I didn't recognize him at first. Short and stocky, he didn't have typical movie-star looks. But his enigmatic energy was dangerously attractive. I had seen *Taxi Driver* a few years earlier, when I had taken my parent's car (while they were away on a vacation) to a screening at the Writer's Guild, even though I didn't have a driver's license and was relatively inexperienced at driving a stick shift.

"Harvey, I forgot to tell you, Susie and I are leaving for Europe next week to get full-time contracts," Yvonne piped up.

Harvey cut her off. "I'm going to Paris next week myself to start work on a movie with Rudolph Nureyev…one of *your* people. God, I hope he can act," he chuckled. "You should both come stay with me in Paris, before you go off on your auditions."

Standing there quietly, I found him captivating, even though I wasn't exactly sure who the hell he was.

Harvey glared at me lustfully while Yvonne gave me a little nudge that said let's get going. "See you tonight," she said. "We'll discuss Paris, and if we can both fit in your hotel room," she giggled, as we bid him goodbye.

"He was kind of flirting with me," I said as we walked away.

"Harvey does that with every girl he meets, especially dancers and models," Yvonne replied. "No big deal."

And now, here I was, sitting on the couch in the den with my mother hovering nearby, wiping her hands on her dishrag. Even in my disheveled state, I waved the phone to shoo her away. I wasn't about to let either of my parents listen in on my conversation. No matter how screwed up I was, they weren't going to invade my microscopic private life.

"Have you seen Yvonne?" I asked Harvey in my raspy whisper. "I've lost touch with her. I've pretty much lost touch with everyone," I said. "I'd like to talk to her when I get better."

"Get better? Are you ill?" he asked.

"I don't think so. I might be; I'm not sure."

"Why have you lost touch with everyone?" he pressed.

"Long story…" I trailed off, hoping he wouldn't notice. Admitting my depression and my situation that seemed inescapable would have been humiliating, so I acted like I was okay.

"Yvonne is trying her hand at screenwriting, and I think she has some talent," Harvey said.

"Wow, that's really cool," I said, acting like I really cared about Yvonne's other talents.

Landing at the airport outside of Paris, we managed to find the right train into the City of Lights, where we'd meet up with Harvey before we shoved off to Switzerland and Germany, countries whose dance companies actually hired American dancers.

We hopped off the train, flagged a taxi, and dragged our heavy bags to the trunk. After muttering a few words in French, I pulled out the little book that had the address of Harvey's Left Bank hotel. We showed it to the driver and were on our way through Paris.

Tired and a bit cranky from the long trip, we looked less than perfect as we dragged our luggage into the elegant lobby. We informed the concierge that we were staying with Harvey Keitel and suddenly we were two Cinderella's who magically had been invited to the ball.

Yvonne and I both came from middle-class families. Our touring with the Eglevsky Ballet, almost always by bus, with overnight stays in Motel 6-type accommodations, was a far cry from this elegant Parisian hotel. The world we inhabited didn't look like this and reminded us that the elegance of the ballet dancer is often, truly a façade.

But there was no façade in my parent's den that unbearably hot L.A. summer. I was sweating and shifted my uncomfortably out-of-shape body on the couch, as I held the phone with Harvey Keitel on the other end. When I first met Harvey on the street in Manhattan, I said to him, "I can't wait to be back on stage. Life doesn't make sense to me without it." Now, here I was, stuck on a couch in my parent's den in the San Fernando Valley. No façade, only this grim reality.

I turned the subject to Yvonne. "Where is she living?" I asked.

"Yvonne's still in New York," Harvey replied. "I'm setting her up with a literary agent at my agency."

"Wow, that's great. She must be really good. I'm really happy for her," I said, my voice trailing off. But not enough for him to end the conversation and say goodbye.

My mind spun back to Paris and the elevator that took Yvonne and me up to Harvey's floor. We were exhausted and rode in silence. We wandered listlessly down the hallway until we found the door to room 322, which was conveniently right next door to Harvey's 324. We entered our small but exquisite room, and Yvonne took note of the adjoining door to Harvey's suite. "I guess Harvey has a ménage a' trois in mind, with that tricky little adjoining door," she said with her usual candor.

"I guess so," I said, acting like it was something I actually knew about and was okay with. We started unpacking our bags, chattering on about how gorgeous the hotel was, and how tired we both were from the long trip. I looked up when I heard the doorway to the adjoining rooms open, and there was Harvey with a big smile on his face.

"Welcome, you two," he said, in his gruff voice.

The phone was messing up my already matted hair. My hands were sweating from my anxiety and unease of talking to, well, just about anyone, but in this case, Harvey. I felt a large wave of jealousy when his words echoed in my ear that Yvonne was "trying her hand at screenwriting."

How could Yvonne be a writer? She was a dancer, and if she wasn't dancing anymore, she should be struggling existentially, right along with me.

"Do you see her?" I asked, truly wondering if they still had a relationship. It had been so long, and so much could have happened.

"We're still close," Harvey said.

It was all cause for jealousy, because in my mind he had been MY SVENGALI, NOT HERS! But what was I jealous of? I had no interest in writing myself. *No wonder she's okay and finding her way in the world. She always possessed more confidence than I had.*

"Hi Harvey!" Yvonne put down her unpacking and ran to give him what looked like a French kiss.

"Hi," I said, peeking up for a moment from my bag. I continued unpacking, not wanting to draw any attention from their little encounter.

Pushing Yvonne's arms gently away, he invited both of us into his much bigger room for a drink. "I want to tell you two about your comrade, Mr. Nureyev, and you've got to see this bathroom."

"Please tell," Yvonne said. "Come on Susie, put that stuff down, I can't wait to hear the dirt." She took my hand and led me through the little open doorway, and whispered to me, "This is going to be fun."

"It's already fun," I whispered back. We're in Paris!"

"What are you two whispering about behind my back?" Harvey asked as he wandered over to the mini-bar in his gorgeous suite.

"Nothing," we giggled. We both sat down on the pastel silk-flowered sofa. Yvonne put her arm around me to seal our friendly and non-competitive relationship.

"Isn't this a beautiful hotel, you two?" he said.

"We wouldn't be here if it weren't for you," Yvonne said flirtatiously.

Shifting in my seat, I felt like I might be interrupting something important between the two of them.

"Nureyev has this thing about him, like a lost little boy, very endearing. He's actually not a bad actor," Harvey said, while pulling out a few bottles of vodka from the mini bar. He placed some glasses on the table before us and emptied each bottle into our crystal glasses.

Uncomfortable and anxious, I felt I needed to add something to the conversation. "I used to run into him at the School of American Ballet, when I was there five years ago. He was always wearing fur until he got into class." I gulped down the cold vodka to soften my anxiety. Yvonne sipped hers delicately.

"Is that right? We'll have dinner later," Harvey said.

Before I could blink an eye, clothes were off, including mine, and the conversation was at a minimum.

"Come over here," Harvey demanded. *Was he talking to me?* He kissed me, sort of, and finished taking off whatever underwear I still had on. Yvonne just watched with a big smile on her face. This obviously was no big deal to her. Harvey pointed to the huge puffy king-sized bed that was just a few feet away. "You two must be tired. Let's take a nap together."

I shyly got on to the bed with both of them. I actually thought we were going to sleep. I was certainly exhausted. I rolled onto my side and away from them, just in case they wanted to kiss goodnight, or something. I pulled the fancy silk sheet over my head and started to roll further and further off to the far end of the bed until I almost fell off. They started to whisper things to each other. "Yeah baby…I want you so much. Yeah baby, do it like that…harder, harder. Do you think your friend is into this?"

I tried to play dead, like a frightened possum with a keen survival instinct. Surely, I didn't sleep. I could barely contain my uncomfortable laughter.

My neck was dripping sweat, holding up my parents' beige, push button phone. I was alone momentarily, and even though Harvey's voice was echoing in my ear, my mind was racing with questions about why he would even call me. It had been almost two years since our encounter in Paris. We hadn't spoken since I'd left Los Angeles for the Cleveland Ballet, when life was good and I was still normal, more than a year earlier.

Had I actually had a rendezvous with Harvey Keitel? That among other things went through my mind as I sunk deeper and deeper into my parent's couch.

Did I like the movies? Did I like to talk to people on the phone? I guess I did, but it would never be the same. I'll never dance again, and I'll never be who I was, and this couch may actually get attached to me. I will

59

never float on air again or feel music the way I had, so very deeply. When I actually do decide to leave my parent's house, they'll have to pry this couch off of me. There will be some kind of tentacles that will grow out of my body, and then a surgeon, will carefully make the separation, without killing me. Or maybe dad will say, "I just want my fucking couch back! Don't worry about that lump attached to it. Just get those cancerous tentacles away from my couch."

"How's L.A.?" Harvey asked, waking me up from my daydream.

"Oh, great. You know…the same. It's home for now."

"Fucking L.A. can never compete with New York."

The plush silk comforter was pushed way down off the big bed and now hung near the crème-colored super fluffy, three-inch carpeting. My head was still draped comfortably with the silk sheet, and my top hand held it in place, as Yvonne and Harvey had sex. I'd never felt sheets like this. They were so light and soft as a cloud.

"What's wrong with her?" Harvey whispered.

"It looks like she's just sleeping," Yvonne said diplomatically, trying to protect her embarrassed friend.

She nudged me gently, still acting as though I'd truly slumbered through their sexual adventure.

"Oh God, did I fall asleep?" I said, with a little fake yawn. "Wow, it seems like I just fell on the bed."

"I hope we weren't too noisy," Yvonne giggled, completely confident about who she was and what had just occurred.

"I didn't hear a thing," I said, faking another yawn.

"I'm going to find something to wear to dinner," Yvonne said, as she got out of the huge bed and glided with absolute grace across the suite to our adjoining room. I followed clumsily behind.

"Come here," Harvey demanded.

"Where?" I asked, wondering whom he was talking to.

"I want to show you the bathroom. It's so beautiful."

The hard tile under my knees was incredibly cold. He held me down and forced his penis into my mouth. I tried not to show him that I was uncomfortable, and sadly wanted him to think that I was actually enjoying myself.

"Pinch my nipples," he said. "Harder." I obeyed. Perhaps I wouldn't have, if I'd had some sense of self. Dancers often don't have a voice to say "no." We're told what to do and do it. We are there for other people's enjoyment, especially if we haven't developed boundaries or a sense of self. I certainly had very little of either, unless I was on stage, or dancing well, in class.

Even though the bathroom was extraordinarily beautiful, I was in some pain with that hard tile under my bony knees. Taking a breath, I

60

peered around the bathroom and prayed that Yvonne wouldn't walk in on us with a big smile on her face. Being an insecure twenty-two-year old, I wanted Harvey to think I was just as wild as Yvonne.

"Yvonne is right next door," I said, gasping for air. I felt guilty, even if I were just acting like this was fun.

"She's really excited that you're in here with me," he said.

"Really," I choked out.

Perhaps I was paying for my free room.

Later at dinner, at a beautiful restaurant, we dined with a couple of the French producers of Harvey's movie. I watched him across the table, feeling uncomfortable with these seemingly confident people, eating heartily and speaking mostly French. I felt surprisingly attracted to him, even with Yvonne there. What an incredibly dynamic man. I picked at the lobster, wondering if these people always ate like this.

My ear was still vibrating from holding the phone for so long, listening to Harvey talk about all the great roles he was preparing for, and his communication with Yvonne. I changed the phone to my other ear that wasn't throbbing.

"Maybe you should come back to New York to see if you want to act. There are some wonderful teachers here that I can turn you on to," Harvey suggested in his charming way.

"When are you coming to L.A. to shoot?" I asked, hoping he would stop prying into my boring life, and get back to talking about himself.

"Not sure yet, but I'm going to do a bang-up job in the new Scorsese film, The *Last Temptation of Christ*. "I was born to play Judas."

"Wow, and what about your accent? I can't imagine Judas with a Bronx accent."

"Scorsese doesn't care about that. He loves great actors. He wants it real."

Early the next morning, I stared up at the beautiful crystal chandelier hanging above my queen-sized bed. Feeling restless and insecure, I quietly got up out of my plush bed, took a quick shower, and packed my dance clothes so I could get to a class.

Yvonne didn't even budge when I opened the heavy door, blissfully sleeping off the wild night in her own bed. I tiptoed out of our exquisite room and down the hallway to the elevator. I floated through the lobby and out to the street. It was so beautifully charming, that old cobblestone. I knew where to go. I counted on my memory and instincts to return me to the professional dance studio that I had visited the year before. I managed to find the nearest Metro to get me to the studio, where I could dance, where I could sweat, where I could finally connect with my soul.

There wasn't an American in the bunch in that creaky old studio with raked floors. There definitely were some Paris Opera dancers there, dancing as though they were on air, even though that old wood floor was sloped towards the front mirrors. I had performed on one raked stage in Europe six months earlier, when I was working with the Hannover Ballet, in Northern Germany. I was one of the sylphs in *Les Sylphides*, on a beautiful, but raked, outdoor garden stage, and it had been difficult to keep from tumbling into the orchestra pit. And now I was struggling to keep on top of my legs yet again, in this French dance studio, watching everyone else move effortlessly.

The chatter in the dressing room, before and after class was decidedly French, and it was clear that everybody else in that fully mirrored and moldy-smelling room was accustomed to those raked floors. Maybe the French kept their floors like that to keep the American dancers away, since they never hired us for their companies.

A charming boyish man came up to me in the dressing room, after that humiliating class, and started talking as though he knew me.

Why is he talking to me? Why is he dressing in front of me? Oh, right, I'm in Europe and our nude bodies are no big deal.

We entered the large, white tiled, community-style shower together. There must have been twenty other nude male and female dancers showering together in a long line of evenly spaced showerheads. I kept my eyes averted and continued to chat with him.

French showers, French doors. I could see my parents talking quietly through the glass separating the den from the living room where they were seated. I turned away from them to not get distracted by their presence.

"Would you like to meet Jack Nicholson?" Harvey asked as I pulled the blanket further up towards my head.

"That's okay," I said. "I mean, why would I want to meet Jack Nicholson?' I trailed off again, staring at the knots in those wood panels.

Maybe I did have some appeal at one time, or maybe Harvey wanted to pimp me out with a bigger star than himself?

The young Frenchman was named Pasquale and his French accent made me melt. He and I left the creaky Parisian dance studio together, chatting as though we actually knew each other. "Where are you from?" he asked.

"Oh, I guess Los Angeles, by way of New York, and last year I danced in Hannover, Germany." We strolled in Pigalle, peering at the peep show posters, and the luscious open markets. The weathered people with babushkas and tattered clothes, bargaining in French, outside on the street seemed so alive. I felt like I was part of an old painting, or romantic novel, as we took in the real Paris.

"And where are you staying, and how long are you staying, and can we have a short affair before you go off on your travels?"

We strolled closer to Harvey's hotel on the Left Bank.

"You have to experience love in Paris. It's the most romantic city in the world," Pasquale said as I shook inside with his idea.

Wasn't I in enough trouble already?

"This is it," I said, thrilled that we had arrived, but wondering why I even let this guy basically follow me to my tentative home. We floated through the lobby, towards the elevator. The concierge remembered who I was, and waved us in as though it was no big deal.

"Fancy, isn't it," I said, as we both peeked into room 322.

"Your friends must be pretty rich," he said, taking off his jacket. "Look at this big puffy bed," he whispered, falling onto the beautiful silk-flowered comforter. "Come here."

I obeyed, falling onto the bed right next to him.

"You seem so different than the American girls I've met." He grabbed me, and pulled me on top of him, softly running his hand along the side of my face. He looked deep into my eyes as though he was falling in love. He ran his hand through my hair, and started to kiss me passionately again, as though he really was in love. What a great actor! You'd think Harvey Keitel would have tried a bit of his technique.

Realizing I could be in a bad situation, I stopped Pasquale for a moment and got up from the bed. I unlocked the adjoining room door and peeked into room 324. Thank God they were gone. I drifted back to Pasquale's arms as directed, and my paranoia subsided. My emotions were as complicated as they'd ever been. I wasn't sure what would happen. Would I be caught? Would Harvey then hate me? Would Yvonne hate me? I wanted to please everyone, but in that moment, I wanted to please Pasquale. Even if I was a bit attracted to him, it didn't really matter what I felt.

Primarily, I was there for his pleasure, for Harvey's pleasure. If I wasn't dancing, my body wasn't my own. And somehow, this was how I got attention. I felt loved for a moment. But I ached to be on stage, where I would experience my deepest self, where I could tell the truth.

I could feel the air-conditioning coming through my plaid robe, and onto my naked feet. It was disturbing that I couldn't point my feet anymore. They were atrophying, and my worked-to-death arches were falling. "Has Yvonne met Jack?" I asked, trying to get my voice above an annoyingly dry whisper, praying that Harvey couldn't detect its diminished sound.

"No, but I'm going to ask him to read one of her scripts."

"Wow, you must really believe in her."

"I do," he said, as though I wouldn't feel a tinge of jealousy.

Maybe I should tell my dad about Jack. Maybe he'll be impressed. Maybe he'll think Jack could come get me off this couch, in case Harvey wouldn't. But dad was nowhere within earshot, and probably wouldn't give a shit about Jack, since he didn't seem to give a shit about Harvey.

Just twenty-two years old and in the romantic and magical city of Paris, I didn't seem to think it was a problem to invite someone I didn't know into a fancy hotel room that wasn't really mine. Even if I wasn't quite sure what I was doing. Maybe Pasquale and I would truly fall in love, just like he mentioned earlier on our walk to Harvey's hotel. Even if I was scattered, and unsure of my bearings, I certainly didn't fight him off, as I'd done a couple of years earlier with the great dancer Alexander Godunov. He was tall and seriously handsome in a light blonde, Nordic prince way. He was a good twenty years older than me and spoke almost no English. Perhaps I was too young or too shy, or too stupid to appreciate his blaring heterosexuality.

I fought Alexander Godunov off! He was a star! Maybe it was all the vodka he drank on our nearly wordless date in New York that repulsed me.

But with Pasquale, there was no alcohol involved, and he seemed so sincere in his intentions. I wanted to make someone happy. I hadn't done that for myself in the dance class I'd attended that day, watching all those dancers move gracefully on the severely raked floor. Whether in a company or not, I judged myself on how class went for the day, every day. I hadn't planned on being picked up by a French dancer after class, but I had. I didn't tell Pasquale about Harvey and Yvonne, and that they could walk in any minute on this encounter. I kept that to myself, praying we wouldn't be caught.

My hand was getting exhausted holding that phone, and my poor shoulder started cramping, but I was too embarrassed to tell Harvey that I was seriously depressed and hadn't moved off this disgusting couch in months.

"So, do you like Jack?" he asked, while I stared into space, my neck and shoulder aching.

"Yeah, I guess so. He's done some great movies. But, so have you." I really couldn't have cared less, but I didn't want him to think I was more impressed with Jack Nicholson than him. I could see my parents get up from the green crushed velvet 70s couch in the living room. It looked like they were going to come in and maybe ask for the phone. My heart began to beat wildly.

"Would you like to come up to his house when I come out to L.A.?"

"Yeah, that would be fun…" I stammered, watching my parents walk right through the breakfast room. Surprisingly, neither of them even acknowledged how long I'd been talking on their phone.

I saw mom get her car keys. She was only twenty feet from me but was acting as though I wasn't even there. She walked past me yet again, without saying a word. I guess dad told her to get out of the house and do something. I overheard him whispering earlier in the day, "Remember Jean, this is our house, not your crazy daughter's, who we should never have let come home."

She started up her 1977 white Mercedes Benz that had a completely different roar than my dad's rumbling sports car.

"Remember the great food we had in Paris?" Harvey said. "I'm definitely going back to that restaurant on my next trip there. Do you remember the name?"

Of course, he'll get to go back to Paris. I never will. I'm never leaving this fucking couch.

"I didn't eat that much. I don't really remember the food, except for that huge lobster," I replied. "You're going back?"

"Probably soon. Are you dancing out there in L.A.?"

"I got fired, and I can't dance anymore," I surprisingly revealed. "I'm not really sure why."

"So, everybody gets fired sometime. It's not really a big deal," he said.

"I guess so."

"Did you stay in touch with your French lover? I wanted to beat the shit out of that guy," he chuckled.

"No," I answered, not really sure what to say about the whole experience.

Pasquale and I had decided to leave the hotel for a little sightseeing when the adjoining door swung open. The color drained from my face. I looked over at Pasquale, who looked a little paler than he had a few moments earlier. "Harvey, this is Pasquale, Pasquale this is Harvey," I stammered, trying to act like we didn't just have sex in the room that wasn't really mine.

"What the fuck is going on here?" Harvey barked as we gathered our clothes in the matter of a minute. Acting as though nothing strange was happening, we dressed and left, sauntering down the hall, towards the elevator. Harvey got in after us. He was fuming, but completely quiet, and looked ready to punch Pasqual in his young and handsome face. He actually followed us out of the hotel and on to that beautiful cobblestone. We both looked back at the red-faced and aggravated Harvey.

I was a bad girl and didn't even know it. I'd finally graduated from bun-head school.

"Keep walking," Pasqual said. "Is that Harvey Keitel?"

"Actually, yes."

"Why didn't you tell me he was your lover?"

"He's not. He's with my friend Yvonne, and it had been convenient to put us both in the one room."

"Was he expecting a *ménage a triose?*"

"No, I don't think so."

I walked a long way with Pasquale, and the great feelings of newfound love were now buried with the threat of Harvey Keitel's wrath. But I was in Paris and I might not ever be here again and, as Pasquale said, "You must experience love in the most romantic city in the world." And, although, I would have liked to spend the rest of my Parisian adventure with a true Frenchman and dancer who was my age, I bid Pasquale goodbye, never to see him again.

I was lucky that the stars lined up for this short but lovely experience. Regrettably, I felt that I owed something to Harvey. He showed a kind of need, on top of all that brutishness, even if he wasn't quite tender, like my French lover. He also showed an interest in my growth as an artist, whatever direction I was going.

Harvey had a full day off of shooting the next day and decided to spend it with me, while Yvonne went to the same dance studio I'd visited the day before. She'd never danced in Europe, as I had the year before, so she needed to find out about those raked floors. Personally, I was in an emotional upheaval, which wasn't uncommon for me, but it had never included a situation as the present–terrible guilt about inviting someone into a hotel room that wasn't mine, and covertly taking my travel-mates boyfriend away.

While Yvonne was off dancing, we decided to visit the Pompidou Museum together, to see if we could mend our undefined yet bruised relationship. He never brought up Pasquale but decided that since I was such a problematic girl, I should become an actress.

"Even if you don't become an actress, it will be a journey of self-discovery," Harvey said, as we studied the great paintings by Toulouse Lautrec. I wandered over to a Degas, familiar with other paintings and sculptures of his from my many visits to The Metropolitan Museum in New York City. His renditions of another world and the pastel-hued ballerinas resonated deeply in me, as did Lautrec's vision of stage performers. I was in heaven seeing this extraordinary art, even if overwhelmed by my confusion about the whole Paris adventure.

"You are exactly like me. You need to explore your dark side," Harvey said yet again. We walked slowly along the rows of paintings, studying and scrutinizing. He seemed to know something that I hadn't truly revealed to him. In absolute bliss over seeing the Impressionists up-close, we arrived at a Van Gogh.

"Wow," I said. "This must have been his dance."

Harvey and I had been on the phone close to an hour when my dad walked right past me, slammed the den door, and headed for the garage. He started up his old Maserati with its guttural and low-toned roar. I traded ears yet again. "No Harvey. I can't come to New York. I just left there. I don't have any clothes that fit, and packing is impossible right now."

Could he see what I'd turned into, and would that stop him from calling ever again? Nausea overwhelmed me as I continued listening to him talk.

"You can come here and study acting. I told you in Paris that's what I thought you should do, and now is as good a time as any," he said.

Svengali was rearing his head again, while I was disintegrating in the town where he got to play different characters and be a movie star.

"I can't leave right now. Maybe in a few months, when I'm better," I repeated in my whippet-thin voice.

If he only knew what I looked like, maybe he wouldn't be that interested in talking to me. He was never my boyfriend, so I couldn't ask him to pay for me to get up off my couch and out the door. He didn't offer to help in any way either. I never really liked asking for anything, something my parents managed to instill in me. Couldn't he hear that it was such a struggle for me to express myself?

"Have you ever read Franz Kafka's *Metamorphosis*?" I asked. "That's what's going on with me right now."

"You've been all over Europe, for Christ's sake. You know what it is to travel. New York is a better place for you to be, really. As I said, there are some great teachers here."

"New York kind of scared me last time I was there," I said. And then suddenly, it was time to go. "Bye Harvey," I said. "Thanks for calling and say hi to Yvonne for me." I hung up the phone, picked up my blanket from the floor, and covered myself. Safe again.

I was experiencing a true *Metamorphosis*. This was everything I'd read about in novels or stories of artists struggling on the verge of collapse. It seemed so much more interesting when it was happening to someone else. I was so intrigued with Nijinsky's published diary when I was very young. His consciousness about everything around him seemed normal to me. It didn't seem crazy; his supposed and famous madness felt tragic and profound, and connected to something bigger, something spiritual.

But, I wasn't famous or adored for my gifts, so how could I be suffering as though that was true? I was just a little dancer, growing bigger by the day, that no one would ever know.

Chapter 10

COUCH

Had it been over five months? I couldn't really tell. I never looked at a calendar to count the weeks or months. I stared at the cream-colored, wood-beamed ceiling with its daunting dark smoke stains, directly above my father's chair. That swiveling leather chair was just to the left of my woolen, plaid, and presently scorched couch. Those visible stains above my head signified my father's long cigarette addiction. The reality of the situation—the disgusting couch and marred ceiling—was softened by a daydream of better times not too long before.

"This is a spiritual encounter," the exotic, dark-skinned man said, staring straight at me in the most curious and beguiling way. He was wearing a long and seemingly real fur-coat. He brought his hand onto my own already fraying and cheap vintage-fur coat. Shocked, because no one in my three years living in the city had stopped me in the middle of a bustling street, as of yet. All of those busy and focused pedestrians pushed by us, hitting us with their shopping bags and briefcases on bustling Fifty-seventh Street, near Fifth Avenue. "This really is a spiritual encounter," he said again. I finally heard the enticing French accent that I initially couldn't quite place. Time stood still for a moment. I breathed in the crisp clean winter air of New York City that was masked lightly with the seductive smell of his very French cologne. He finally took his arm off my torn coat and said it again. "This truly is a spiritual encounter…you must have a coffee with me."

I looked at him without the usual blinders that got me through long days of subway riding, and keeping to myself, until I would reach the safety of any ballet studio I was dancing in. I lost my tiara for a moment, in this intriguing Frenchman's gaze.

Suddenly, my father's resounding voice woke me from my stupor. "Find something else to do, or I'm throwing you out of the house!" he said as he yanked the *Los Angeles Times* crossword puzzle that was dangling from my hand. His voice awakened me from the daydream of my first real love.

Then he proceeded to tear that crossword section into little pieces, right in front of my eyes.

"Please don't," I cried, picking up the roll of scotch tape I kept nearby because of dad's habit of shredding that part of the paper, my temporary distraction from mental anguish. "I'm learning new words. I thought you wanted me to be educated!" I stuttered, as I taped my crossword puzzle back together.

"This is not your private mental institution and this little vacation of yours is going to be over very soon," he said, as he poured his third or fourth martini of the day. Cigarette smoke wafted around us as I struggled with those tiny pieces of newspaper. He turned on the television to the evening news. I coughed from his cigarette smoke and stared at the yellowing stains on the ceiling.

Finally, dad broke the silence with a suggestion on how to end my bleak situation. "You should move to a kibbutz in Israel and see what it's really like to work. "Dancing isn't real work, you know. Performers are kind of like circus people."

"Thanks," I said. He was pretty much criticizing the last five years of my life. Somehow, my depression allowed his stinging comment to drift right by. If I was still dancing I would've gotten up and left the house, or moved right out. But, instead I resumed taping my crossword puzzle, ever hopeful I'd complete it this time.

A few days later, my father, fueled by his desire to get me out of the house, drove me to the Jewish Federation. I peeked over at him as we drove in silence over Laurel Canyon to the Mid-Wilshire District. He looked happy, almost content. I couldn't wait to get back home. I stared out the windshield and laughed at his ridiculous idea of me moving halfway around the world to a place where I could do some kind of manual labor among young Jewish people.

We parked in the huge parking lot behind the ten-story building. Dad decided to wait in the car, so I could suddenly feel independent. I entered the steely modern building in that ugly green dress and some Earth shoes mom lent me; again, something to wear that I hadn't chosen.

Being on the verge of her own nervous breakdown, mom succumbed to dad's wishes, but not without some argument. But, secretly, she knew that my acceptance on a kibbutz was most unlikely. She seemed relieved though that I was at least off the couch and out of the house.

I stood outside the door to the office suite, turned the doorknob and stuck my head inside.

"Come in, come in," said the European-sounding receptionist behind the glass window.

This is such a joke! She's going to figure out I'm not even Jewish!
Even though my grandparents raised my father as Jewish, he was only

familiar with the Passover and Chanukah celebrations that he experienced before joining the army at eighteen. He was a complete rebel when it came to religion and even married mom in a Catholic church in Baltimore. My grandparents attended their only son's wedding with no complaints about his dismissal of their religion. He'd actually converted to Catholicism to make the marriage official. I filled out the form that the receptionist handed me and waited.

"You can go in now," she said, within minutes of my arrival. "Bring the form into Mickey. He'll be your counselor."

Counselor?

Mickey was small and wiry and dressed conservatively. He looked at me with empathy, somehow reading my depressive state. I felt like I was at least twice his size, even though we were probably close in weight, and probably about the same age. I tried to be honest with him and it seemed he was trying to be honest with me too.

I told him that I wasn't really Jewish, even though my grandparents were. I also told him I'd never lived in any kind of communal situation and had no desire to leave the country. When he closed the folder containing my paperwork, he gave me a look of compassion. I could tell my father's idea wasn't going to work. I bid Mickey goodbye, relieved that I wasn't going to be making any trips to Israel.

On the drive back over the hill, to the den with the smoke-stained ceiling and smelly woolen plaid couch, dad's excitement at the possibility of me leaving and eventually working out of the country was weirdly disconcerting. I shut out his predictions of my new life on a kibbutz and drifted back to a happy time in my life.

The cool winter air whooshed across my face. I truly was a city girl. New York's cool air elicited a certain kind of kinesthetic joy in me and made me feel truly alive. It was so different than the more mild L.A. winter. "Would you like to have a coffee?" he asked in a most entrancing way. He truly had woken me from my ballerina-with-blinders-on trek on Fifty-Seventh Street.

"I really can't, but…" I stammered, nervous, even if this charming man with his lovely smile appeared fairly harmless.

"Oh, come on, this truly is a spiritual encounter." He seemed terribly confident that I would acquiesce and he smelled so good.

The cool air and sights and sounds of the city woke me from my dancer's routine. I decided to give myself a brief break from the daily discipline of dancing all day and locking myself in at night to read something I thought was important, like Vladimir Nabokov–Lolita was a favorite–or Dostoyevsky. I loved those Russians, even though the character names were often hard to pronounce and even harder to remember.

"You must be a ballerina," the Frenchman said as we walked west on

Fifty-Seventh Street. He was slight, average height, with dark curly hair, and dark, kind eyes. He looked and sounded sophisticated in a European way and possessed a kind of energy that just bounced right off of him "How'd you guess?" I laughed, as we passed Freed of London. "I was on my way to buy some new pointe shoes," I said, pointing up at the famed sign hanging outside on the second floor.

"You're all pretty easy to detect," he chuckled. "Where are you from?" he asked, as we walked side by side on the bustling street, passing my initial destination.

"Oh…Los Angeles. But I feel like I'm from New York. This feels like home to me. I've been spending summers here since I was fourteen. I moved here permanently when I was 18, three years ago.

Would you like to stop here?" he asked. His fur coat was blowing in the light breeze. I put my hand over the gaping hole in my own vintage fur coat, hoping he didn't notice this embarrassing sign of being a poverty-stricken young dancer in New York.

"You mean The Russian Tea Room?" I asked shyly. I stopped and stared at the famous gold and red doors. It looked like a palace entrance or part of a set in a romantic fairytale ballet.

"Of course. Why not?"

"Okay," I said, wondering why anyone would stop at The Russian Tea Room for a cup of coffee in the middle of the day, when there were things to accomplish, like perfecting my ballet technique. I was used to the Greek coffee shops that were everywhere in New York in the 1980s and affordable on my meager budget. But I went with it, enjoying this moment of reprise.

"Do you realize I haven't even asked you your name?'

"I haven't asked yours either."

"I'm George," he said.

Was I falling for the accent, the sincere brown eyes, or just the fact that he was drawn to me and had boldly stepped up to the plate? Whichever it was, I was falling fast.

"It's so nice to meet you, I said, as we entered those fanciful doors to The Russian Tea Room. "I'm Susan."

"Ah, Suzanne."

As we drove back home, dad stared at the windshield with a determined look. "You're going out tomorrow night on a date," he announced. "Before you move to that kibbutz to better your life, and really know what it is to work."

"How do you know I'm moving to that kibbutz?" I asked. "Maybe they won't take me. I told that counselor that mom's not Jewish, you know. I put it down on the form."

"Jesus Christ, what's wrong with you? You should've said she was.

"I thought you didn't like people to lie," I said, wiping the sweat from my upper lip.

"You couldn't figure that little thing out?" He lit another cigarette, probably his twentieth of the day.

"You always taught me not to lie." I brushed away the smoke, but it came right back like a cloud over my head. "I guess they're not going to take me on the kibbutz," I said, relieved that I wouldn't have to leave my couch.

"Maybe they'll make some kind of adjustment since your grandfather's office is right down the street, and they know him," my father said as he flicked ashes out the open window.

"Why do you bother flicking the ashes out the window when they always blow back inside?" I brushed them off my arm. "And, by the way, why all of a sudden do you think I'll be fine on a kibbutz?" I coughed up more of the seemingly endless smoke.

"Because you have to go somewhere and I think you need to work!" You need to learn what it is to get your hands dirty." He flicked that cigarette butt out the window.

"You do have an ashtray, you know," I said.

Driving in the hot and smog-filled afternoon, I couldn't wait to get back into my sweat pants and robe, and beneath my blanket. Once dad got up our long driveway and into the garage, we opened our doors simultaneously, and got out of his car. We walked toward the house in silence. Mom's Earth shoes were uncomfortable and walking was painful.

How was I going to work on a kibbutz?

And then dad started in, perhaps to distract me from lying down, yet again.

"Remember, you're going out on a date tomorrow night," he blurted. "I showed Benito's assistant your picture and he can't wait to take you out. I think you should see if someone would put up with you for a night."

My life in this self-imposed prison was truly becoming a horror. Dad was trying anything–a date, working on a kibbutz–anything to get me out of the house, to snap me out of this unnatural state. He didn't consider my spiritual death to be real or fueled by my loss of dance. Perhaps I was making him feel like a failure as a parent, but mostly, my deteriorating presence was disturbing his peace.

"You're setting me up with a car mechanic?" I groaned as dad opened a couple of the wooden shudders. They were normally closed to keep the stifling heat out and the air-conditioning in, hence no light, and the prison effect. "I don't remember anything about agreeing to a date with a car mechanic!"

"You think you're some kind of a queen? I did tell you."

"I don't remember."

"You're going," dad said, as he turned on the light. He snatched the

L.A. Times from the couch to search for my crossword puzzle. He tore it from the paper and tossed my saving grace into the garbage can. Desperate to take off the ugly green dress, I trudged upstairs to my room to find my sweats.

"I'm not going on a date with someone I don't know," I repeated as I came downstairs and back into the den.

"You're going! "I don't care if I have to go with you!" he said, lighting up yet another cigarette. "You're getting off this fucking couch or I'm going to throw you out on your ass."

I got under the smelly crocheted blanket, trying to hide from this harsh interaction. Then he uttered his painful truth. "Someone is crazy enough to take you out, and I need peace for one night."

"I haven't even seen any of my real friends," I pleaded, as though I truly had something to do.

"You're going! It's all set up, and you have no say in the matter," he said, taking another long drag on his cigarette.

"HOW CAN YOU DO THIS TO ME?" I screamed. "I'M STAYING HOME!"

I returned home at 3 a.m., numb from the cocaine I snorted with Arturo. To appease my father, I did take a shower and managed to wash my hair. I even put on a little mascara, after digging it up in an untouched make-up bag at the bottom of one of my dresser drawers.

Practically stumbling into my childhood bedroom with the white, pink, and blue mini-flowered wallpaper, I pulled down the white eyelet bed cover, got into my fluffy queen-sized bed, and stared at the white ceiling.

I felt so fucking awful. That creepy date wasn't my idea. I was just blowing in the wind with nowhere to go and nothing to say. The coke certainly didn't cure my depression even if that pushy guy stuffed into slick pants, a polyester flowered shirt, zip-up short boots, and a couple of gold chains was convinced it would. The absurdity of it was astounding, especially since it was all set up through my father. All I felt was nausea while he grinded on top of me. I stared up at his ugly, smoke-stained ceiling, wondering when he'd be finished. I had no voice to say: "No thank you, maybe next time." It's not like I was attracted to him. I was just following orders like any good ballerina.

"How was your date?" dad asked early the next morning, staring past me at the breakfast table.

"It was okay. I had a nice time," I lied with absolute gloom, shuffling away to refill my coffee cup. I fumbled my way back to the breakfast room, slid my heavy chair from the table, and sat down again. I put my cup down, stood up and pulled my chair back out. "I think I'll go back to bed for a while."

"You must be exhausted," mom said, putting her hand over mine for a brief moment of absurd empathy. She was completely unaware of the hideous evening I spent snorting coke and getting dry-fucked by a car mechanic in tacky clothes.

"What the fuck can she be exhausted from?" dad said, interrupting our moment. "She lies down all fucking day long!" He threw his morning paper down and got up from the table. "And don't you dare search for that crossword puzzle!"

I shuffled off to my bedroom and crawled back into my bed so I could hide away a little longer. I drifted off to yet another daydream of the life I once had. Staring at my ceiling there was the image of the beautiful brownstone on Seventy-Fourth Street off Columbus Avenue that George and I moved into only weeks after I'd met him on Fifty-Seventh Street.

George decided his ultra-modern high-rise apartment wasn't quite appropriate for our new life together. There were five flights up to our small but charming, brick-walled penthouse. At twenty, I was finally experiencing what it was to really be with someone. George owned his own business in the health food industry and was doing remarkably well. He even helped out many of his family members who were struggling financially. His small group of eccentric friends would gather weekly at our apartment. It was often Shabbat that we celebrated.

As an Orthodox Jew, George's life was full of ritual: Shabbat meant no electricity or work from sundown on Friday, to sundown on Saturday, as well as no travel and no exchange of money. And even though his religious rituals were completely foreign to me, I experienced a sort of domestic bliss. His joy about life itself was intoxicating. I helped cook our macrobiotic dinners and loved playing hostess to his French speaking, much older friends.

One of his best friends was William Dufty who had written *Sugar Blues*, and had collaborated with Billie Holiday on *Lady Sings the Blues*, and was a bit of a celebrity at the time. Bill would traipse across Central Park from the Fifth Avenue palace of his ex-wife, Gloria Swanson, barefoot, smoking one of his skinny dark cigarettes. He'd announce himself on the intercom, run up those five flights of stairs, still barefoot, and immediately start in on a diatribe concerning Gloria, and their divorce. He never wore shoes!

It was a time of absolute bliss. I had nothing to worry about except perfecting my ballet technique and learning to be with people who communicated in a different way than me. My new European friends often addressed me as either Suzanne or Mignon. I was the *Dear One* at a truly blessed time.

There was the possibility that George and I would eventually get married. Six months in, he even called dad in L.A. to see if I'd convert to Judaism. But my dad, being my dad, told him, "I don't think she gives a shit about religion." Besides, something that good wasn't going to last forever. And it didn't. No matter how happy we were together, I still ached to perform and couldn't just be in class twice a day without actually preparing for an actual run of a ballet. I couldn't continue with a life solely based on his rituals. I needed my own that included the sacred space of class, rehearsals, and the theater. I needed to travel to Europe to get a full-time job doing the only thing I knew how to do. Ultimately, I needed to dance more than I needed to share in someone else's life.

Chapter 11

EUROPE

Virgil Paleru and Susan in Hannover, Germany, 1982.

Was it possible that this person I'd become, this person that couldn't get up from her parent's couch, had already lived with two different men? Was it possible that I had lived and danced in Europe? That I had once carved out a life for myself in New York City, away from my La-La Land home? Embedded in that couch, it seemed I'd never done anything in my twenty-four years. But the reality was I had.

"We have a way of fixing that," my profusely sweating landlord, Bruno, said. I stood there, dumbfounded by his disgusting flirtatious manner. His office, not too far from my studio apartment, was a disorganized mess, strewn with papers, rusty file cabinets, and loads of dust. The family of roaches didn't seem to mind human intruders. They didn't even scatter when I retreated a couple of steps to get away from his leering stare. There were underarm stains on his blue coffee-stained shirt and drool running down his chin. When he stepped even closer in my direction, I took a few more steps away, suddenly aware of his intentions.

"We can take care of your late rent."

"That's okay." I turned toward the door.

"Don't be like that," he said as I slammed the door behind me and bolted down those dirty stairs, onto Seventy-Third Street. "You really think you're something!" he yelled down that stairwell. "People like you don't deserve…"

I was on the street, headed for the subway downtown, never to return to my studio apartment.

Good Bye New York. I'm on my way to Europe. I am going to get a job.

After a pretty amazing year together, and the most love I'd ever shared in my life, we decided to separate. George wanted a traditional wife and children, not a dancer who would go anywhere to perform. Life needed to move on for both of us. Hence, the tiny one-room apartment that I lived in for a few months before going to Europe. I needed to get back in shape after severely injuring my back, performing sometimes two *Nutcrackers* a day in Chicago. The stage's subfloor was concrete, not sprung, and with all the endorphins dancing on stage always ignited in me, I ignored the agonizing pain that had crept into my back. With a bulging disc and sciatica, I refused to stop performing and completed the entire run. Even though I could have collected workers' compensation, and gone back to New York to be with George, I needed to dance, in pain, or not.

The relationship was inspired and hopeful, with evenings full of laughter, theater, music and art. Every evening was a celebration of some kind. I was never happier, unless I was dancing full-time, but I wasn't.

In Europe, I felt I could get a full contract so I could take care of myself financially. Plus, I wasn't cut out for waitressing. I was too shy to ask people whether they wanted their burger medium or medium rare, and what dish they might want on the side. I would shake just coming near people to ask, well, anything. Speaking above a whisper was a challenge and, somehow, I believed the people I waited on must have found me completely incompetent.

Nonetheless, I carried on, got myself to my job, my chiropractor, to the YMCA to swim laps, and into ballet class twice a day.

I knew from my contacts in professional classes around town, German and Swiss companies sometimes offered contracts. I was told that sometimes, only sometimes, those ballet/opera companies hired Americans. At almost five-foot-eight I was too tall for most American classical companies of the time, except of course for the New York City Ballet. But that ship had unfortunately already sailed when had I left the School of American Ballet at seventeen, and with it my true opportunity as a Balanchine dancer.

Goodbye New York! Goodbye dear, wonderful, George! Thank you for putting up with an obsessed dancer that did truly love you. Your great smile will never leave my memory, nor will your kind heart and brilliant sense of humor. You taught me what it is to laugh, and what it is to love another human being. Thank you for showing me the potential for love and life. Time to move on.

After my horrific encounter with my landlord, I crashed at my friend Patrick's apartment for a couple of months while my back healed. Once well again, I was on a plane to Europe, my first trip abroad.

In London, my hands shook as I tried to use the huge black payphones that looked and worked nothing like the silver ones I was accustomed to on the streets of New York. Having no idea how much it cost to make a local call, I fumbled through my wallet to find some British coins. I opened my little black address book. Even though it was a cool October day, a drop of sweat fell right on the page, blurring the number. I dropped the strange looking coins into the slot, and started dialing, hoping for the best.

"Hello?"

"Hi, this is Susan. Nagmeh told you about me, and that I'd be coming to London for a couple of days. I just got in…" I stuttered.

"Yes, we have the date and time of your arrival right here," a woman said. "We're close by; wait at the front of the station. We'll see you."

She hung up. I wiped the sweat off my face and figured I was in good hands. My New York City friend Nagmeh, who I'd danced with in the Eglevsky Ballet, was a warm and kind girl, and a terrifically gifted dancer. Her Persian family had fled Iran in 1979 during the Revolution and had homes in various parts of the world. Lucky for me that her sister and her husband were willing to put me up for of couple of nights in their London flat.

An hour later I settled into the small freezing room with a tiny pullout cot that was made up just for me. Stranger in a strange land, but all would be okay as soon as I got to class, as soon as I got to dance. Thankfully, I knew where to go.

After unpacking a few things, brushing my teeth, and throwing freezing cold water on my face, I settled into my cot and crawled under the covers, chilled to the bone from the early fall weather of London.

I'd finally arrived, had made it, even if I was going to have to be a bit of a vagabond for a while.

The next morning I grabbed my dance bag, stuffed in a leotard, tights, legwarmers and my flat ballet shoes, and was out the front door, hailing one of those huge, black London taxis within minutes.

"The Pineapple dance studio," I told the buttoned-up and friendly driver, "It's near the Haymarket district, I think."

"I know exactly where it is," he reassured me.

Off we went into the London fog. The grey skies didn't bother me. I was prepared for them, having already spent three years away from the

Southern California sunshine.

After exiting the cab onto the old cobblestone, I looked around at the unfamiliar but glorious architecture. London felt just right and I wished it could be my new home. *Everybody speaks English!* But, there was nowhere for me to dance. The Royal Ballet didn't hire Americans, unless they trained there, just like New York City Ballet didn't hire Brits. The training was so different for both companies.

Once I got into the dance studio, and the pianist started those first few bars of music, I was home, and all the anxiety of getting to a new country was relieved. As long as I could dance, all would be okay.

Getting ready to leave after the class, a twenty-something dancer with a heavy Irish brogue chatted with me in the dressing room, noting that she'd never seen me at the studio before. I could barely understand her English with her accent, but managed to convey I was on my way to Germany and Switzerland to look for work. She immediately offered that her American boyfriend danced in Hannover, Germany, and that one of the female corps dancers had picked up and left, just a few days earlier.

"You should go there immediately," she said. "I know they'll hire you."

She looked at me with her beautiful green eyes and I knew she meant well. She seemed so strong and grounded in a way that I wasn't, and she bubbled over with a kind of joy that made me feel welcome in this new, old world.

"Why don't you audition?" I asked, figuring she might like to live closer to her boyfriend and have a dance job at the same time.

"I'm in nursing school here, until I can get a job near him," she said. "I have no desire to be professional. I just love to dance. You need to get the ferry from White Cliffs of Dover and then a train through Belgium. It will take at least ten hours, but you need to go now, seriously."

"I was hoping to stay here a little longer, and then travel and audition a bit," I said.

"If you start auditioning now, you might not get a contract until next year. They need someone right away."

I guess she saw my desperation or was just an angel on my shoulder. I thanked her for her advice and said goodbye. That night I bid my hosts goodbye and off I went on a long and lonely trip to Hannover.

I was the only passenger aboard that train. The conductor was a gentle, unassuming middle-aged guy with whom I felt safe. He spoke to me about his family for almost the entire hour-long trip to the coast.

When the White Cliffs of Dover were in full view from the train window, I couldn't believe my eyes. I pulled my journal from my bag to record their majesty. I couldn't believe how lucky I was to have this extraordinary experience, trying in my clumsy way to write about what I saw before me. The friendly train conductor escorted me to where I'd wait for the ferry to Ostend, perhaps worried I might miss my connection. And before I knew it, I was on the long train ride to Germany. I was happily on my way to get a job.

The first day I auditioned, I got in. The sweet young Irish woman I'd met in London had apparently told her boyfriend, Geoffrey, that "An American girl is on her way to audition, so say hi to her if she gets in or not." And he did.

Geoffrey made me feel completely welcome into this new family of forty or so classical dancers, all with very different training. He was short, stocky, and had the determined look of a prizefighter from New Jersey, which was where he was from. It was helpful that I could understand his English much better than his girlfriend's. He'd been there for a year and was determined to leave after the finish of this particular season, for a better company, he told me secretively that first day.

It was a surprisingly heterosexual company, with dancers from all over the world. There were four actual couples, which was somewhat unusual in the American ballet world, all trying to make lives for themselves in a country that had money to support the arts but lacked their own classically-trained dancers. We only had three or four actual German dancers in the company. And two were over forty, ancient in ballet years. Basically, they were just creaking along, collecting their paychecks, horribly injured by the constant grind of keeping up a technique. The German government supported their artists, so they could be employed until they retired or were made to retire.

Our principal male dancer was a short, stocky Turkish guy who could jump and turn like no one else. His wife, who he had brought along from Turkey, was an extremely tiny yet voluptuous corps dancer with a sketchy technique. There was a British couple with kids, who had danced there for ten years, both, still in the corps. One of our principal females was a lovely American dancer, married to a German soloist who was also surprisingly impressive.

Almost immediately I made friends with two young British women in the corps. Bunny, the company gossip, had introduced herself to me the first day. She and the other young Brit, Elizabeth, had a kick watching me get frustrated by the German directions for my first rehearsal of the opera *Aida* only two days after I had arrived. Along with a few other corps dancers, we all performed the very next night as fairies, in beautiful long tulle tutus, flitting in and around the towering opera singers. In between their dramatic singing, they'd whisper loudly, *Rechts…links…* and chuckle at the new dancer, me, who had no idea which direction to flutter about in after having had only one rehearsal. I was basically filling in for the mysterious girl who'd jumped ship only a couple of weeks before.

Even if the opera singers had a ball making fun of me, I was thrilled to be safe, and employed in a decent company with a gorgeous state theater.

It was all so different from my New York dance experience. Dancing for the opera didn't really require much ballet skill, and before leaving for Europe I'd worked so hard to improve my technique, after healing from my back injury. I was strong, and I needed to perform, like a racehorse that needed to run. Everybody assured me that I'd get to dance in the three ballets scheduled for the year, but my restless spirit wanted more.

Within a month, on a day off, I traveled to Berlin to audition for the Berlin Ballet. After my audition, which was basically to take a company class, the burly and handsome artistic director invited me to his fancy office where he asked me in his German-accented English if I was employed.

"I just signed a contract in Hannover and I'm a little frustrated having to dance for the opera so much."

"You should have come here first," he said. "We're a bigger company, with more ballets and more performances in the season."

"Well, I'm happy to move here right away," I said, my heart fluttering with anticipation.

"I'd love to hand you a contract, but once you sign a contract in Germany, you can't break it.

"But…"

"I'm so sorry. Maybe next year," he said, staring through his rose-colored sunglasses.

I got up from my seat, kicking myself for being so naïve. I wished I had given myself a chance at a bigger company. I had gone to Hannover for safety and was now tied to my contract with a sad and dejected heart.

Virgil was a tall and dashing soloist from Romania who I noticed when I first arrived in Hannover. He had a great technique and I was impressed, but not interested. Somehow, he hadn't introduced himself until he came up to me after class, the day after I got back from Berlin.

"Where did you go?" he asked in his unfamiliar accent.

"Oh, just a little sightseeing trip," I said, not wanting him to know I went off to audition. I'd never spoken to him before so I was surprised he knew I had been away for the day.

"Bunny told me," he said, running his hand through his dark wavy hair. "She knows everybody business. Want to have a coffee in the canteen?"

"Okay," I said, unsure of his intentions and why Bunny, who I'd entrusted with the information about my secret trip, would tell on me.

Geoffrey, the boyfriend of the Irish girl I'd met in London, had an easy rapport with most everybody in the company; he came up to us and gave Virgil a little nudge. "How come you like all the American girls, even though your English sucks?"

Virgil took a hold of him and gave him a friendly knock on his head.

81

"You should have introduced us. You speak American."

"Sorry," Geoffrey said to me. "I thought you were still getting over your last girlfriend."

Virgil glared at him as though he was interrupting something important.

"You took her place," Geoffrey said. "She went back to America to get a better job, smart girl."

Virgil gave him another disconcerting look, took my hand and escorted me to the canteen.

"Bye guys," Geoffrey chuckled, leaning his head down the stairwell. "Don't do anything I wouldn't do."

We sat down at one of the long community-style tables and Virgil asked me what I wanted.

"Just a coffee," I said, knowing we'd be rehearsing in half an hour and couldn't dance with food bouncing around in my stomach.

"Back in a minute," he said. "I have to eat something."

I looked at all the life happening around me. Opera singers in grand costumes on a dress rehearsal break surrounded me. They were eating hearty meals, drinking all sorts of alcohol, and communicating in a foreign way. Not only were they speaking mostly in German, they all seemed so animated and dramatic and drunk. How were they going to rehearse so inebriated?

Virgil returned with two sandwiches, a coffee for me, buttermilk for him, and pulled out a chair opposite me. "I have ulcer, so I can't drink coffee; too much acid." He lit up a cigarette and took a long sensuous drag, then bit into one of his cheese sandwiches. "Want a bite?" he asked. "They make good sandwich here."

"I'm okay."

Exotic and attractive, his dark wide-spaced eyes drew me in. I sipped my coffee, trying to figure out what he was saying in his broken English, wishing that I could eat something too.

"Where are you from?" I asked. "I don't recognize your accent."

"I'm from Romania," he said. "It's shit country. I love it here."

"Is that kind of like Russia?" I asked.

"Ceausescu is shit dictator. My country is very poor."

Between bites of his sandwiches and sips of his buttermilk, he took long drags on his cigarette while we struggled to communicate. Besides the loud clutter of plates, glasses, and people getting in and out of their chairs, it was a dichotomy of spirits, with the huge opera singers nearby having no problems whatsoever expressing themselves. Our quiet dancer voices were nearly drowned out by noise.

Virgil put out his cigarette, took one last bite of his second sandwich, and said, "Let's go…we have rehearsal in ten minutes."

The moment we arrived in the dance studio, Virgil went one way and

I went the other–and there was Bunny, right in my face.

"Did he put the make on you?" she asked.

"No. We just sat across from each other with very little to say."

"That's how it starts," she said. "I'd watch out if I were you."

Virgil began his warm up at the barre, taking note of the prying young British blabbermouth, and gave me a warm smile. Soon enough, we were all dancing, doing what we did best.

He drove me home, or managed to talk me into driving me home, and then escorted me up the stairs and to the front door of my charming sublet that I would only have for another week.

"Thanks so much for the ride," I said, opening the heavy black wood door. "I'm so glad we've finally met."

"Aren't you going to invite me in?"

"Well, I guess, for a minute," I stuttered, wondering what the hell else we could possibly talk about since his English wasn't that great, and I couldn't speak French, German, or Romanian.

"You like my Mercedes?"

"My mom has almost the exact same model in Los Angeles. I'm from there."

Before I knew it, we were on the couch, kissing. He certainly was fast, yet surprisingly gentle. He seemed completely comfortable with his heterosexuality. I guess I was too, hence the seduction. I wasn't used to dancers being sensual with me. All my guy dancer friends back in New York were gay, and loved discussing art and culture, and who made an appearance at Studio 54, or Max's Kansas City the night before, and their boyfriends of the moment.

Virgil and I connected even better without words. I guess you could call it good chemistry. It wasn't that strange, considering both of us were used to living and expressing through our bodies. When we finished, we did talk a bit; he didn't just run off. He said he liked me, plus, he had those sad eyes that had seen too much, or certainly more than I had in my young life. He even suggested that he might get to partner me soon. "I have to teach you more Bolshoi technique," he said. "So, you can become soloist, and then you will be my partner."

"That sounds great," I said. The thought of him being my partner was certainly enticing. We were both tall. He'd be able to reach my long arms when I was on pointe. It seemed like a good plan.

Within a week, Virgil talked me into moving into his tiny, cement-floored apartment, on the fourth floor of the state-subsidized building he'd been living in for two years. He'd actually been living there with the girl who'd left the company, the other American, and he was lonely. He knew that I needed a new place to stay since my sublet lease was ending. Somehow, it was convenient for both of us.

Hence, my new insight into the life of a dancer from a Communist country who had known real deprivation. I liked hearing about Virgil's life, and it helped that his English was improving. His formative years were so different from mine, growing up in the San Fernando Valley amongst a certain amount of American privilege, except that we'd both been dancing since we were kids. He basically grew up an orphan, separated from his family at twelve to receive his very strict classical training.

"Ballet is shit life," he'd tell me almost daily. I think he really meant it. He danced because it was all he knew how to do and had enough talent to get where he was, not because he truly loved it. It really was just a job for him.

He didn't tell me everything right away, and I don't think it was because his English was limited. After cohabiting for a few weeks we came home together from a rehearsal one afternoon and the phone was ringing off the hook. "Don't answer it," he said.

"Okay," I said, as we entered our sparse apartment.

"Don't say anything," he urged, as I dropped my heavy dance bag in the living room. He picked up the telephone receiver.

"Hello," he said in Romanian. (I'd learned a few words, by then.) He waved the phone at me, silently mouthing the words, "Don't say anything."

I grabbed a piece of marzipan from my bag, unwrapped it, and stared out our one window looking out into the courtyard. There wasn't even a single bush.

Virgil's life was more complicated than I ever imagined. First, he was married. Second, he had children. I only found out this information because we had come home at the same time that day. Since he had a soloist position, we didn't always rehearse or finish at the same time, except this fateful day. Somehow, he managed to get his wife to call at more opportune times for him like when I was rehearsing with the rest of the corps. So, he was able to keep his family a secret until now.

I nibbled on my marzipan, staring out the window, wondering what the hell I'd gotten myself into. When he hung up I asked, "Is there a reason why whomever you were talking to shouldn't know that I live with you?"

"Yes. I have wife in Romania. She's actress."

"Now you tell me," I said, standing there, a wide-eyed twenty-one-year-old.

"I'm never going back. Romania is shit country. "Don't eat marzipan. You're dancer."

Accepting the reality I'd created for myself, I tried to enjoy the domesticity of our life together, and even helped Virgil pick out the gifts he sent to his family in Romania. The gifts were necessary items; things they couldn't afford or just weren't available there. The authorities apparently rifled through those packages and items would go missing. His wife would call the next day crying that she "needed her cigarettes and shampoo. They took almost everything, all the toys for the kids."

Even though I'd been there only three months, I knew I had to get out of Germany. I couldn't continue living with a married man, even if Virgil tried to convince me he'd never see his wife and children again. Most importantly, I wasn't in love, and I wasn't dancing to my fullest potential. But I had to finish out my contract. So, I carried on, wishing my life was somewhere else. Somewhere that I could dance more.

A few weeks later I made a desperate call to George, just to say hi and be reminded of his joyous, beautiful voice. We'd been apart almost a year by then, but I knew he'd be happy to hear from me, even if he was in a committed relationship. Virgil wasn't home. The time was right. There was no way I'd let him listen in on a conversation with my ex-boyfriend who didn't know my new situation. So, with apprehension and a bit of excitement, I picked up our heavy German phone and dialed. I almost fainted when he answered after a single ring.

"Ah, Chéri. I knew it was you."

"You did?" I said, trying to hide my tears of loneliness.

"I knew you'd call sometime. Do you like it there, my Chéri?"

"Well, I miss New York...my friends...you."

"I'm coming to Paris next month for business. Come stay with me."

"I can't...I mean...I'm working," I insisted, while aching to be near him.

"I'm staying at the Hotel de Crillon," he said. "It's the most elegant hotel in the world. Don't you get a day off ever?"

We talked a bit longer, and his *joi de vivre* started rubbing off on me, even if I was incredibly torn as to what to do. My leaving for a couple of days would spark Virgil's paranoia and jealousy. Although Virgil controlled me, I also leaned on him for a certain amount of stability.

When he got home that evening, I told him that I'd be taking a short trip, and that he shouldn't worry about anything; I was completely over George. I also reminded him of his own marriage. I convinced him that George and I were just friends at that point, which was actually true. That fact didn't stop Virgil from being a jealous twenty-seven–year-old with his own set of abandonment issues.

When I got to Paris, after a ten-hour train ride, George was waiting for me at the most beautiful hotel in the world. I walked into the suite, dazzled by its elegance, so happy to see my first love. Exhausted, I fell onto the big plush bed, weeping with happiness.

"Ah Chéri," he said. "My sensitive *artiste*." His warm and beautiful smile made it seem as though no time had passed.

But it had. Things had changed for both of us and our beautiful life together was marred by so much time spent away. The magic was over, or

I wasn't capable of being with two men, even if it was just for a night. I never thought for one second that I would need to get back to Virgil, but I did. So, the very next day, after taking in a few sights of incredible Paris, I went back on the train. With no small amount of tears George and I bid each other *adieu*, never to see each other again.

A couple of months passed uneventfully, except my parents decided to take a trip to Germany to see their only daughter. They had no idea that I was on my way out of the company, but dad had always wanted to see the castles, and for some macabre reason, the concentration camps. He had been a history major after all, obsessed with Hitler's rise and fall. So, it only made sense that he should visit the country where it all took place. I was a great excuse for their late spring expedition. Plus, dad mentioned that he could, maybe pick up a nice old Mercedes Benz really cheap and ship it home.

I set them up to stay with an Australian opera singer, jovial John Pickering, who I'd become fast friends with after performing in *Orpheus in the Underworld* together. He had a nice big solo and I was one of the cancan dancers. It was probably the most fun I had dancing in an opera, earlier in my contract. Being the generous artist that he was, he offered his place up for a few nights. Dad couldn't have been happier.

Although John had a nice big flat on the outskirts of Hannover, I was a little nervous about my parents seeing my own living situation, but, of course, they had to see the set-up. So, after a matinee performance of the ballet, *Copellia*, in which I was one of the peasant girls and Virgil was the male soloist, we invited them over for a visit.

Even if they were impressed with the gorgeous theater we had just performed in, they were shocked by our small and cramped living quarters. By the lack of a shower in our bathroom and the cement floors and plastic furniture.

Even though my parents knew that I lived with George for a year in New York, they'd never met him, or come to visit. This was the first time they saw me cohabiting with a man, and one from a communist country, no less. They didn't know that Virgil was married with two children, but somehow, they had a hard time disguising their feelings in front of us.

Mortified by what I viewed as my parent's judgmental behavior, I talked dad into taking us out to dinner the next night, so that they could make up for being so rude to Virgil. I didn't want him to feel bad about my parents' inability to approve of him, or me for that matter.

At a Greek restaurant near our apartment, Mom picked at her food, while we ate quietly. Then she broke the uncomfortable silence with one of her zingers. "I thought you didn't like dancers," she said. I almost died of embarrassment right there, having told her already that Virgil understood English very well. "Funny that you ended up with one."

"Jean please," dad said, chomping on a lamb chop.

"You could still go to college, you know," mom added. I buried my head in Virgil's shoulder, aching with shame.

Virgil was now my anchor to reality, my anchor to what I was–a dancer looking for love from pretty much anyone. It was clear that my parents weren't ever going to be there for me emotionally, no matter what I did, no matter who I was.

We drove them to the airport the next day and bid them goodbye, both relieved that the ordeal was over.

A month later my contract ended. I had no desire to renew it, even if Virgil wanted me to stay. "You'll be soloist in one more year. I promise you," he said.

Two weeks later I was on my way.

"I don't know where I'm going to dance, but I'll find something," I said, as he loaded my two bags with all I owned into his Mercedes.

We drove in silence to the airport, neither of us knowing what to say.

"You'll be back," he said, helping me unload my luggage.

"I don't think so," I said as we hugged goodbye.

Even though Virgil and I had been together less than a year, it was hard to leave him. There was some love there, of course, some co-dependence. He was the second man I'd ever lived with, after all. And even if he wasn't the great romancer that George was, I felt safe with him, protected.

Chapter 12

PUZZLES

Los Angeles, 1984

It had been six months. I couldn't drive anymore, or to put it more
realistically, dad wouldn't let me get behind the wheel. He didn't trust my
odd behavior. So, on yet another sunny hot day, mom managed to get me
back into that ugly green culottes dress and into her car.

We were going to get some crossword puzzles and word games at a
nearby Von's market. I had run out of puzzles and there was nothing to do
to occupy my mind. I didn't really want to go anywhere. The depression
had completely overtaken me but getting up from the couch and out the
door, even briefly, was supposed to be a good thing. It would be my first
time out since that disgusting date with Arturo and the weird trip with dad
to the Jewish Federation.

Mom was happy I was out of my sweat pants and not lying down. In
the car all the things I hated about suburban L.A. were right in front of me.
I loathed the strip malls that were all over the San Fernando Valley. I had
become a sophisticated city girl in my years away from Los Angeles
suburbia.

We drove in silence down the long driveway. My discomfort with
being in my own skin and out of that house was palpable, but I needed to
offer some sign to my parents that I was really okay. As if just getting out
of the house meant that was really true. I peered out the window to see
what still existed on my hometown main street. Most everything looked the
same, and then, there it was; my old dance studio that was still run by my
teacher, Natalie–my ballet mom. I could never tell her what had happened
to me. She'd never understand. She had still expected great things from
me, even though I'd fucked up at barely seventeen, leaving Balanchine's
school. She knew all about that, since I'd come home to recover from my
sprained ankle and finish high school.

But my current horrifying condition must be kept a secret. I felt a
wave of summer heat and even more discomfort as we passed the white
building with the black awning and the old sign that read: Natalie Claire's

Ballet La Juenesse. I had absolute shame at having ruined my life only blocks from the ballet studio that had once given me one.

"Do you want to take class later?" mom asked.

"No, that's okay. I don't really feel like it."

"Natalie would love to see you. She used to always ask about you and how you were doing, when you were dancing. I still run into her at Gelson's occasionally."

"I don't think she'll understand," I said. "You haven't told her I'm home, have you?" The anxiety that my old ballet teacher might know the truth of my condition was overwhelming. My shame was crushing. "Can we not talk about this?" I pleaded.

"She's had a couple more face-lifts since you last saw her," mom continued. "She always wears those big sunglasses to hide the bruises, but she likes to stay beautiful. I don't know what's happened to poor Michael. She's probably still berating him for his drinking, and his weight. Very sad."

We passed the market and the drugstore and the other familiar establishments, finally pulling into the huge strip mall parking lot. "Do you want me to come in with you?" mom asked.

"No, I'll be okay."

I didn't want to feel any more humiliation, having my doting mother alongside me, so I pushed open the car door and stepped onto the hot black asphalt. Any pride I might have had was gone. Yet, in this San Fernando Valley parking lot there was a glimmer of a brand-new life. I had actually left the house, even if mom had to drive.

Shuffling into the huge Von's market, I felt paranoid, out of place and physically uncomfortable. My initial instinct was to rush back to the safety of mom's car. Shoppers pushed big carts filled with food for their families. People chattered about things that seemed inane. Life in the San Fernando Valley felt absurd to me. How do people do it? Did they not realize how painful it is to be alive? Why were they having so much fun in a stupid, fucking market?

Wearing that ugly green culottes dress with the elastic waistline stretched to accommodate my new size, I carried on as though I'd never danced a step in my life, completely disconnected from my body, my once sensitive instrument. I approached the aisle with the crossword puzzle and word games books. Dad had effectively gotten rid of my *L.A. Times* crossword puzzles to get me off the couch, so the word games would have to suffice, for now, anyway. The fluorescent lighting was a fierce assault on my now sensitive eyes, but I carried on, blinking and hoping no one noticed me. I picked up a few different puzzle books and moved on.

Just put one foot in front of the other.

Finding the candy section, I picked up a large bag of Peanut M&M's. I carried a stack of puzzle books and my bag of M&M's to the checkout counter and waited nervously while the shopper before me purchased what looked like groceries for an entire family. I turned my head from side to side like a nervous bird, paranoid that I would see someone I knew, or worse yet, that they would see me.

Anxious about just being out in the world, I bought all of my supplies so I could go home and retreat to the couch. But I wasn't done. I needed to open a bank account for the unemployment checks I had received since being fired from the Cleveland Ballet. The five envelopes stacked unopened in my bedroom and were now in my purse. I shuffled out of the market and was struck by a glaring sun that blocked my view of the Bank of America only a few yards away. Walking the short distance was daunting, but I needed to do it now.

I can do this. Just put one foot in front of the other.

The bank lobby was a whole new story. A long line of people stood waiting for a teller. I was again in close proximity to other human beings who had lives, things to do, and responsibilities. And then, there she was.

It was Marta from high school who used to dance too. Not professionally, but in gym class. The people ahead of me finally finished and, even though I looked down at the ground, I felt so exposed, so naked. She was waiting for me behind the bank teller counter with a big recognizing smile. I walked slowly towards her.

"Hi Sue," she said kindly.

She actually recognizes me? Cringing with embarrassment, I choked out a "Hi Marta," and numbness raced over my entire disgusting body. What was I supposed to say? *Hi Marta, I'm in the midst of a mental breakdown, so please don't notice I'm here depositing my unemployment checks into my new account that YOU have to open for me. I've been hiding out at my parent's house for six months, and I really don't want to leave my makeshift hospital ever again.*

"Call me; it would be so nice to catch up."

"Ok." I took her number in my sweaty hand. Yeah, right. I certainly wasn't going to reveal my soap opera to an acquaintance that knew nothing about me. Besides, she had a real job, working in the real world, which was completely foreign to me. There was nothing I could explain to her. Plus, I was in no place emotionally to understand another twenty-four-year-old's dilemmas. The irony was how dirty and stringy Marta's hair used to be in high school. She was the one who looked like she needed help. Now, it appeared she had it together. How did she manage this masquerade?

Slinking back to mom's car, I opened the car door, and pleaded, "Let's get home, please."

"I'm so proud of you," she said with some empathy. "We should do this again."

We drove up the driveway to a disconcerting sight. A couple pieces of luggage were sitting there, unattended, and they looked like they were mine! All of a sudden, dad burst out of the house and started to open the wrought-iron gate. The sound of that old gate scraping the asphalt had become familiar, a comforting sound, knowing that one of my parents was finally home, and would be some company to relieve my loneliness. But now, the sound was daunting. I looked out the car window, and instead of opening the gate for us to drive through, dad opened it just enough to get one of the bags through. It looked like he was going to put my luggage in mom's idling car! I got out and started to grab one of the bags from him.

"She could still go to college," mom cried.

"She's leaving now, and I don't care where she goes!" dad yelled, yanking the bag I was holding and dumping it in the trunk.

"We can't do this to her. She's our only daughter!" mom cried.

"I don't care if she's Princess Grace, She's leaving my house today!"

My mother and I managed to get the two bags out of the trunk, and then dad and I fought over them physically. I almost broke his thumb in our tussle over that luggage.

I needed to get back to that couch and start in on those crossword puzzles. I needed to get back to my safe place, and disappear again.

Dad followed me up the short flight of stairs, through the den, past the breakfast room and finally to my bedroom where my bed was still unmade. "You've been living on your own for six years now, and you will continue to in whatever way you can," he said, rubbing his injured thumb. "We're helping you become an invalid, and I'm not going to be responsible for that crime," he added while I unzipped a suitcase. That grating sound scared me even more than it had a few months before when I had first moved home. It now seemed more final. I was never leaving this house.

"I have nowhere to go. I can't dance," I blubbered while unpacking my red corduroy Norma Kamali snap-front outfit that I'd never fit into again.

"You've done this to yourself, and I don't know why," mom cried, as she joined the dysfunctional scene in my bedroom. She helped me put my cherished size six clothes that once completely hung on me, and now I could barely squeeze into, into the pine closet. Dad marched down to the den, unable to deal with two emotionally devastated women.

"She needs help!" mom reminded him as he settled into his king's chair for a cigarette and gin martini. I was a symbol of mom's failure as a parent, but she still didn't want to let me go. She knew at the deepest level what a mental institution was like. She wasn't going to let me suffer that, and still enjoyed to some extent taking care of me in my damaged state. It gave her a purpose, even if her own life had been horribly interrupted.

After finishing my unpacking, I went back to the den and watched dad take the pimento green olives off the toothpick in his martini glass. He popped one into his mouth and sipped his drink. I sat next to him on the wool plaid couch, feeling awful about almost breaking his thumb.

"I'm sorry. I didn't mean to hurt you. It's just so hard."

"I told you not to come home, right?"

"I know, but I didn't know where else to go…to get better."

"You're clearly not getting better," he said. "Want my other olive?"

Chapter 13

THE DEAL

My parents made me an offer I couldn't refuse. The deal was to get a job, any job, and in return I could stay at their house until I made enough money to move out. So, without much thought—more like obeying orders—a few days later, I dragged myself into the shower and scrubbed the dirt and sweat off the body I no longer felt connected to. It didn't even bother me anymore that I was fat. I didn't care. I certainly didn't want to go back to being a constant exposed nerve, fearing everything inside and around me. I had no desire at all. Looking into that bathroom mirror, whoever I once was, had completely vanished.

After my shower, I squeezed into my now skin-tight jean dress and those same damn Earth shoes, so I could search for an office job in the San Fernando Valley. If I got lucky, maybe I could find one that would allow me to hide and not run into any of my former high school classmates or any of the people who expected me to be having a wonderful, artful life, although, I was doubtful anyone in their right mind would hire me.

Dad was now saving the *Los Angeles Times* want ads for me. In his view, a job in the real world would solve all of my existential angst.

Even though I was sparkling clean, I felt like a zombie getting into the car yet again with mom. In L.A. where everybody drives, it was embarrassing that I couldn't get myself anywhere on my own. Full of shame, I sat beside my determined mother in silence for what seemed like forever, before we arrived at an address on Ventura Boulevard. Overwhelmed with dread of the world outside of my parent's den, I stared at the huge office building, where the job I was applying for was located. Mom turned off the ignition. "Do you want me to come in with you?"

"No, I'll be fine," I said, acting as though that were true. Humiliated, I shuffled towards the glass and steel building. I had absolutely no desire to be on display to this world, or any world for that matter. My School of American Ballet days were long gone, and this impersonal building symbolized the failure that was my life. I was an automaton checking in with the security guard. I got into the unwelcoming elevator, to ride up to an unwelcoming office on the fifteenth floor where I'd have to act as though I had some skills to offer those who had adjusted to the mundane life of the office worker. This was it. What a joke.

Closing the heavy door behind me, I stuttered "Hi," to the young receptionist, whose job I might get, if I could manage to get past this interview. She handed me a clipboard with the inevitable form. I sat down on the pleather couch and began to fill it out. No big deal. I'll get through this one. My eyes started to water when I got to the section that said, "Any History of Mental Illness?" Even though I had never been diagnosed, I wanted to jump up and say to the sweet receptionist, looking at me as though I was okay, "Can't you tell?"

I watched him pick up the phone in the breakfast room. I knew what he was doing. He wouldn't stop nagging me about getting some kind of job in the last few weeks. I hadn't as of yet nabbed one and he wasn't pleased. My visit to the office building on Ventura Boulevard had been futile. His anger and frustration were mounting, his alcohol consumption increasing, and his behavior towards me might be considered frightening to someone else that wasn't in a zombie state. Our deal wasn't working.

"Hey Chuck, you think my crazy daughter could come in and do a little typing for you?" he pleaded. "She's not educated, but I think she could probably figure out some filing."

There was a desperate look on my dad's face, but I couldn't quite hear Chuck's response to his ridiculous request. He knew I had never been a secretary!

"I've got to get her out of this house or I'm going to lose my mind," he chuckled, while clipping his fingernails, trying to make light of a situation that was becoming increasingly bleak.

By now, accustomed to his rude conversations and pleas right in front of me, I continued on with my crossword puzzle, literally glued to the couch. If I still possessed a sense of self, I would've gotten up off the couch, and gone somewhere, called a friend, done anything. But, having virtually zero self-esteem allowed me to listen on, as if whatever he said about me was true. Sadly, part of it was.

"No, she isn't dancing anymore," he said. "She got fired from her last dance job and can't seem to do anything else. I told her to stay in New York, but she wouldn't listen. Maybe she'll learn something from your girls there," he added, with another of his sarcastic chuckles.

A few days later, to appease my frustrated dad, Chuck hired me.

For that first day of work at Chuck's office, I moped listlessly into the shower, and put my skin-tight jean dress on, after mom handed it to me. I still couldn't even choose an outfit for myself. Still, it was an assault to squeeze into my old clothes. Dad was driving me this time. I was getting out of the house, so maybe I'd just get better all of a sudden? We drove in silence all the way to Van Nuys.

"Don't fuck up," he said, as I opened the car door.

"Thanks for the ride. See you later."

"I'll be here at 4:30. Be ready, and don't make me wait."

"I'll be here, don't worry." I slammed shut the heavy car door.

Dad roared off in his fancy sports car, and I entered that rundown office with a fake little smile on my face. I opened the door slowly to find two secretaries hunched over their typewriters.

"Hi, I'm Susan. I'm supposed to help out."

The two other young women looked up simultaneously with a similar sneer. "Hi," they both said, and got right back to work.

Quietly wandering around, I started checking out the cabinets, and messy files everywhere, figuring I could get started on neatening up the place. I truly had no idea what to do. I'd never been in any kind of business office before, except for a doctor's here and there and the few interviews I had endured over the past couple of weeks. Chuck didn't seem to have an eye for decoration, or didn't care, so I started putting things at right angles, as though that would make the ugly office look better.

The two girls looked up from their typewriters and simultaneously said, "We'll be with you in a minute. There might be some things for you to file."

"Oh, that would be great," I said, hoping they didn't notice how uncomfortable I was.

"Maybe a letter or two to type," they added.

"Great," I said, as though I knew how to type.

Finally, I was handed some kind of written letter to type up. I managed to insert the typewriter paper but it was entirely crooked. I couldn't figure out how to make that damn page straight. I didn't even know how to put paper in a typewriter! One of the girls came over and helped me, so I was on my way. Completely distracted by my dismal situation, I found it hard to concentrate, but kept pounding on those keys with my perfectly straightened piece of paper, as though I knew what the hell I was doing.

The sound of the other two typewriters buzzing along was disconcerting. I felt completely out of place and unnecessary, but mostly, I felt so uncomfortable in my body, which had once flown across stages and belonged to me. I had once controlled it in a way that made life worth living. I expressed my deepest emotions with my body. Now I was a huge lump in an ugly office in Van Nuys, California. I was now, officially, nobody.

Out of the corner of my eye, I noticed the other two secretaries checking out my skills while they typed on without a care in the world. My sweaty, un-manicured fingers tapped the keys every ten seconds, mainly because I was so incredibly distracted. All I could think as I typed, or filed some folders full of paperwork, was how absurd this was, how absurd those secretaries watching me were. I craved to be buried back in my couch.

All the paperwork I filed, and the letters I managed to type, assaulted my soul. This wasn't the world of art and beauty I once knew. Where was the nuance? Where was that deep connection to a higher force? Where was the Prokofiev?

The two secretaries tried to be sympathetic, but they also whispered behind my back. "Chuck's just helping Bob out because she can't get a job anywhere else," said the one at the other typewriter. She was even chubbier than I had become and seemed absolutely fine with it.

"Gee, I wonder why she can't get a job anywhere else?" The skinny one laughed abrasively while speed typing a message from her boss. I might have been crazy but I wasn't deaf. I carried on with my work as though I knew what I was doing, distracted by the absurdity of life in the real world.

We celebrated Secretary's Day while I was there. Chuck took us all out to Tony Roma's, a popular Van Nuys restaurant, for a feast to celebrate our contributions to his law practice. It was incredibly uncomfortable slopping up greasy ribs that were a specialty of the house. I just couldn't keep up with those happy people. I felt the distance, the absolute separation. I tried to make nice while indulging in those famous ribs.

The four of us sat together in a big red leather booth with a faux wood table in the dark lighting that was popular in restaurants at the time. This was a place I'd been to with my parents when I was an adolescent; the ambience was a reminder of my disdain for all things tacky. I was a world traveler. I'd dined with Harvey Keitel in Paris. I'd been to The Russian Tea Room in New York City with George. I had once experienced class and taste. Now I didn't feel good enough to sit with these people because my secretarial and communication skills were so terribly lacking.

As the lunch at Tony Roma's droned on, I blurted out a laugh, acting like I was having a good time while spilling barbecue sauce all over the bib I wore. How terribly fitting for a twenty-four-year old infant. I just smiled with sauce running down my chin. We walked out of the restaurant carrying the beautiful roses that Chuck had bought for all of us. My shame and embarrassment was overwhelming.

Those professional and oblivious secretaries could only handle a week of my failed attempts to please my father. The day that I was fired I climbed back on the couch, ready to hide again. I actually longed for my all-consuming pain that had been briefly interrupted by my week at Chuck's and the weird Secretary's Day. I never wanted to act like everything was okay in front of anyone ever again. I couldn't make myself fit in the work world, and the check that I soon received was meaningless.

Mom couldn't take it anymore. She had to do something. A few days later, she made a call. I listened in agony, mom's plea to her good friend Maryanne, announcing it all, practically crying to her best friend, sharing her secret about my disturbing condition. Maryanne knew all the positive things that had happened in my young life. Now, it was mom's turn to reveal the ugly truth about "what being in the dance world has done to my daughter."

Maryanne's daughter, Ileana, and I had gone to Marymount, the all-girls Catholic school, when we were very young, and although I lost touch with Ileana in the sixth grade when I transferred to public school, mom and Maryanne stayed close. They loved shopping and lunching together, gossiping about their husband's misdeeds, and children's accomplishments. Now, with obvious shame, mom revealed her only daughter's failure.

Mom's eyes lit up. "Oh, you know a good psychiatrist? I'm sure that's what she needs, although Bob couldn't agree less."

Dad stood there, listening too, but couldn't take it anymore. He grabbed the phone from mom and said, "It's just a job in the real world that she needs. I'm not paying for some fancy psychiatrist, Maryanne, so don't…"

Mom grabbed the phone back." Don't listen to Bob."

He grabbed it back, and said jokingly, "I tried to get her to move to a kibbutz."

She took the phone back again. "Can you give me the phone number?" She scrambled for a pen, tore a piece of paper from a pad, and then scribbled the number for the psychiatrist that Maryanne recommended. They said goodbye, and dad glared at me, like I was the bane of his existence.

"Don't you dare make an appointment for her," he said. "If you do, she's paying for it."

In a rare act of defiance, mom picked up the phone and made an appointment for the very next day.

Chapter 14

MEDS

Jean and Susan, Los Angeles, 1982.

"I'm so glad we're doing this," mom said, as we drove down the long driveway. She wore a nice dress and a bit of make-up for this special appointment to find a cure for her only daughter. We drove in silence through Beverly Hills to Century City where the doctor's office was located.

We parked in the large and imposing multilevel concrete parking structure. I opened the passenger door, got out, and looked around. I was on Mars. Peering through the car window, I could see mom pulling out a book to read while she waited. "You can come with me," I mouthed through the closed window.

She rolled down the window. "I thought you wanted to do this by yourself," she said.

"I don't want to do this at all," I admitted.

She opened the heavy car door. "Let's go. You're finally going to get some help."

My thighs burned from rubbing against each other on the trek from the garage to the great doctor's office. I had on no make-up, but was as clean and fresh as I'd been since that absurd date weeks before with Arturo, the car mechanic.

We arrived at suite 712.

Can I just run away now? No...you can't run. You're too fat and completely out of shape. Your feet will hurt too much.

I opened the heavy, wood door and an annoying bell sounded. Perhaps it was to alert the receptionist that another crazy, neurotic patient had arrived.

"Can you sign in?" the young blonde receptionist requested.

I picked up the pen, and signed my name. We took seats along the wall and mom took her book from her purse.

"The doctor will see you now," the receptionist announced.

"Wait for me," I said, as I walked toward the doctor's private office, feeling like I'd better not screw this up too.

I peered at the balding fiftyish stranger with a hopeless, resigned stare. The distinguished-looking psychiatrist looked back with what seemed little interest and signaled with his pasty white hand for me to me to sit in the leather chair across from him. I obeyed.

He pulled out a yellow-lined writing pad, ready to take notes. "Your mother says you are experiencing some kind of a depression."

"I guess." I slumped in the chair.

"She says that you were a dancer. Is that right?"

"Yes."

"And that you lived in Europe and New York?"

"Yes." I wondered if that were still true. It seemed like such a long time ago. I looked up from my lap where I'd been studying my sausage fingers. He stared at me disapprovingly.

"Can you paint a picture of yourself with words?" he asked, his mouth barely moving.

"I was a dancer and I'm nothing now. There's really nothing to me anymore," I whispered.

"There must be something you can talk about pertaining to your dancing." His eyes appeared cold and his mouth still seemed immobile. I couldn't see any of his teeth. He started tapping the pen on his yellow pad as though he was already sick of me.

"No, there's really nothing. I don't really feel anything anymore," I whispered again. "I feel blank."

It went on for at least another half hour, the doctor prying, and me, incapable of opening up, feeling uncomfortable and full of shame, wanting to get home to my couch so I could just disappear.

"I won't be able to treat you unless we put you on some medication," he said, making it all seem very final.

Boy, that was quick.

"I won't be able to get to the root of the problem, if you can't speak to me at all. Can you just say something about something?" he asked, tapping again in his annoyed fashion. He swiveled his fancy leather chair back and forth a few times, waiting for some kind of response.

"I can't."

"Something? You are part of your recovery. I can't do it all for you."

The leather chair under me was feeling sticky and I just wanted to lie down. Clearly failing again, this was probably my last chance to rise out of the ashes. "I stopped dancing and there was nothing left. I just don't care about anything, and I don't know if I want to get better. The world seems like a shitty place to be," I whispered, as sweat dripped down my uncomfortably chubby body.

The fifty-minute hour was nearly over.

"I'm going to write a prescription for you that I think will help you at least get to a place where we can help you through this," he said, as though he couldn't wait to get me on some drugs and away from him. I stared out the seventh-floor window, wondering if anything would ever help me out of my hell. The sunny office and those tall glass windows felt as assaulting as the doctor was.

"There's no point in us meeting if you don't take it," he said, forcing a little white paper into my sweaty hands. I stared at the little letters. They meant absolutely nothing to me.

Getting up listlessly from the sticky leather chair, I brushed myself off. I'm sure mom was hopeful that I'd walk out of the office like my old, spirited, dancing self. When my hand reached the metal doorknob, I peered back at the doctor and saw him jot something down on his yellow pad. The door closed behind me, and I gestured to mom that we could leave. We wandered down the sterile hallway and into the elevator in complete silence.

The big metal doors opened and there before us was an elevator full of people, laughing and having a good time. They all had on beautiful clothes and their white teeth shined. I just stared, frightened to step inside, self-conscious beyond belief. Mom interrupted my moment of paranoid observation. "How did it go?"

We exited the elevator and walked towards the parking structure. I didn't want to answer her in front of all those people so I was silent for what seemed forever. After what seemed another eternity we reached the safety of her car. "Are you going to tell me how it went?" she asked.

"He can't work with me unless I take this," I said, showing her the prescription for the anti-depressant, Tofranil.

"So, let's go get this filled, if that's what he thinks," she said with an absurd delight. "I'm sure he knows what he's talking about." She turned on the ignition and backed out of the parking space.

"He's kind of cold," I said, as we drove down the winding concrete ramp of the parking garage.

"I'm sure he's fine. He just wants to help you." She paid the parking attendant and off we went, back to the San Fernando Valley to fill the prescription and return to the house and the safety of the couch.

"Maybe he's not a good doctor," I said, staring at the urban landscape of shiny Century City.

"He can't work in Century City if he's not good," mom said while peeling back into the mid-afternoon traffic.

Before swallowing any of those little yellow pills the doctor prescribed, I decided to look them up in the *Merck Manual of Diagnosis and Therapy*, that trusty medical reference book that sat on the shelves of my parent's home because mom was a nurse. Rifling through the pages, I came upon my prescription and was completely taken aback by the description of its possible side effects and the symptoms it was supposed to treat.

Tofranil: Prescribed for clinical depression; endogenous depression; major depressive disorder.

THAT'S NOT ME!

Side effects: Obesity, loss of libido, increased heart rate, dry mouth, confusion, drowsiness, constipation, possible suicide.

NO FUCKING WAY!

I walked into the kitchen and handed mom the bottle. "There's no way I'm taking this shit. That doctor wants to fuck me up even more than I already am."

"Take it. You need it," she said, handing me a glass of water. "You'll feel better and get back on track."

"You didn't happen to notice the side effects listed in the *Merck Manual*?"

"They don't affect everybody the same way," she said, sounding like she actually knew what she was talking about. She grabbed her dust rag in the laundry room, avoiding my need to dismiss the recommendation of the doctor, who was nothing more than evil even though he'd been so highly recommended by her good friend. "They just have to list the worst possible things that can happen. Please take them," she pleaded. "I just don't know how else we can help you."

So, I took them.

After a week, I put my meds on the kitchen counter and whined to my poor, stressed-out mother. "All I can feel is a dry mouth."

She continued mopping the tile floor, then went to the bucket to squeeze the mop out, barely noticing me.

"I told you that doctor was full of shit. I still want to kill myself."

"You never told me you wanted to kill yourself."

"Isn't it fucking obvious at this point?"

She put her mop down, grabbed the bottle, and studied the label. "It's supposed to take at least two weeks to take effect. Here, read this," she said, handing it back to me. "You're supposed to go see the doctor next week...when you're better."

"This is bullshit. I'm not going to get fatter than I already am," I said, with a newfound conviction. "And what if I meet someone?" I said. "I'll have no libido!"

Like I even cared about my completely non-existent sex life! But for the first time in months, I started to speak up for myself. Sex was another hush-hush matter with mom, so why would she care if I ever had sex again. The answer is, she wouldn't. No matter how old I got, I would always be a virgin to her. Now, I was just a crazy, depressed virgin.

I stomped away in disgust, as though I had somewhere better to go. As though I was going to put on a pretty sundress and go to the mall, or the beach, or to a summer art class, or a lunch date, or a job that any normal young woman closing in on twenty-five might have.

As I shuffled back towards my bedroom, I stepped into our 1940s tile bathroom, and peered in the mirror above the sink, barely recognizing my puffy and scarred face. In my hand was the yellow-and-gold-colored bottle still containing a few weeks worth of the medication that would supposedly create a less depressed mind. I twisted open the little white plastic top and dumped the remaining little yellow pills into the toilet and flushed. I got a thrill at the sight of each and every little pill disappearing.

That was it. I was done destroying my poor parents and myself as well. I was repulsed by what I had turned into. I'd killed the ethereal creature that I'd worked so hard to become. I'd done it all to myself. I had willed myself into this mental state and now I was going to have to dig myself out of it. No one was going to help me, but me.

It wasn't their responsibility, their fault. I needed to let go of the idea that they were capable of fixing me or loving me in this damaged state.

I stepped into my bedroom, my head spinning with anticipation. Buried in my underwear drawer, I found one of my old journals. It had been two years since I had written in the old composition book that had once been my constant companion. Relieved that I hadn't thrown it away, I read and re-read what went through my little ballerina bun-head. My journey may have been young and naïve, but somehow, I was always thinking, what's our purpose on this planet? And why do we feel all of these conflicted emotions? I was obsessed with trying to understand the meaning of things, even though my only desire, truly, was to dance. Perhaps it was a need to express myself with words, in whatever clumsy way I could, and that journal had been there for me. In these last excruciating months, my curiosity about the world and other people had crept away. I hadn't written a word. I was a closed off shell of a human.

How could I have been so different not so terribly long ago?

The empty pages at the back of that journal might be the one place to figure out why I was such a mess.

I opened a new page and wrote:

I'm never going to that psychiatrist again. It's time for me to help myself.

It had been two years since my travels to Europe, when I'd jotted down my feelings, thoughts, and observations. I had been busy dancing and traveling and now for way too many months, lying inert on my parent's couch. This was either the end, or a beginning for me. It was time to get out of the hole I had dug. I didn't know exactly how I was going to do it, but it was time. It was a conscious decision to live or die.

Truly not wanting to believe, as both my parents did, that my brain chemistry was the only thing that was keeping me this way. I felt what I was going through was a spiritual death, and that was something my parents could never truly understand. They blamed my mental breakdown on my inability to be flexible or cope with life's ills. They blamed it on, *the crazy world you've lived in*. But I had chosen to live in any world that wasn't theirs, any world that would offer me love or a sense of self. And the only world I knew was taken away. Or did I take it away from myself to prove them right? Prove to them that I would never succeed?

Now that mom figured out that she couldn't heal me herself, she uncharacteristically asked me to call my old friends. My dad was all for that; again, anything that would get me out of his house would be acceptable and possibly brilliant. I didn't want to call any dancers from the Cleveland Ballet and humiliate myself even more. Plus, they were all dancing somewhere, doing what I could have been doing. There was no way I would tell any of them that I'd completely fallen apart, gotten fat, and was too depressed to get back in shape to audition for another company.

Despite the moments of clarity, my still disoriented brain needed any new voice to penetrate the walls I'd put up. I needed to hear the voice of anyone other than my parents. Finally, I decided that it would be okay to call my old high school friend, Lynne. I knew her number by heart. And she just happened to know that I'd had some crazy times with my parents before the shit really hit the fan. We had kept in touch off and on since junior high, and she knew about the first melt down/depression that I'd experienced seven years earlier when I moved home from New York, and abandoned my scholarship at the School of American Ballet to finish high school. She was aware of my sometimes-fragile hold on things.

Mom stood by, and pleaded, "Please do it. You need to get out. You need some fresh air. Please."

A couple days later, Lynne drove her little white Toyota over from

Pasadena. She was a scientist, a true non-conformist, and struggled with her own issues that were completely different than mine. But, we'd always had an easy communication, and for some reason, I knew she'd understand. I believed she'd at least be compassionate, even if she couldn't help me out of this hot mess.

I opened the front door and we stood staring at each other for a moment.

Maybe she doesn't recognize me?

Then she gave me a big hug. She didn't say a word about my physical change. I was, of course, worried she might judge me, especially with her arms wrapped around my non-dancer body. But it appeared she wasn't going to. She was Saint Lynne.

It felt good to finally reconnect with a human, especially one that had known me for so long, and one outside my dysfunctional family. I invited her in for a second so she could say hello to my parents. Dad had a playful relationship with Lynne and loved making fun of her, thinking she could take it. I was certainly anxious about what he might say, considering how sarcastic he'd been with her in the past.

"Hi Lynne," mom gushed as she walked into the front hallway, wiping her hands on her dishrag. Throwing the damp red and white cloth over her shoulder, she gave her a big hug. I was embarrassed that mom looked so haggard, even if I looked worse. Her hair was untouched, and she had those old cleaning clothes on, and again was without a stitch of make-up. She truly was getting as bad as me. At least my hair was still long, even if it was matted. "We're so glad you could get here. She needs some fresh air," she whispered to her, as though I wasn't standing right there next to both of them.

"Well that's exactly what Sue and I are going to do," Lynne said. "We're going to the L.A. Reservoir for a nice long walk."

"Maybe you can just dump her in the water and see if she can remember how to swim," dad chuckled. He was walking towards us from the breakfast room, his ivory cigarette holder dangling from his left hand. He was wearing his oil-stained work-outside-in-the-garage-clothes and didn't look much better than mom.

"Bob, please," mom moaned. "Don't be so cruel."

"Hey plumber," Lynne remarked. "I'm not dumping anyone in the reservoir, and haven't you grown up a little since I've seen you? You've certainly had enough time."

She called my dad plumber in response to his once snide remarks to her about her curvaceous bum (fat ass is what he actually called her), when she was sixteen. It was certainly out of place, but Lynne adjusted to his comments and would have some fun getting back at him, even then. Plus, without his suit and tie, he kind of looked like a plumber.

"Looks like you don't have a fat ass anymore," he remarked, getting at least one jab in.

"Some people think it still is," she retorted, flowing easily back to the fun they used to have with each other. "It's so nice to see you, too!"

"Thank God you don't have to help her with her science and geometry today," dad said. I just stared into space, as though his sarcasm didn't affect me. "Although, maybe you could help her with one of her crossword puzzles," he said. "She works on those all day; can't finish them, of course."

"Lynne, you look good," mom said, looking into her deep blue eyes. She was clearly trying to avoid dad's comments. Then she blurted out, "Will you take care of her?"

I thought I was going to roll up in a little ball when mom came up with that hapless statement. Lynne grabbed my hand. "Sue doesn't need anyone to take care of her. Bye," she waved, grabbing my arm to escort me out of the house.

"Don't let her drive," dad chuckled as we turned towards the door.

The sun assaulted my eyes as we walked out the front door. We continued down the red brick path, down the driveway and onto the quiet suburban street where Lynne's car was waiting. My parents were standing in the doorway looking worried. It was hard to read if they were happy that I was getting out of the house, or just concerned.

Getting into her little white Toyota, we both waved goodbye to my apprehensive parents. "God, that was hard," she said.

"Can you imagine eight months of living with that?" I said, slamming the car door shut.

"Your dad won't stop, will he?" she said, turning on the ignition. "But, you gotta love him. He's pretty damn funny. Eight months?"

We drove quietly towards the reservoir. I looked over at her clean and pretty clothes and wondered what it would be like to fit into my nice clothes. It was as though she had some secret to life. She seemed so strong and independent. She could drive wherever she wanted. Her hair was clean and her teeth sparkled when she smiled. How did she figure out how to live in this world?

After parking, I shook with trepidation as I got out of the car, worried how I would survive this trip to the real world without the safety of my couch. So far, none of my experiences out there had been very good. Not one trip out of my parent's house had made me want to jump back into life.

What would Lynne and I talk about? Would I be able to make it around the reservoir? I knew it was a super long trail.

We made it to the gate at the path entrance, and I avoided the eyes of the other joggers and trekkers. Seeing normal people having a good time, laughing, was going to be even more daunting. It would remind me, again, how fucked up I really was.

"Your parents are making you seem worse than you are, I bet," Lynne said as we walked through the partially open gate. I had to really squeeze through. Lynne didn't.

"Actually, they're not," I said, as we walked along the asphalt path.

"It's beautiful here, isn't it?" Lynne remarked as we trekked along the path, not even noticing the joggers flying past us. "It is strange though that you're not dancing. You've never not danced."

"When I got back from the School of American Ballet, I stopped for a month." I mumbled. "But my ankle was sprained then. I bounced back so fast, though. It seems so long ago."

"You did. I remember, so, why don't you go back now?"

"I can't."

My thighs started to burn from rubbing against each other on this trek in the urban wilderness. There was no lightness in my movement and I felt terribly uncomfortable. I was tired after ten minutes and wanted to lie down.

"Hey, let's pick up the pace a little," Lynne, said, probably sensing my discomfort.

"Okay. I'll try to keep up with you, I mean, you were a swimmer and all that."

Acting as normal as ever, Lynne revealed a new kink in her own life that was probably more excruciating than I could imagine. "Wendy got back from living on the streets in Alaska. She's been diagnosed as schizophrenic."

"You're kidding, right. You mean your sister?"

"Yep. It's so sad. She was so smart."

"So, is she ever going to be okay?" I asked, as though that was even a remote possibility.

"People don't recover from schizophrenia. It's pretty devastating. And she has to take these meds that made her gain like eighty pounds. You wouldn't even recognize her."

"Are you helping her too?"

"What do you mean, too?"

"Well, you're here helping me."

"Sue, I'm not helping you. I'm just taking a walk with you."

"A doctor put me on medication. I threw those little pills down the toilet after a week."

"Why? You don't hear voices, do you?"

"No… is it worth it?" I asked. "I mean living." Breathing in the semi-clean morning air, I brushed damp hair from my face. I pulled some strands over the picked-at welts on my face, shamed by my now adolescent-looking skin.

"Of course, it is," she said with the cheer of a young person who was genuinely finding her way. "I'm not sure it is for Wendy, though. She'll probably be in an institution for the rest of her life."

Silence as we walked further down the path.

"Sue, you've got to snap out of this. You don't want to end up in one of those state-assisted homes like my sister."

"Don't worry, my mom's never going to let that happen. She'd rather take care of me herself," I joked, trying to make light of my endless soap opera. My heart pounded and I huffed and puffed as we came to the end of the long walk. Sweat dripped down my entire body and my thighs felt like they were forming little blisters from rubbing together. My make-up melted off my picked-at pimples. The beating sun was assaulting and I couldn't wait to lie down again. I'd never float on air again.

Lynne appeared as though she'd done absolutely nothing. Not one drop of sweat on her face or body.

"Oh God," I whispered in my gravelly, barely audible voice. "It's going to be like *Whatever Happened to Baby Jane*? I'll be stuck with mom in an old house somewhere, and we'll both never leave. I'll be Joan Crawford to her Bettie Davis and we'll shuttle each other around in wheelchairs. My dad's so right. I see the whole scenario ahead, because I'm too fucking chicken to off myself."

Lynne drove me home. "You're going to be okay, Sue," she said. "You were a beautiful dancer, and you just think you failed. To everyone else, you've succeeded. You should get back in class, anyway. That always saved you."

Peering through the car window, I looked into her beautiful blue eyes, and wondered if I'd ever be happy. "Hey, can we walk together again?" I felt like I'd just run a marathon, but I knew I had to start somewhere.

"Of course, we can," she said. "We're friends forever, Sue, no matter what."

"Thanks." I turned to re-enter my parent's house, my now, not-so-safe, prison.

My mother had still not given up the idea that a medical remedy might fix my self-destructive behavior. This time it was a homeopath, recommended by Maryanne, the same friend who referred me to the awful psychiatrist in Century City. So again, we climbed into the car and off we went. The empathetic grey haired and cool hippie doctor suggested: "It might be better if your healing happens outside of your parent's home. You need to hear your own thoughts."

Embedded in my parent's reaction to my condition, and still craving the affection I never got, I could barely think or speak for myself. The homeopathic doctor prescribed some little white homeopathic pills for depression. Fearlessly I took those pills and fearlessly I shared with her my devastating fall from grace in only one session.

Survival instinct was finally kicking in. It's not like I hadn't had many opportunities to get away from the house I was now hiding in. It's not like my dad hadn't tried everything to get me to leave. But some inner voice reminded me that my soul wasn't safe there anymore, and that it was time to rise up out of the ashes that I had created.

The day after my walk with Lynne, and a few days after my appointment with the homeopath, I walked into my bedroom and tore open the last few of my unemployment checks. Suddenly, I felt rich with the possibilities of a short trip, anything that might relieve my constant inner pain. I also had that check from Chuck, my dad's lawyer friend. I was rich! Just wanting some kind of relief was a huge step. Just thinking that there was something beyond what I'd been living through these past eight months was a sign that the homeopathic medicine was maybe working.

Years before, experiencing depression after a seasonal contract had ended, my psychiatrist in New York had advised me after only a visit, *You're a dancer and you need to dance. Your brain is used to the endorphins that keep this kind of depression at bay*. And I listened. Then. Within weeks, I was back on track, swimming first, finally getting back to class, and performing once again. I needed to move then, and I needed to move now, or I would die a slow and meaningless death. So much of my life had been spent with other people, either rehearsing, or in class, or on stage. Bingo! I needed to connect with the energy of other humans. Perhaps my dad was right about that kibbutz six months earlier.

Just focusing on finding a place to go gave me a reason to get up in the morning, although I didn't have to do much investigation. Maryanne sent a brochure for a healing spa in Temecula, California, called Alive Polarity. It arrived within a couple of days. I looked it over. I liked the regimented schedule, and after minimal consideration, I decided I would go for the whole month. It would cost three thousand dollars, which was all the money I had. The same day that the brochure arrived, I called the no frills spa to make my reservations. In four days, I'd finally be on my way, even if dad had to drive me.

Dad looked happy behind his cool Ray Bans as he drove me to Temecula, about ninety miles southeast of L.A. I wasn't really a desert kind of girl, but at this point anything outside of the sphere of my parent's house, even an igloo, might help.

After a quiet two-hour drive, dad parked outside the entrance. He got out of the car and opened the trunk. "You know you're not moving home when you come back, so you better get it together."

I heaved from the trunk my bag containing only some clothes that mom had lent me, clothes I could fit in, and said, "I know. Thanks for the ride."

As I walked up the path to the front entrance, dad got back in his car and tore off down the block-long driveway, the sound of his engine, trailing behind.

I walked through the big wooden front door carrying my one bag. Two people at the check-in desk welcomed me with great warmth, as though they knew me. They escorted me to my bungalow that I'd share with one other woman. These two monk-like healers made me feel like everything was going to be okay. One of them handed me the schedule, even though I already knew the whole rigmarole. "Welcome to Alive Polarity," they said in pleasant unison.

With excitement, I perused the schedule, even though I already knew what was ahead for me. Every day was quite regimented: 6 a.m. nature walk; 7:30 a.m. vegetarian breakfast; 9 a.m. therapy; 11 a.m. yoga; noon vegetarian lunch; then spa treatments, tennis or swimming in the afternoon; 6 p.m. vegetarian dinner and reading, socializing in the rec room, ping pong or walking for the rest of the evening. Of course, I had the option to not engage in any activities. There wasn't a television or radio anywhere to be found.

"It will be quiet and peaceful," they uttered simultaneously, and then floated out the door.

I stuck to the regiment like the trained dancer I once was. My discipline still existed. Slowly, I began to enjoy the morning walks, the therapy, meals, and nightly chats with my roommate, a kind mother of three children. Every day I came out of my shell a little more. Not hearing my parents' opinions was a good beginning. My anxiety began to diminish.

Diving into the Olympic-size swimming pool, covered in my mother's red-and-white striped bathing suit, I assumed all eyes were on me, my décolleté on view for the public. But, of course no one was even looking. Nobody there cared that I was once a dancer and once looked more like a preteen adolescent than a fully developed woman. Once in the water, I'd swim away the discomfort I felt with my chubby body. And those endorphins were starting to kick in.

Every day I felt a little better, a little clearer. My spirit started coming back. I never thought for one minute that I wanted to be buried back on my parent's couch. All that occupied my mind was learning to live in the moment and finding out who the hell I was without the veil of ballet. I was recovering.

Through my therapy sessions at the retreat, I discovered that the strand that I dangled on for way too long had been broken. I was going to have to find my own voice, without dance, without the barres, the mirrors, and the music, without the only thing that had made my life worth living.

On this month-long trip away from my parent's home, I discovered that maybe I wanted to try my hand at acting. It was still the theater, the place I knew so well, the place I felt my inner life and my truth. It was where I felt my power and my presence, even if my voice rarely rose above a whisper. Those voices from Dennis Nahat of the Cleveland Ballet, "Have you ever thought of becoming an actress?" And of course, Harvey Keitel, who had suggested a couple of years before, when we were in Paris, "You need to explore your dark side," kept bouncing around in my now healthier brain.

Perhaps I was doing that all along?

The healing month over, dad drove back to Temecula to pick up his new daughter, undoubtedly carrying the hope that I was never going to hide away at his house again.

Waiting in rapt attention at the entrance to this desert paradise, I heard that familiar roar of his car at least a block away. And then, there he was, my skeptical dad. He opened the shiny maroon door, still holding his ivory white cigarette holder with his lit cigarette, and mumbled, "Hello."

Taking my bag cautiously, he plunked it in the trunk and slammed it shut. I waved goodbye to my few friends from the retreat and got into his gleaming sports car.

"You lost some weight," he said as he turned on the ignition, and backed out of his parking space.

Peering out the front window at the rural paradise, my last stop before the beginning of my new life, my new retreat friends waved goodbye. And then we roared down the long road, passing that great big pool, the tennis courts, and the neatly lined palm trees.

"So, how was it?" he asked, taking a long drag on his cigarette.

"It was really great," I said, truly meaning it. "I mean, I feel better, and I think I'll get a job."

"That's good. What kind of a job?"

"Oh, anything. Maybe waitressing or something."

"Well, that sounds appropriate, since you're such a shitty secretary."

We both laughed, realizing how true his statement was. I took in the sights, observing the beautiful desert flowers, trees, and cactus alongside the road. "I think I want to study acting," I whispered, my old vulnerability still intact.

"You've got to be kidding. Where are you going to act?" he said, as we drove towards the highway.

"I don't know. I'm just going to study."

"As long as you get a job and find a place to live, you can join the circus if you want," he said, lighting up another cigarette.

We got on the great big open highway and headed towards Los Angeles, my heart aching with joy. I was alive again and the wind coming at me from the open window felt so good on my face.

"Thanks dad. Thanks for letting me spend some time there."

"You paid for it," he said, taking a long drag on his cigarette.

"I know, but you could've sent me to a mental hospital instead."

"You would've snapped right out of it when you saw how fucking crazy everybody else was there," he chuckled.

"Maybe. I might've gotten worse, though," I said, knowing that probably would have been the case.

"That's what mom seemed to think. It was all an act, wasn't it?"

"Actually, no." I said with a surprising amount of conviction.

We revved down that open highway, the darkness that had completely enveloped me since being fired from my dream job, since losing my identity, was gone. I was never going back to live in that house that had eaten my parents and me alive, ever again.

And, I didn't. Within two days I moved in with my jazz dancer friend from high school, Juliette, and her mother. Juliette and I shared a twin bed for a couple of weeks at her mom's Laurel Canyon home, our long arms and legs hanging off the sides, laughing our way to sleep. Dad couldn't have been happier but mom still fretted at every move I made. She still wanted to be my nurse and wanted me to move back home.

Within another week I got a waitressing job, in the San Fernando Valley. Dad was thrilled that I was getting on my feet, so he kindly covered a down payment on a used car for me. I stepped off my dancer pedestal, joined a gym and started daily aerobics classes and reacquainted with a few old friends. I even started dating. In another month, I got a roommate and an apartment. I was on my way.

Somehow, my parents began to accept me as a sane but unusual person. Mom would remind me often, "You could move home, and go to college. You can study acting there." But I knew I could never live there again, and the last thing I needed was another psychiatrist handing out meds. I had to get strong, and with that, had to separate emotionally.

Sadly, I never stepped back into a ballet class again. I ached for it, missed it, but knew deep inside that I couldn't go back. I needed to know who I was without the stage, before I ever went back on one again. At twenty-five, it would take me a year to get back in ballet shape, and then another year to get into a company, just to be in the corps. I didn't have that kind of time, and I needed to make a living. And, I had no desire to be a ballet teacher who still wanted to be on stage. I'd seen too much of that in New York in a ballet class I often attended at Carnegie Hall. The forty-year-old ex-dancers struggling to execute steps that were so easy for the twenty-year-old professionals seemed tragic at the time. Those once-almost-professionals somehow seemed drained of all life force.

Certainly I could have gone to Las Vegas and been hired as a show-dancer. I was tall, had breasts and long legs. I could move well. But that just wasn't ever going to be me. It was all the way or nothing.

Chapter 15

WAITRESS

Naomi Goldberg and Susan at Venice Beach, 1987.

1987

For the next two years, everything was new. Every person I worked with, every old friend I saw, every event I attended, was new. I had been transformed, and surprisingly, everything I did had a feeling of excitement and adventure. I was finally a working woman and my dad was incredibly proud, even if he had a fabulous time making fun of my job slinging hash. Mom had a hard time adjusting to the healthier, happier me, but was doing better. Perhaps the drama I had bestowed upon her for an entire eight months took attention away from whatever her own problems were; she never actually shared them with me. Instead, she'd beg me to move home, so I could save money and go to college, and reminded me, "We're always here for you."

But I knew that my reliance on her or my father for anything would always end in some kind of victimization. I think dad was trying to tell me

112

that all along, before I moved back home to fall apart. The positive thing that came out of my spiritual death was that my desire to rise up and learn a new art was incredibly strong. Depression wasn't my cover story anymore, and I had that naïve hope that everything was gonna be alright.

New occupation: waitress at a 1950s-style eatery, Larry Parker's Beverly Hills 24-Hour Diner to be exact, working the 11 p.m. to 7 a.m. shift. I was new there and getting used to the grind of working for a living, not on stage with other dancers, and certainly not wearing a tiara. This would be my third waitressing job in the two years of not dancing. I'd gotten fired from the first two.

There was a big talent agency nearby so some of the celebs would stop by for a meal in the comfortable and unpretentious atmosphere. The food was decent. The actor Mickey Rourke always had a beautiful young actress or model with him, and I would act like they were no big deal, while almost spilling coffee or a milkshake all over them. I ached with envy to be that special person with him, or at least in that echelon. But I was just a waitress, never to be a ballerina again.

I wore a short white polyester zip-up uniform and a red apron that had "Larry Parker's 24-Hour Diner" written on it. That apron was full of checkbooks and pens and covered with ink stains because I never closed the caps on the pens. Always in a hurry to make sure the toast or bagels wouldn't burn, the milkshakes got made, and to pick up my orders on time. I worked in fear of being yelled at by one of the short-order cooks for doing something wrong.

I didn't look too bad, but at size ten, I was four sizes larger than my once anorexic-looking ballet body. I was voluptuous and not yet comfortable in my non-dancing skin, but I'd come to accept my new reality and was learning how to serve and how to communicate without being obsessed with my own art. What I now ached for was some kind of love in my life, and even though I had lived with two men when I was a dancer, my dating skills were still pretty juvenile.

Between waitressing jobs, I nabbed some work as an extra in the movies but grew tired of the sitting, the constant waiting, and not getting to be one of the actors. By the time I got the job at Larry Parker's, I was surviving on my own–learning new ways of performing and spending some free time with Naomi, my good friend from the School of American Ballet. She still danced with a special exuberance, but no longer for a ballet company.

She'd come to L.A. after being scouted by a TV casting director in San Francisco, when she was performing with The Flying Karamazov Brothers, one of her performing jobs when transitioning out of ballet. Before that she had danced with the Pacific Northwest Ballet, in Seattle, while I was dancing with the Cleveland Ballet, so in some way, we'd taken similar paths–except for the nervous breakdown I'd recovered from, and her recent degree from Barnard. We reconnected as though no time had passed.

Naomi worked intermittently as a substitute teacher, but in our off hours, we'd trek down to Venice Beach in some comfortable baggy clothes, carrying a big boom box and a couple of hats for collecting money, so we could do some improvisational dance, and hopefully take home some cash. I had already given up dancing professionally ever again, but Naomi was a free spirit with a newly earned modern dance education and wanted to have some fun with her old dancer friend–me.

"I can't dance anymore," I complained as we trekked up the boardwalk, taking in the clean ocean air, to find the perfect place to set up our makeshift stage. We settled into one of the gazebo-covered cement quads and dropped our heavy bags.

"Of course, you can," she said as she searched for the right music for us to start our little performance.

"I can't point my feet anymore," I added as Naomi brought out hats from one of our large duffel bags.

"Do you think anyone cares that you can't point your feet, Susie? Just feel the music like you always did. We've got tennis shoes on anyway."

"But it's been almost three years and I don't feel like a dancer anymore," I moaned, as I started to move my arms, mirroring my oldest dancer friend who still poured everything she had into movement in space, and the joy it brought to herself, and others.

"No one will know. Just dance."

I started to move at the pace of the music and within a few minutes people had gathered around to watch. I jumped and turned as though no time had passed, even though three years is forever in ballet years.

"Join in," Naomi called to the onlookers. At least twenty people stood around, dressed in t-shirts, shorts, hats, and all things tourist. Surprisingly, a few people even stepped in the little arena that Naomi and I had created and they started to move and dance.

"Hey! You guys are pretty good," I heard from the crowd of onlookers that weren't yet dancing. "Can we join in?"

"That's what the sign says," Naomi said, pointing to our little painted sign that was leaning against the dirty metal trashcan. In big blue letters, it said: Ballet Girls. Come Join In. "You have to! It's good for your health and for your soul!" The sweat poured down her entire body as she continued to move to *Under the Boardwalk*, the old Drifters song, with me keeping up and doing the best I could.

I hadn't learned to improvise when I was a dancer (except of course, during my disco days at Studio 54 when I was seventeen), but it came pretty naturally. Just moving to music was a nice change. Just being happy was a nice change. And clink went the money into our little straw hat.

Sometimes there were actual bills. We were making money!

"You girls must be professional!" Clink.

We danced on the Venice Boardwalk Saturdays and Sundays when more people were out and about. We had found our calling, at least for the summer months in 1987, and it was absolute joy, no matter how out of shape I felt. Completely covered in a loose turquoise jumpsuit, sweat would roll down my nose, and my breasts would bounce, now that I had them. I truly had no physical stamina, and I hated that I couldn't dance the way I once had, but it was still a good thing. It made showing up at the restaurant and serving people seem okay. This was my calling for now.

"Keep going," Naomi yelled, the moment I moved to the wooden bench to take a break. "We can't go home empty-handed, can we?"

The beach was a nice change from all my years in urban settings, always hurrying to class, the theater, or to hop on some kind of public transportation. I was alive and happy to be on the planet and getting used to being unfound.

My life now consisted of dancing on the Venice Boardwalk, slinging hash in Beverly Hills, and slowly becoming immersed in the world of great playwrights, as the lessons in my acting classes began to take hold. My first entrée was to observe at the famed Actors Studio, in Hollywood. I'd dated a couple of actors from there, and somehow, they managed to get me invited to become an "observer." I didn't even have to audition, a saving grace because using my voice in any way, except to take food orders, was still a challenge. I was a complete novice at the late age of twenty-six, and even if I was excited at the prospect of becoming something new, acting paled compared to my connection to music and dance. Considering the grueling hard work and sweat it took to dance well, acting seemed like doing nothing. I had grown used to the sweat and a pounding heart as a reminder that I was truly accomplishing something. But I was determined to figure it out.

Through my Actors Studio connection, I was referred to Susan Peretz, a well-known teacher who was handpicked to teach by Lee Strasburg and Al Pacino, with whom she'd worked on the film, *Dog Day Afternoon*. I fumbled my way along in her classes, learning Method acting, a technique that many great actors had studied, starting in the 1950s when Marlon Brando and so many others made acting real. Getting in touch with one's own emotions through relaxation and sensory exercises was the basis for creating a character from the inside out.

My state of emotional paralysis had finally left and I was in a true metamorphosis. And even if using my voice was strange, I still possessed a need to please with my presence. I still possessed the duality of complete insecurity in mundane matters and feeling more present when on stage.

Every waking moment was a new adventure in looking, listening, and trying to feel what a character lifted from the written page might feel in a situation or place completely foreign to me. I had an arsenal of emotions stored inside, so the minute I'd sit down amongst my peers for the beginning of class sensory exercises, the tears wouldn't stop. This wasn't acting, of course, but, being in touch with all of one's senses and emotions is a great start for beginning actors, and apart from having a bit of presence, that was something I possessed. I just needed to learn how to use all of those feelings while in someone else's shoes and not be afraid.

None of it was comfortable. I had no true voice yet. None of it felt as instinctual as dance once did, perhaps because I started dancing at such a young age and was still inherently shy. But I kept on, knowing that struggle was part of learning any art and I reveled in this new struggle. I must have worked on Nina in *The Seagull*, by Anton Chekov for a year in class, never to really soar or find how to get in her shoes, or speak those beautiful words.

But I was learning, and my other new obsession, just like Nina, was to find true love.

It was around 3 a.m. when I came to his table. His date was a woman who looked at least ten years older than me, and a few years younger than him. They were both laughing when I arrived. They said they were entertained watching me take orders from the table full of Brazilian soccer players.

"Can I take your order? I'm sorry that took so long." I wiped the sweat and grease from my face.

"My bride will have the lox, because you know how pussies like fish," the man said in a sexy Eastern European accent. His exact words went right over my head, but I was taken by his offbeat charm, and his dark blonde resemblance to the greatest male dancer of the time, Mikhail Baryshnikov.

"Okay, the lox with what?" I became even more nervous as he stared at me with the most beautiful and tormented green eyes I'd ever seen. I wasn't quite sure where he was from, but he looked at me as though he wanted me.

"And I'll have vodka in carafe," he said with his accent and incredible sexuality that was starting to melt the Cover Girl off my face.

"We don't serve vodka here, and it's actually past serving time in the bars," I said with false confidence.

"Well, my little princess, why do you think we're here?" *Doesn't his girlfriend speak?*

"There's no alcohol. I'm so sorry." More sweat beads formed above my quivering lip.

"Okay, my princess, do you think you could make chocolate milkshake for me? And the lox plate for my bride."

I wrote down the orders in a perfunctory fashion thinking that what he said about his bride was incredibly obnoxious. Why didn't SHE give me her order? He probably guessed from watching me serve those young soccer players that I was new at the job, and a bit tentative. I stuck my uncovered pen back in my ink-stained apron and walked towards the order line to pick up my orders. But I almost fainted from my quivering attraction. It was like a light went off inside my body that blinked *I need you.*

"Are you going to pick up these fucking plates, or do we have to watch you melt all over that sleazy guy at table four that's on a date," Enrico, the line cook, barked. I approached the disgruntled cook with my false confidence. At least eight hot plates were waiting for me. Feeling overwhelmed by all of the distractions, I nervously picked up one of the hot plates.

"How do you know he's on a date?" I said, stacking two more plates of cheeseburgers, and greasy French-fries. "And how do you know he's sleazy? You're just jealous," I whispered as I turned away, jiggling four plates and all.

"He was in here a few nights ago with a different woman. Michelle waited on him, and gave him a piece of her mind "Enrico said, stopping me in my tracks.

"Oh, Michelle is like that. She's Israeli," I reminded him about my new roommate who I'd met only a couple of months earlier. She was in law school at UCLA, and had opinionated rants about, well, pretty much everything.

I was on my way to deliver plates to the rowdy young men at table fifteen.

"Are you ever going to make milkshake," he said as I passed table four.

"Almost there. I'm getting to it right now."

"We're enjoying your performance," he said seductively. I stood there feeling completely insecure, with sweat and grease running down my face. I wanted to blurt out to him and his extremely attractive date, *I used to be a ballerina. I'm not really a waitress in a stupid 50s diner. I'm just doing research. This isn't the real me.*

"He's a Russian comic; don't take anything he says seriously," said his date, a confident brunette.

Finally, she speaks.

"Oh...um, how long are you staying?" I asked.

"Grieshcka will be here for as long as they let him," she said. "He loves America, and the great service in restaurants, and the pretty girls he gets to flirt with. He's actually famous in some circles," she chuckled.

I looked him over as inconspicuously as possible, not recognizing his face from anywhere. The Russian comic Yakov Smirnoff was popular at the time, but this particular Russian had the refined features and shaven

117

face of a prince from a storybook romance.

That old buzz of romantic excitement was newly planted in me with this strangely intoxicating man. It was as though I was talking to someone from my past–*maybe Balanchine*? I finally had some hormones in my no longer starved body. Mostly, I felt alive again. Uncomfortable as it was, I still had that old dancer vulnerability.

"Would you like to go out sometime?" the man asked while paying his check only twenty or so feet from his date who was still in the booth, looking so cool.

"Oh, I thought you were on a date. It seemed you were," I said demurely, trying to hide my excitement that he might actually be interested.

"What does it matter? I find you very attractive, especially with grease running down your face. In Russia, we like our women little dirty."

"Russian comic, right?"

"Actually no. I'm doctor. Psychiatrist. I'd like to help you."

I shyly laughed at his ridiculous comment but took his card anyway.

"I'll call you," I said, as my whole body shook with nerves and insecurity, and twisted desire.

And I did. I waited a day, not wanting him to think I was too excited, or interested, or that I needed him to save me. I ran into Michelle's room confiding in her that this was it. "I've finally met the love of my life." And then I walked back into my room, which was actually the living room and dialed. My hands shook, picking up my push button phone. When he answered and seemed happy to hear from me, I almost fainted.

"I knew you'd call," he said in his intoxicating Russian drawl. His charm, and my own imagination, made me feel as though I was really talking to Baryshnikov.

A week later, on a hot and balmy evening, I frantically prepared for my date with this intriguing Russian. After a nice long shower, I grabbed my worn-out snap-front white blouse, and my black short culottes. These items weren't very sexy, but would cover my fat, anyway. One could never be less than anorexic in front of Mr. B—he wanted to see bones. I was beginning to sweat in anticipation of more sexual energy being exchanged. After all, while serving him, our chemistry felt like it could burn down a small village, at least mine did.

Stepping into my clothes without looking into the mirror, I pulled out a light wool black jacket that mom had bought for me a few weeks earlier. I considered wearing it, even though it was abominably hot out. I thought it might make me look a little thinner. *He'll never believe I was a ballerina. I'm way too fat*, went through my distorted mind.

Michelle exited the kitchen where she was cooking a fancy Israeli dish. The heat and spicy smells wafted down our little hallway. She walked past me and laughed at my exhibition of anxiety. "Are you seriously going to wear that jacket, Sue? I mean it's very nice and I know your mom just got it for you and everything, but it's like a fucking sauna in here."

"It's not as hot outside," I said, as I put the beautiful long jacket over my cheap and lighter clothes now damp from my nervous sweat. I walked to the bathroom mirror and studied my reflection. "That looks much better, doesn't it?"

She followed me like she really wanted to take care of me, and I saw her reflection in our medicine-cabinet mirror. "Why you're like, going out with this guy, I'll never know," she said in her Valley Girl way. "And why you need to appear, like, dressed up, is like another mystery to me. He's probably going to be as boring as all the other ones." Her strong voice and maternal nature made her seem older and wiser than me, although she was twenty-five while I was already an ancient twenty-seven.

"What other ones?" I asked, as though I had never been on another date. I brushed out my long brown hair and grabbed some make-up to conceal a pimple that I had picked at in a fit of anxiety. "I can't believe I have a fucking pimple."

"Listen Sue," Michelle grumbled, still standing behind me. "This guy doesn't even deserve to, like, go out with you. I don't know what you're like so nervous about?"

I applied the last dab of mascara and turned to her. "I'm a nervous person. That's what my acting teacher told me. I don't know…I'm just a mess!" I tore off the jacket. I marched back to my closet to find another top, but stuck with the short culottes since he'd mentioned how nice my legs were when I'd waited on him. I grabbed a black shirt with long sleeves and a wide boat neck that would accentuate my wide shoulders, and make everything else look a little smaller, and slipped it over my head.

"He's a doctor, you know. I bet your parents would like for you to go out with a doctor!" I said to Michelle and laughed.

"All Jewish parents want that, but not one like him." She hovered over me in my closet. "He's a sleaze bag. I've waited on him, and he always, like, reeks of alcohol." She was picking up my white blouse from the floor when we heard a knock on the front door.

"Oh my God, he's here! Do I look okay?"

"You're fine," she said. "Don't forget your jacket."

"Right," I said, as I put my arms through the lined woolen sleeves.

"Why are you always in black?" Michelle asked.

"I hate color. Anyway, I'm in mourning for my life," I laughed, alluding to my work on the famous Russian playwright's words.

She gave me a quizzical look, not knowing that famous line from Anton Chekov's *The Seagull*, and pushed me towards the door.

"I can't go," I said.

"You're going, even though I, like, hate this guy."

Chapter 16

GREGORY

Gregory Raiport

"So, are you really a comic?" I asked, truly curious what this enigmatic Russian, who was bringing out my dancer passion, did for a living. When he'd left his date to pay the check the week before, the card he handed me read Dr. Gregory Raiport. Was he a doctor, or a comic? Anyone could make a personal card and say they were a producer, or director, or for that matter, a doctor. I'd received a few of those business cards, only to find out those guys were complete scam artists, just trying to pick up girls, promising them a part in a movie that didn't exist.

His rapt attention kept me from staring at the overdone decor of the old red-walled restaurant we were seated in on Sunset Boulevard in Hollywood. Huge gold vases everywhere overflowed with plastic and silk flowers. This place looked like a stand-in for a fancy Russian wedding or funeral, and as a Russian, he represented the entire artistic world to me. I took it all in, with wonder.

"I'm psychiatrist in Russia, but here I'm lowly psychologist," he explained. "I haven't taken stupid American test yet. Why bother? I'll just be working for rich, disturbed, American cows," he added, staring into my eyes. I was strangely intrigued by his absolute disdain for my culture. He had those tormented Russian eyes that said they knew something deep. Here, finally, was the passion and complexity missing in my life!

I kept my hands glued to my seat, just as I was told to do in my acting class. I didn't want to knock anything over and humiliate myself.

"You can come in for free psychological evaluation," he slyly commented.

I couldn't keep myself from giggling at his seductive humor and was lost in his gaze. Feeling completely naked, and so in touch with my absolute submissiveness, I truly felt like I was on a date with someone from my old life.

Dressed in a blue designer jacket, his dark blonde hair fell over one of his light green eyes. I ached to place my hand on that bit of hair so I could see both of his tortured eyes. He looked just put together enough to be a professional of some kind, but still carried an aire of titillating danger about him. He smiled for a second then brought up his arm to wave the waiter over. "Where is fucking waiter? I'm starving."

He resumed flirting with me until the decrepit waiter arrived. He was decked out in his black-and-red Russian attire with gold and shiny stitching, The two of them spoke as though they were at a private KGB meeting, leaning towards each other and whispering in Russian. They seemed to know each other–or maybe they were making some kind of a deal? Looking at me again, as though I was his queen, he asked, "You like vodka, no?'

"Yes. I mean, that's fine."

"The waiter thinks you're very beautiful. He would like to take you out."

"But…" I stared at him, dumbfounded and insulted that he'd even bring up that remote possibility. But, in a twisted way, his bizarre comment made me even more attracted to him. How was I going to get through this night with myself intact?

When the waiter brought the giant carafe of vodka, I protested about the size, and he actually winked at me.

"See, he likes you," Gregory said.

Silence settled over us as the waiter poured the clear liquid into our glasses. My Russian prince gave me another charming smile and put his hand over mine as it rested on the table. "You're not nervous with all these Russians around you, are you?"

"No, I'm okay," I said, my hand beginning to perspire.

"I think I make you nervous. That's good."

"I didn't know vodka came in carafes," I said, as I took my hand from him to take a sip from my glass.

He continued to stare at me with a sort of smoldering desire. He took a long slug from his glass. My face flushed hot. "Did you say something to our waiter about me?" I asked.

"Of course not. Drink up my little pet. You need to catch up. Vodka is like water for Russians."

I picked up my glass and took another sip of straight vodka, cringing from the pure alcohol taste. He'd already finished an entire glass, while I searched for words. He was calm and in control, as I shifted anxiously in my red leather seat. He touched my palm again with his beautiful manicured hand.

In Russian, he ordered some unidentifiable food that was still unidentifiable when it arrived fifteen minutes later. "This looks fantastic," he said as our waiter Dmitri removed a silver cover from a large platter. "Give Serge my congratulations. I think he now knows what he's doing," Gregory chuckled.

Dmitri winked at me yet again as he removed the silver tops off more platters. He whispered to Gregory in Russian and patted his back with a large fleshy hand that resembled the bone-in-meat dish steaming before us.

"Serge is old friend from Soviet Union. He's free now, like me. Eat."

Staring at the food as though I was still a starving ballerina, I was sure Gregory could see me planning how I was going to avoid eating. It truly looked disgusting. No wonder Russian ballerinas were able to stay so thin. Russian food was obviously not for binging.

In New York, I had only eaten thinly sliced lox on thin brown bread those few times George and I went to the Russian Tea Room when I wasn't a thick, struggling, actress/waitress, sitting in a red booth with an enigma who was fueling my desperate and twisted desire.

Since working at Larry Parker's 24-Hour Diner, my diet had changed completely. Burgers with everything, blue cheese dressing on salad, pancakes, bacon and eggs, bagels, shakes, and French fries, had become my menu. I refused to count calories there. Still, something in me wanted this Russian to see me as the ballerina I once was–the starving, delicate, and Russian-seeming ballerina. Surely, he'd have appreciated me more then. I watched him eat ravenously, as though he hadn't seen food in weeks.

"You don't like Russian food, Suzankah?"

"It's great," I said, moving my fork around my plate.

I didn't want to insult him, so I took a bite of the awful looking stroganoff and almost gagged. Trying to act as though I liked what I just swallowed, I watched him spoon one thing after the other onto his huge golden plate. I picked up my fork and moved the stroganoff around some more.

He spooned up some red caviar and guided the spoon towards my mouth with a huge Jack O' Lantern smile. "I know you must love caviar, Suzankah!"

I smelled those fish eggs coming my way and knew before I even opened my mouth, how much I was grossed out by caviar. My father ate it on crackers almost every day as a snack. "So, what's it like in Russia? I've never been there," I said, nearly dry-gagging on the spoon he practically forced into my mouth.

"Of course, you haven't. Why would American girl who doesn't like Russian food want to go there?" he said. "It's Communist country."

"I know you're not going to believe this, but I was a dancer, and I always wanted to study there." I peeled the napkin from my lap and as delicately as possible, wiped my mouth. A few red eggs had dribbled into my white napkin, so I delicately stowed it to the side, hiding the evidence.

"You mean you wanted to be orphan? Because anyone who studies with Bolshoi will always be orphan." He spooned some sour cream on more caviar and rolled it into a blini, then took it all in one bite.

"I really was a dancer."

He looked like a cartoon character, barely taking a breath from eating and drinking. The few sips of vodka I had were beginning to make the room a little fuzzy. I drummed up the courage to boast about my inspired past, to at least let him know I was once cultured. "I studied at the School of American Ballet, in New York City, under George Balanchine. It's hard to get accepted there, just like the Bolshoi is in your country. Alexandra Danilova, one of your comrades, was my mentor."

"I'm impressed, Suzankah. One would never know." He was definitely getting drunk. The carafe of clear liquid was half empty by now.

"Really, I was."

"You're too voluptuous to be ballerina," he commented while swallowing a big bite of the meaty-hand-looking dish. Dmitri came back to check on us and gave me another wink.

"It's been almost four years. I'm studying to be an actress now."

"Actress…I know many actresses, don't I Dmitri?" He poured the remainder of the vodka into his glass. "Should I order one more?" he slurred. "Perfect timing, Dmitri. She would like one more."

"No, really. I'm fine."

"Don't listen to her. She drink like fish, and she's actress. You like actresses."

Dmitri gave me another flirtatious smile and whisked away our empty carafe to be filled again with more vodka. I silently excused the extravagance. I was floating on some kind of made-up cloud.

"I'm actually working on Chekov in class."

"Actresses come in all sizes," he laughed.

"So, what's it like growing up in a Communist country?" I asked, getting away from the actress stuff.

"I grew up in Georgia," Gregory said, referring to the Soviet Republic.

"Is that Communist?" I asked, immediately realizing I had just screwed up and he was going to think I was an absolute idiot.

"Ah, thank you Dmitri," he said as the new carafe of vodka was placed on our table. He poured himself another full glass and gestured to fill my own. I gave him a flirtatious smile and delicately placed my hand over the top of my glass.

"I'm okay."

"You are not okay. I can tell. You need some sessions with me in my office."

"Sessions?"

"I'm psychiatrist, remember?"

I giggled girlishly at what seemed a bit like a joke, even though he certainly embodied the title of doctor. "Balanchine and Baryshnikov are from Georgia also," I said, trying to change the subject.

"They are both orphans as I am, but I never went to Bolshoi."

I felt slighted by his dismissal of two of the greatest artists of the twentieth century and took a little sip of my vodka.

"Is your family still there? I continued with what seemed a normal question. I wiped a little sweat from my lip as Dmitri arrived to take away more plates and to take our dessert order.

"You didn't hear, you COW! I AM ORPHAN! I have no family!" He looked at Dmitri and calmly said, "She's like pretty cow, no?"

Did he just call me a cow? His words were fuzzy from the alcohol and that accent so I was hoping that he said something else.

Still looking at Dmitri, he made his pathetic request. "We'll have the strawberries Romanov. And stop drooling over my girlfriend. She's virgin, and I know you want to fuck her, but she's mine. I've got myself a fat ballerina!"

Then he downed the rest of his vodka.

Twenty minutes later we were in his car, and on our way. As we drove towards his home, the city lights sparkled while I continued to float on a cloud of adolescent love. I was convinced he was the one. A bit dizzy, I got out of his red Mercedes and followed behind, up the pathway to his duplex in Beverly Hills. With great charm, he invited me in. He set the car keys upon the white tiled kitchen counter and opened a cupboard above the sink.

"Would you like some more vodka?" he asked. "You don't drink much, do you, my zaftig little ballerina."

I wasn't impressed with his beige-carpeted, beige-walled apartment. Yes, it was clean and tidy, but it wasn't elegant in the way I had fantasized, the way I knew Balanchine lived. The brown couch was a bit worn, especially for a Beverly Hills apartment. The chrome-framed generic prints of flowers and reproductions of famous paintings that decorated the walls were not something that Mr. B would ever choose. And there he was, strutting toward me with that bottle of vodka.

I was falling in love with a man from the world I once knew. It didn't matter that he was now drinking MORE vodka. I took a little sip from the glass he brought to me. I cringed again from that awful taste.

"Thanks."

God, this night could go on forever and I'd still be in bliss. He might have called me a cow at dinner, and he might not believe I was once a dancer, but he was so tragically deep, so tormented, and so much like Uncle Vanya, the doctor, in Chekov's play. I'll be his Elena, and we'll fall in love behind my ancient husband's back. It had been so long since I'd truly lost myself in something.

He walked over to the stereo and picked out some music.

How did he know I loved Prokofiev? That was it. I just couldn't hold up anymore. The tears I worked so hard to evoke in all my Method acting classes just poured out naturally. I didn't need to hold on to an imaginary orange or apply imaginary make-up while looking in an imaginary mirror to evoke my deepest feelings.

So, is this what real acting, is? Or, is this my real life? Or was it just the Prokofiev?

The last years of my life as a dancer, the only thing I loved, flashed before me.

"You have such a Russian soul, Suzankah. You are just like us."

He did notice. Was it the tears, or did he sense something in me that was like THEM. The people I so admired.

"Can I kiss you Suzankah?

"Yes," I said, truly wondering why he'd waited so long.

It was pretty good. Not great. Passable. They say it's in his kiss, but for me, it was that longing/ passion/suffering, that he was releasing in me. *I probably can't have him. He's much too smart, and definitely too handsome for me.*

He represented everything I'd been reading about for years, and somehow, what I missed from my life as a dancer. And, if I could cry in front of someone on the first date, didn't that mean we were destined to be together? If it was a struggle to get him, didn't that make it worth waiting for.

"Would you like to see the rest of apartment?" he cavalierly asked, giving me his beautifully defined hand.

Sex with the wrong person, or at the wrong time could ruin it all. And I didn't really want him to think I was easy or free, as he called American women, earlier on our bizarre date. My chattering brain told me: *I might*

126

want to marry this guy. I better not go, but I gave him my hand. But then I let go as he continued on. Through my blurred vision his lone figure soldiering toward the bedroom looked like a Salvador Dali painting. Three seconds later, I made a sharp left into what looked like an office.

There must have been a thousand books on the shelves that lined most of the walls in that office. Everything looked dusted and tidy. I was dazzled by the familiar titles: Jean Paul Sartre's *Nausea*; Vladimir Nabokov's *Lolita*. They were my favorites. There was also Ernest Hemingway's *For Whom The Bell Tolls*, Dostoyevsky's *Brothers' Karamazov*, and short stories by Chekov. Even if I wasn't impressed with the furniture and décor, I was with the literature. There were books in Russian that I didn't recognize. I imagined Nikolai Gogol's *Diary of a Madman*, hoping I wasn't now with the protagonist of that book.

The drab apartment came alive with great literary artists and now my questions about him being literate and educated were answered. *Bingo! He must be.* I came around to the large wooden desk near the open doorway and saw piles of books in French, sitting near a covered typewriter. *He reads French too*! I walked over to a lone empty shelf, near a small window that was open a crack. Upon it several Hallmark-type cards were displayed.

Happy Anniversary To My Dear Husband was the first one I found. I didn't dare open it to see possibly his name. *Okay*, I thought. *I'm not going to pass out.* There were more, unfortunately. *Happy Anniversary To My Dear Wife*, and *Happy Birthday To My Dear Wife*. I didn't dare open either of those, in fear that I might find his name signed at the bottom of those tacky cards.

This can't be! He must be borrowing this apartment. It can't be his. He'd never have let me in here if it were his place! Or he didn't mind me wandering in to see the greeting cards displayed fully on his or HER desk! And, where is she? Try to keep steady and don't freak out. Shit! I thought I was going to marry this man!

"So, is your wife French?" I asked, sauntering into his bedroom.

"Yes, in fact she is," he answered as he pulled down the covers to the king-sized bed.

Is he lying or joking, or just tormenting me? Be cool and act like it's no big deal.

"Why didn't you tell me you were married?" I inquired, moving closer than I should have.

"You never asked."

"I just assumed, since you asked me out."

Oh my God, the cooks at Larry's were right. He is sleazy. He definitely drinks too much, but maybe he was as nervous as I was on our first date. Maybe he's just eccentric.

"My wife travels a lot. She's author and on book tour. Come to bed, my zaftig little ballerina. You must show me some tricks." He patted the fluffy bed.

Oh my God! He called me a ballerina! Rewind. Did he call me a zaftig ballerina? Rewind. Did he call me little? Rewind. Zaftig means fat. He does think I'm fat! He's so right.

"Why am I here?" I asked, truly wondering, considering all of these circumstances that were driving me batty.

"Because you like me."

"Is it okay if I ask how long you've been married?"

"Of course, it is, Suzankah. Isn't this nice bed?"

Dizzy from the alcohol, and not even aware that he didn't answer my question, I crawled inside the fancy sheets with most of my clothes on.

I was near him, oh my God. Maybe we could just cuddle. I was finally close to my Chekhovian doctor. Now he's truly going to know how fat I am, but this may be my only chance. Maybe I'll die young, but happy. Maybe she'll come and murder us both. She certainly has the right. Maybe this really isn't his apartment, and those Hallmark cards are for someone else!

I ran my hand along his handsome face and then my fingers through his hair. It would be okay if I died right here. He was so beautiful and was breathing so close to me. It felt so right to be there and yet so wrong. He smelled of the very French Vevetier, the same scent George used to wear. I absolutely loved that smell. There was nothing better on a man. And he seemed so clean. Not like the Russians I'd been reading about. His absent French wife was so very lucky to have him, but what the hell was I doing in their bed?

Chapter 17

COWS

I let the phone ring a few times before I picked it up the next morning.

"Hello," I said, in the sexiest voice I could muster.

It was Gregory and he sounded sober, yet still as Russian as he had the night before. My heart began beating wildly. *I can't believe he's calling me! I knew it; he likes me too!*

"Suzankah, you left earring in bed last night, and maid found it. I had to make up whole story, so she won't tell my wife."

He really is married and that was his apartment! I shouldn't even be talking to this man! What is my problem?

"Oh, I'm so sorry. I didn't even notice that I lost it."

"Of course, you didn't. You're too much in love, aren't you, Suzankah?"

"I don't know that," I stammered, embarrassed that I'd been found out.

"I'm doctor. I know these things. Would you like to see me again?"

How do I keep cool here? He likes me, and it was okay to cry in front of him, and I am going to marry him, and he's going to tell his wife gently that he's fallen in love with someone else, and he's so sorry that he's made this awful mistake by marrying in such haste. They'll get their marriage annulled, and she'll be happy to move on to a more appropriate partner that truly deserves her. He needs to be with someone who truly understands a Chekhovian doctor. That would be me.

"I want to take you shopping," he suggested, interrupting my fantasy thought train of our new life together.

"Isn't your wife coming back?" I asked, momentarily jumping back into reality.

"Let's go shopping on Melrose," he said without answering my question. "There's famous store there I think you will like."

He drove over in his Mercedes, The same car from the evening before. I shook with excitement. This was newfound love—the kind I needed—desperate, somehow. Finally arriving at the top of the stairs, I opened the front door as though I wasn't interested. I was trying hard at the cool and collected thing but it was not working well at all. He stepped in like a gentleman and was startled when my roommate Michelle walked out of her bedroom to say hi.

"Oh hello," he said. I practically melted at the sound of his voice. "You didn't tell me you have roommate. Don't I know you?" he asked with a look of recognition.

"Yeah. I waited on you at Larry's a few weeks ago. Remember, you asked for vodka at, like, 3 a.m.? I'm going to work," Michelle whispered to me. "You guys have the whole place to yourselves."

"You're very good waitress," he commented. "Not like Suzankah, here. She drop plates and has fight with cooks, but looks sexy in polyester uniform. She likes to show off her pretty legs, don't you, Suzankah?"

Michelle gave me that tough Israeli–Valley Girl look and gathered her things to get on her way. She'd warned me about *This crazy Russian guy that comes into the restaurant late at night with different women all the time.*

"Bye guys. Don't do anything I wouldn't do," she laughed. The door slammed behind her and we fell into each other's arms. I ran my hand along his face. He dreamily looked at me with those sad Russian eyes.

"She's tough girl, your roommate. She should be cop."

"She's Israeli. A bit rough around the edges, but she's a great roommate. She likes to clean and is an amazing cook."

"Good for us both," he slyly remarked and then leaned in for a kiss.

We were soon walking hand-in-hand down the street that had some of the best vintage clothing and furniture stores in Los Angeles. The year 1987 wasn't a time of shopping for me. Not only was I just trying to pay my rent, cover acting classes, gas, and phone bill, I had an expensive habit of getting parking tickets. I had no health insurance, no car insurance, and having new things really was of no importance to me.

We entered the store Gregory had boasted about, the one he claimed was famous. I went one way and he went another. The 1940s rattan couches and chairs with big and colorful Hawaiian flowers caught my eye. A few minutes later he was standing beside me, holding something small and distinct, and possibly affordable. He seemed completely unaware of other people walking by. We were in our own little world in this dusty vintage store.

"Do you like these cows, Suzankah?" he asked, while opening his beautiful Russian hand to me. "They're salt and pepper shakers. I notice you don't have any on your dining table."

The cows again! He has an obsession or something.

"They're very nice, but I don't really need them. I love these chairs, though," I said, taking a seat in the low-slung 1940s rattan chair.

"Suzankah, I know you want them."

"You don't have to buy me anything, really."

I wandered around the store admiring the handcrafted chotchkies, hoping he'd follow me. It felt so nice to be with a man. It had been five years since I'd lived with Virgil, in Germany, and more than six since I'd lived with George in New York. I'd been single for what seemed an eternity. I felt suddenly whole because I had a man. He liked me. I was part of a couple. And, he was a doctor. He was intelligent. He talked about philosophy and science, and Dostoyevsky. He claimed that *Notes from the Underground* was the story of his life. My parents would be so proud that I was with someone who was educated.

Walking from the store onto Melrose Avenue, I breathed in the clean air. It was one of those rare days when L.A. looked and smelled like a tropical paradise. He walked out of the store and sauntered toward me with a big Jack O' Lantern smile. "Look what I got for you, Suzankah," he said slyly, pulling the two cow-shaped salt-and-pepper shakers from his pocket and handing them to me. My eyes widened. I was stunned.

"You stole them?"

"Why do you think that?" he chuckled, acting like it was no big deal. "It's America. They owe me," he said with the confidence of a man who might have worked for Don Corleone in *The Godfather*.

My stomach dropped. I had shoplifted a total of once with my friend, Lisa Lockwood who was now dancing as a soloist for American Ballet Theater. We were in the Northridge mall and, well, it was a cool teenage thing to do at that time. In our amateur venture, we ended up in a police station, waiting for our parents to pick us up, cringing with fear and shame. After our handcuffs were taken off, we decided to rehearse an entire ballet right in front of the cops while they booked us. We relieved our anxiety as they looked on in wonder. I doubt they'd ever seen two fifteen-year-olds dance an entire Balanchine ballet around their desks.

But on Melrose Avenue I tried to hide my absolute discomfort with this unscrupulous Russian. "I told you I didn't need them," I pleaded.

"Don't you like them, Suzankah?"

My heart was beating way too fast. "Yes, but..."

"It's fun to see what one can get away with. You should try it sometime."

Why did he seem so relaxed? He had just committed an actual crime.

"Let's go get some food," he said. "I'm hungry. That's enough shopping for today."

We entered the huge Ralphs Market on Beverly Boulevard. He ordered some very expensive lox at the deli and told the bald man working the counter to, "slice it very thin." Moments later I saw him slide the package of Nova Scotia lox into a side pocket of his jacket.

We waited in line to pay for the eggs, bread, milk, and vodka. The milk and eggs were for his wife for later, and the rest was for us. I didn't want to eat in front of him. I still felt fat, especially since he reminded me of my ballet days, but he was hungry.

"I can't believe you walked out of the market without paying for the lox," I said, trying to act like I was accustomed to shoplifting men.

"Wasn't that fun? I do it all the time. You buy a few things and never walk out without bag."

"I thought you were a doctor. Can't you afford food? Or salt and pepper shakers?"

"You're so naïve, and so charming, my angel."

"I thought I was going to have a heart attack both times," I said, but I was mesmerized by his chutzpah to commit petty crimes right in front of me.

"Such a gentle soul you are. You're so Russian, Suzankah."

Why does this guy know how to say all the right things to me?

"Suzankah, you need to relax. People steal every day. They just do it in different ways."

Walking quietly to the huge parking lot, not quite hand in hand, I looked at him when we reached the red Mercedes. He gave me a twisted smile and we got into his car. We drove silently to my nearby apartment. Michelle was at work so we'd have the place to ourselves.

We walked up the white-painted stairs to my second-floor apartment, and I tried to conceal my joy of connecting with a man to whom I was insanely attracted. Since my relationship with Virgil in Germany, which only lasted the year of my contract, I'd only had a few short affairs. I wasn't even attracted to any of those guys who would pick me up after one of my night waitressing shifts. They all left after one night, leaving me curiously devastated. In my recovering-from-ballerina mind, I thought those anonymous men, actually liked me.

Opening the door to 2C, my heart raced with the anxiety of being intimate with him again. It had been so long since anyone acted as if they liked me. I went to the kitchen to get plates and glasses for our cozy lunch.

I tried to steady myself as I entered the dining room. His presence made me so fucking nervous. He was some kind of a drug. He knew himself. I didn't. He had control. I didn't. He got up from the table, gave me that wide twisted smile and pulled out a chair for me as if I was a princess. I set the plates, glasses, silverware, and paper towels on my cheap dining-room table.

"You really don't feel bad about stealing that expensive fish?"

"Of course not," he said, unwrapping the stolen lox. "Let's have some vodka, Suzankah. Let's celebrate."

"Celebrate what?" I asked as he poured vodka into one of the spotted water glasses.

"Your love for me, and perhaps mine for you."

Oh my God! He's in love with me, too. I can't believe how lucky I am! I shook inside, planning our new life together. "What about your wife?" I asked, picking up my glass of straight vodka. I took a stinging sip.

"It's complicated, as I am and as you are, my little rabbit."

I took another delicate sip from my glass. He drank from the bottle. "There's an extra glass here," I suggested, holding it up to him. "I know they're not very nice, but I actually purchased them."

"Maybe I should get you some new glasses. I can get them cheap," he said, taking another slug from the bottle of Stolichnaya.

I wondered if he always drank like this.

He stared at me with those beautiful eyes, partially covered by that strand of dirty blonde hair. "Let's go to bed, Suzankah."

"Aren't you picking up your wife at the airport later?"

"I am, but I'm here now with you. I know you want my big Russian cock."

How many colors of red could I turn? I wasn't used to men referring to their penises. I struggled to hold in my absolute embarrassment. Yes, I was obsessed with him, but why did he have to mention his penis?

The Russian thing was happening all over again. I knew intrinsically that I just wasn't enough. How could I truly deserve someone so mercurial, so handsome and so worldly? One of the definitions of "passion" is "suffering." It all just fit so well. Not only was I going to relive my passion and suffering as a dancer, I was going to learn what it was like to see the world through an authentic and tortured Russians' eyes. I was in absolute agony already. This truly must be love!

When he left abruptly after our sexual encounter, without a kiss or any kind of affection, maybe I should have gotten the message that he might not be my Prince in shining armor.

But I didn't.

"Wait here, Suzankah," he said as he climbed out of his car. I mean her car. His wife's car. I finally found out that the Mercedes wasn't his. He didn't even have a car. I sat in that red 1985 Mercedes so he could break into his Beverly Hills apartment, or what was once his Beverly Hills apartment. It had been three months since our first date and he no longer had the keys because his wife had finally thrown him out. They weren't divorced yet, just separated. I waited patiently in that car on that dark street for a half an hour. I still ached to be near him. It's not like I didn't have anything else to occupy my time. I was working diligently on Chekov in my acting class, but I still waited and yearned for our stolen moments together.

Though most of my friends questioned my sanity to wait for a guy like this, especially since he was married, I was committed.

"Waiting makes one appreciate any glory one receives in life," said the great composer Igor Stravinsky. I was definitely waiting.

133

"I got some vodka, bread, and cookies. Bitch doesn't have much food in there," he said as he climbed back into her car with me. She was away again, on yet another book tour, but still lent him the car until she returned.

Michelle, my tough roommate, was so clear on his intentions that she wouldn't allow him in our apartment, for fear of him messing it up and making me crazier than I already was. My neediness became unbearable for everyone around me. For me, in my still, recovering-from-ballerina-naiveté, I truly believed it was love.

Chapter 18

HOPE

Sitting at a terminal at the Los Angeles International Airport, I struck up a conversation with a conservative-looking young woman next to me. She was also waiting for her boyfriend's plane to arrive. Gregory had called me the day before to ask me to pick him up, and I was only too happy to oblige. It didn't matter that it was the middle of rush hour traffic or that I had to miss my acting class. He needed me. He needed my help. And I needed him.

"Where's your boyfriend coming from? I asked, admiring her pulled together look and long, flowing, fairy-like blonde hair.

"New York City," she said, while going through some paperwork in her briefcase.

"Mine too," I said. "It seems his plane is late or something."

"Mine is coming back from one of his motivational lectures that he gives periodically around the country. He's a doctor," she said.

Over the loudspeaker, I heard the announcement that the flight from JFK had arrived and passengers were disembarking at Gate 27. I stared into the distance toward the gates and when I turned my head back, the woman was gone. Where did she go, I wondered? I rose from my seat.

Then, all of a sudden, there she was, walking towards me with Gregory, a sweet little gallop in her step. She looked happy and contented, the way I wanted to be. She looked like a fairy from Shakespeare's *Midsummer Night's Dream*. Gregory walked his usual slow and tenuous pace, not quite keeping up with her. They were such an odd couple. They definitely didn't fit together. The airport terminal blurred as they approached. I blurted out something incomprehensible and they stopped in front of me. Then, SHE INTRODUCED US!

"Hello," Gregory said with great charm, as though he'd never met me before.

I took his arm assertively. "Can we talk?"

"Suzankah, don't make scene. I made mistake."

"We're going to take a little walk," I said to the bright-eyed little fairy. She didn't seem to mind.

"Take your time," she said, as though I was no real threat.

He looked upset as I dragged him away from her, but I was going to at least try to express myself without rocking the boat too much. If I went overboard, I might not get to see him again.

"You can't remember how many women you called to pick you up at the airport? Who is she?" I asked, holding back tears of jealousy.

"Nice girl, very smart. Her name is Erin. I like that name because it's little bit like boy, but she's very much girl, as you can see. She looks conservative, no?"

He likes her name because it's like boy? He must have had a few vodkas on the plane. He was slurring.

Erin walked up to us and took his arm. "Are we going?" she asked, as though I weren't there.

"Um, Erin, excuse me," I said, still trying to hold back tears. "He called me yesterday to pick him up, and that's why I'm here," I said, as though she was the real girlfriend.

"He called me early this morning. Are we going, Grieshcka? I have dinner waiting."

Oh my God! She cooks! No wonder he likes her more. I need to learn how to cook, and maybe then he'll appreciate me.

"Suzankah, I forgot I called you yesterday. I'll go with her and have some dinner, and then come and sleep with you, my proud little angel. Go home. I'll soon be there."

Is she okay with that? Going to my place after is okay with her? She might be as weird as he is. He has sex with her and then sleeps with me. She is definitely more desirable. She's thin, and it looks like she probably has a job that isn't slinging hash. He may even respect her. Oh god, I love him so much. I'll wait for him.

I walked away as though it was okay, as though I deserved what just happened. A strange strobe light effect blurred my vision as I made my way back to my little red Honda. Exiting the overwhelming airport was challenging and I drove around the terminals twice before I found the freeway turnoff. I cried on the long drive home back to West Hollywood, to my little apartment that felt so empty without him. He treated me just like his wife.

"I'm here Suzankah. Your prince has arrived," Gregory slurred.

Was I dreaming? I lifted my head; my bedside alarm clock said 3 a.m.; two hours after I'd dozed off while reading, yet again, *Notes From The Underground*, by Dostoyevsky. Gregory had given it to me a couple of weeks earlier with specific paragraphs underlined so I'd understand who he really was.

Rubbing the crusted tears from my eyes and cheeks, I tiptoed to the front door. I didn't want to wake up Michelle, in case I was just hearing things. There was also the possibility that I wasn't dreaming and my prince had arrived. I unlocked the door and opened it a crack. And there he was, as though nothing disturbing had occurred at the airport a few hours earlier.

"Erin dropped me off. Wasn't that nice of her?"

"How was dinner?" I whispered.

"Brilliant. You should learn how to cook, Suzankah. I'll come over more often and you won't feel so sad."

"Don't talk loud, please. Michelle is asleep like most people at 3 a.m."

"Aren't you going to invite me in, Suzankah? I'm freezing my balls out here."

"This is L.A., Gregory. We don't freeze here, remember?" I whispered, trying to make him believe I was at least sort of funny.

"Let's go to bed, Suzankah. I'm tired, and I have nowhere else to go. I'm orphan, Suzankah."

I opened the door quietly and watched him shuffle like an old man toward my bed. He took off his clothes and pulled a little black sleeping mask out of his jacket pocket. Then he took out a bottle of prescription pills. I was used to his vodka bottles and had seen him light up a crack pipe a couple of times, but hadn't yet seen any prescription pills in his possession.

"Okay, almost ready," he said, placing that ridiculous mask over his eyes.

"Do you need some water for your pills?"

"Do you mind, Suzankah? You know how hard it is for me to sleep. Insomnia is terrible thing."

I poured some water into the slightly spotted glass. What did it matter? He had that stupid mask on anyway. He'd never see them.

"Here," I said, handing him the dirty glass of water.

"You are angel," he said, swallowing a couple of pills.

I asked what he was taking.

"Valium, Suzankah. I can get you prescription, you know. I can get you anything you want. It would help you." He crawled into my bed as though everything was okay. I watched him fall sleep. He was at peace and I was tortured. He didn't even kiss me good night. I opened my book to see what else I could learn about this intoxicatingly bizarre man.

Chapter 19

CANCER

I was in my apartment, waiting for a call from Gregory. It had been a week since we'd spoken, so I was getting ridiculously anxious, almost like a drug addict without her fix. Suddenly the phone rang. Finally. I picked up the receiver, slowing my breath, trying desperately to not sound too excited.

"Hello," I said.

"Hello," said the female voice on the other line.

Damn! Why can't he call me? Where is he?

It was my mother. She hadn't called for a while, thankfully. I needed a break from our usually heated phone conversations with her view of my poverty-stricken life, coupled with her constant criticism of pretty much everything about me. Her words came out in a rush, considering my focus was truly on the man that I couldn't have.

"I have some bad news. Now don't get upset. I know how you are."

"I'm listening."

"Your father has inoperable lung cancer."

"What?"

"Your father has inoperable lung cancer. He might have a year."

She didn't just say that. I'm having a very bad nightmare, and if I think hard, I'll snap myself out of it. Rewind. Your father has inoperable lung cancer.

"Are you listening?" she asked. A deafening ringing overwhelmed my ear.

Heavy tears welled in my eyes. I let out a guttural scream. Michelle, who was getting used to my crying jags over Gregory, rushed in from her bedroom to see what the hell was wrong. This sound was different. It came from deep in my gut. How could I go on without my father?

The thought of never hearing dad's strong and beautiful voice again was unbearable, and how was I going to be able to handle mom without him? He was able to shut her down when she bothered me about my lifestyle or my appearance. She had a habit of commenting on my weight whenever she saw me. My dad protected me from her cruelty. He stuck up for my independence.

"You used to be so beautiful" she'd say. It was always nonchalant, as though it wouldn't upset my fragile hold on life. "What's happened to you?" she'd ask, as though I had become a drug addict or a hardened criminal just released from jail.

Jumping back to the unbearable moment, I reconnected with mom's pained voice. "Your father is going to die, and I don't know what's going to happen to you."

"Why don't you just worry about him right now?"

"Why do you want to be an actress? Is it because you didn't make it as a dancer?"

"Why are you asking me this now!"

"Because when your dad dies, I don't know who's going to take care of you."

Michelle was standing nearby, curious and stoic. "I'm so sorry, Sue," she said. "I really like your father. I mean I love his voice on the phone anyway. He makes me laugh."

I went back to the phone, wiping my tears. "I'll see you soon, mom."

Two weeks later, after my dad had a lung removed, I walked into the familiar smelling den, with the pine walls and beams, and the couch that I'd almost ruined four years earlier. Mom had it re-upholstered, but it still looked pretty much the same. It was never easy for me to visit, even though my apartment was only eight miles away in West Hollywood, where I had a life completely separate from theirs. I told mom I couldn't stay long. "I have to be at Larry Parker's by five 'o'clock."

"Dad is resting in the bedroom," she said. "They took that whole black lung of his out." Mom had worked at Children's Hospital in the cancer ward and had seen many children suffer and die from the disease. She'd seen death. Nurses have to be tough, and mom was certainly that. She put on her best nurse's front and took care of my dying father in the best way she could.

"I'm going up to see him," I said and walked sadly to their bedroom.

Peeking in, he seemed to be resting peacefully but didn't look like himself. He hadn't lost his hair yet but appeared frail and powerless, something unthinkable for my tough-as-nails father. I could see the outline of his diminished frame under the bed cover.

"Don't argue with your mom, please," he begged, in a crackling, barely audible voice. "I'm too tired."

"You heard us in the den?"

"Of course." "Thanks for coming. I know how busy you are with work."

I looked at what had been my parent's bedroom for the past twenty-one years. We'd moved to this house when I was six-years-old, and it held such checkered memories of my life. It still had the same smell that brought up the pain of the past.

"Can I get you anything?"

"Yeah, a few years to live," he said sarcastically.

"I love you dad," I choked out, trying to hide my tears.

"No tears. I'm going to beat it. I promise."

Despite his hopeful tone, my father was completely inert. I looked around the bedroom and spotted the framed pictures of my family all taken by him. He loved to shoot us candidly, somehow needing to see life as it really was in his photography. Dad's perfectly engineered Nikon camera allowed him to capture the inner lives of his family, and the people that shared his love of trapshooting. There seemed to be no façade in his observations. He saw us as the real deal.

"When you come back, please don't argue with mom," he pleaded. "She's doing the best she can. This is harder for her than it is for you."

Dad recovered from his lung-removal-surgery and went back to work at his office in Van Nuys, part-time, with one lung. His legal work gave him purpose and seeing his secretary every day gave him another reason to be. She'd grown used to his sarcasm over the years and had learned to appreciate him for who he was. Twenty years is a long time to work for someone, and dad's illness affected her too. She stayed strong and by his side through all that was to come.

Dad supposedly gave up smoking, but according to my brother, Mark, he'd sneak one or two a day outside in the garage when mom wasn't looking. He had to work with a breathing tube to develop the oxygen capacity of the existing lung, and he'd still sneak outside for a smoke! Considering dad's forty-year, two-pack-a-day cigarette addiction, I felt blessed that I wasn't an alcoholic and never picked up the smoking habit. But, without the veil of ballet, or now, a character to play, I was leaning towards masochism, without even knowing that's what it was. And, instead of the cold and dank atmosphere that had created Russia's great artists that I so admired and so ached to become, I was surrounded by sunny, suburban bliss.

A couple more weeks into dad's recovery, we had another visit in the pine-walled den where he was sitting in his swiveling king's chair. Thankfully, he wasn't having a cigarette. I stared up at the smoke-stained ceiling. He interrupted my dismal thoughts. "Hey, what the hell are you looking at?"

"Just wondering if we should repaint that ceiling, now that you don't smoke anymore."

"Mom will do that when I'm dead."

"It would look so much nicer," I said, trying not to acknowledge his blunt statement. "You're not going to die, remember."

"I might have a year, if I'm lucky."

"I'm taking Gregory to my high school reunion. What do you think?" I asked, trying to avoid the subject of his imminent death.

"Everybody is going to be married with children, and will have real jobs, or careers, and you're going to walk in with that degenerate, and a slinging-hash, job."

"I thought you liked him," I said, not registering his biting insult about my job. His words never hurt as much as mom's. They always had a tinge of absurd sarcasm that allowed me to laugh at myself and everything else.

My parents had met Gregory only once, about a month before dad's cancer diagnosis. I brought him to Thanksgiving dinner, and it was basically a good time, as dad showed no signs of being ill. Dad acted like he liked Gregory. Maybe he was just happy I was with a professional, or anyone, for that matter.

My gaze still searched the ceiling in my parent's den when dad jolted me back into some version of reality. "I just want you to have someone who might be able to take care of you," he commented, as though he knew that Gregory's psychology practice was failing, and that his divorce was pending.

"I'm just happy I'm not in a mental hospital," I said, reminding dad that I could laugh off my recent, not so great mental condition. "I don't really care what I appear like to anyone, really."

"You were never going to go to an institution," mom piped in, entering the den with her usual dishrag over her shoulder, acting oblivious to the eight months I spent on their couch.

"Jean, would you shut up," dad said. "Why do you always have to open your big mouth? She's doing fine, and she can take care of herself, even if she has shitty taste in men."

"I don't have shitty taste," I said, defending Gregory. "He's a doctor. You always wanted me to be with a doctor."

"Bob, she'll do whatever she wants to do," mom said, never happy to be left out when she could throw in an insult or two. "You know that. That's how she is."

"He's really not that bad," I demurred.

Maybe they did see how rude Gregory was at Thanksgiving dinner. Maybe that's why dad warned me not to bring him to the reunion. At least Gregory didn't say, "You need to obey me," in front of them during that joy-filled Thanksgiving gathering. I thought he had put up a pretty good front, compared to his normal behavior with me.

It was only my perceptive grandfather who saw through the façade.

Passing the stuffing down to my step-grandmother, Grandpa whispered, "What a wise ass." My step-grandmother gave him a strange look, thinking perhaps he was talking about his only son, my dear father. We all continued to pass the cranberries, stuffing, mashed potatoes, and string beans around, as though there wasn't a mad Russian at our table. Then, Grandpa expertly cut into our Thanksgiving turkey, the professional carver that he was.

Getting ready to leave for work, my foot nearly out the den door, mom chimed in another one of her astute observations. "Those Russians are all alcoholics," she said. I rolled my eyes back, signaling my own disdain for her disdain of pretty much everything I did.

"Bye dad," I said with an aching heart.

"Bye," he choked, and went back to his book on World War II.

I opened the den door and made my grand exit, back to my little red Honda, back to my own personal struggle.

Chapter 20

REUNION

The dress that mom bought for me, so I would look okay for my 10-year high school reunion from North Hollywood High, was long and black with silver buttons up the front, and a low-tiered waist. I didn't have the proper dress shoes, and I didn't want to pressure her for another purchase, so I wore my trademark black western boots. I thought they looked cool with my long black dress.

I didn't listen to dad's advice about bringing Gregory. I was actually proud to have a man with me, not a twenty-something boy. He looked pretty dashing when dressed up, and he certainly was capable of carrying on long conversations in English. He'd be fine if I left him alone for a minute to catch up with a long-lost friend. I thought having him on my arm would be impressive, and I needed someone there to make up for not being a dancer anymore. That's what everyone would have expected, I imagined. But surely, no one really cared. Everyone would have his or her own dramas and expectations for the evening.

We walked hand in hand down the long red-carpeted lobby at the Sheraton Universal Hotel. We had taken his wife's red Mercedes-Benz yet again. Cars matter in L.A., and even though I wasn't caught up in the material world, I didn't want to drive up in my ancient Honda.

I'd lost my ethereal-ballerina, floating-through-air quality, and felt more like a grounded Russian shot-putter walking with my prince down the long mirrored hallway to the ballroom, where the reunion would take place. Couples walked by, but I didn't recognize anyone. Loud conversations briskly glided past us. My head spun with over-stimulation. I stopped by a huge crystal vase that held a bouquet of tiger lilies and roses and took a deep whiff of their glorious fragrance.

"Suzankah, you're slowing us down. Don't you want to show me off to your friends?" Gregory asked with his usual confidence. "That's why you brought me here, isn't it, my little rabbit?"

Still reveling in the beautiful aroma, I looked at him with my usual submissiveness. I was still so dangerously attracted to him, no matter how absurd his comments were.

"I'm going to get drink, Suzankah. Would you like one?"

As he walked away, I suddenly felt so alone and cold from the air-conditioning. Should I follow him? When I finally caught up with him we argued about him leaving me there standing alone. He ordered a Stolichnaya from the bartender.

"You need to relax, Suzankah," he blurted, turning to me with a glass of straight vodka in his hand. "I have Valium here if you'd like one. In fact, I think I'll take one myself." He set his drink on the bar and pulled out a prescription bottle from his beautiful navy jacket pocket. Giving me one of his Jack O' Lantern smiles, he shook a couple of tiny blue pills into his open hand and swallowed them with his vodka. "They have lots of free booze here, Suzankah. Aren't you going to have a drink?"

"Sue!" Marlene yelled, only a few feet away from the bar that was making me terribly nervous. *Would I have to peel Gregory off the floor and drag him to the car by the end of the night? Maybe I shouldn't have brought him. Maybe dad was right.*

I turned away from Gregory and gave my old friend a big hug. It was so comforting to see Marlene's big-dimpled smile. "I didn't know you were like going to be here. I thought you might, like, still be in New York," she said, reminding me that even though she'd also lived in a few interesting places, she was still a Valley Girl. "I think I got, like, one letter from you since you were living in Europe."

"I haven't danced in four years," I whimpered, suddenly worried about where Gregory went and what he might be doing. "Are you still working for *Rolling Stone*?" I asked, admiring her long green dress, strappy sandals, and super skinny arms. She looked like the one here that might have once been a ballerina.

"Yep, but I moved to Nashville. I'm just visiting family while I'm here for the reunion. You're not dancing! That was, like, your entire life, Sue!"

We both glanced around the grand lobby when Gregory re-appeared, drink in hand, teetering and slurring his words. "Aren't you going to introduce us, Suzankah?"

"Nice name," Marlene said. "Sue, you didn't change your name, did you?"

"Gregory, Marlene, Marlene, Gregory," I said, tentatively, praying that he wouldn't say something ridiculously embarrassing to my friend I hadn't seen in years.

He took her hand and gave it a Russian-Prince kiss.

"Let's go inside," Marlene said, looking at me strangely.

"Would you like a drink?" Gregory stopped her, as though the bar was his own.

"A white wine spritzer, thank you so much" Marlene said, still acting suspicious of the man, standing so close to her.

We waited while he ordered her spritzer and a white wine for me. Then we all walked in together into a sea of people that I still didn't recognize. Finding our table, there was my only high school friend I'd contacted when I'd had a breakdown four years earlier. Lynne had taken a few walks with me at the Hollywood reservoir when I so needed support. She was Saint Lynne.

"Thank God you're finally here," I said to Lynne as Gregory pulled my chair from the table, like some version of a gentleman.

"Thank God you're here," Lynne said. We gave each other knowing smiles. She worked in a lab at USC and functioned in the real world, but she was never terribly social. She was as uncomfortable there as I was, even if she had her life seemingly together. But I had Gregory, my shield from the world that I didn't quite fit into yet. "I'm proud that you got here," she said sincerely, not taking note of the curious man by my side.

"Aren't you going to introduce us?" Gregory slurred.

"This is my old friend Lynne. She's in science too."

"Are you doctor?" he asked in his best flirtatious manner.

"Actually, no," she said, looking disgusted by his very presence. "Did Sue tell you that I was a doctor? Hey Marlene, it's been, like, forever."

"Who is Sue?" Gregory asked.

Both Marlene and Lynne giggled at my boyfriend's dismissal of my name.

"Let's go to the bathroom," Marlene piped in. "I need to pee. Does anyone else?"

"We just sat down," I complained.

"I have a peanut-sized bladder."

"Me too," Gregory slurred. "But I have big cock."

"Did he just say what I think he said?" Lynne whispered as I turned a few shades of red.

He's really going to do it. He's going to ruin my time here. I gave him a subtle dirty look that I thought he might understand, and he gave me his twisted Jack O' Lantern smile. He then got up to escort Marlene to the bathroom.

"Excuse us, Suzankah."

Lynne watched them leave the table, shaking her head in disbelief. "Jesus, Sue, are you sure you're in love with this guy. I mean, I don't think he's very good for you."

"Probably not, but he's so...I don't know...."

I watched the two of them drift and prayed that Gregory wouldn't try to accost Marlene in the women's bathroom. I prayed he wouldn't slip and fall on the tile. I fretted as I sat there with Lynne, wondering what he would do next.

By the time they returned to the table, they were talking like old friends. Lynne and I were catching up, and I was tipsy enough now to ignore Gregory's behavior. He bid Marlene goodbye and left our table to inexplicably wander around.

"Why did you bring him?" Marlene finally asked, sitting back down at our table. I scanned the huge ballroom and caught sight of Gregory chatting up people I didn't even know, as though he knew them. I saw puzzled expressions on the faces of the people he tried to talk to.

Would someone call the police on him? Would I sit in absolute embarrassment while he was taken away in handcuffs?

"I'm madly in love. Can't you tell?"

"Sue, I think he might be crazy and you should be careful," she said. "He was talking about someone he wanted to murder to get some money. His wife's uncle? I think the name was, like, Bernie Cornfeld. Sue, he's married!"

"I know, but they're separated."

"You didn't tell me he wanted to murder his wife's uncle," Lynne piped in.

Bernie Cornfeld was a millionaire financier and playboy who Gregory had met at some Hollywood party with his wife. He lived at Grayhall mansion in the heart of Beverly Hills and was connected with the Hollywood elite. Mr. Cornfeld was not Gregory's wife's uncle. That was just one of his many delusions that he himself believed.

My mind drifted off to a few days earlier when Gregory and I had taken a little trip to his private post office box in Beverly Hills where he'd receive those absurd, *Murder In Five Easy Steps*, manuals.

"Yeah, he gets these manuals in his post-office-box, with mapped-out methods of murdering people," I admitted. "It even has pictures! I'm not sure if it's a joke book. It actually has these stick figure diagrams with literal directions on the side. It's pretty funny."

"Sue, that's not that funny," they both said in unison.

The clanking of glasses and the loud chatter was becoming overwhelming.

"I think I'm going to go," Lynne said. She pulled her straight-back-cushioned chair away from our huge round table. It slid so easily on the plush carpet.

"Let me go get you a margarita," I suggested, downing the rest of my white wine.

"I'll stay a little longer, but I'm not drinking," she said. "I don't want to wind up wandering around talking to people I don't know, like that insane Russian doctor you brought."

"How the hell can he be a doctor?" Marlene asked as I got up to get Lynne the drink she didn't even want.

146

"He worked with the 1976 Olympic gymnastics team…psychological motivation," I said, peering at the green and pink floral carpeting. "I mean the Soviet teams. He's writing a book about it with his wife. I mean ex-wife. They're separated. He told you he's a psychiatrist, right?"

As I marched down yards of plush carpet, I pondered my relationship to Gregory, and why I was always drawn to older men. I thought of Anais Nin, and the wonderful essays and diaries she'd written about her affairs with great men. I adored her stories about Henry Miller, and her frequent trysts with the intellectuals and bohemians of the time.

The handsome blond surfer types brushed past me. I barely even noticed, so lost was I in my worry about what Gregory might do next. He was intelligent and funny in a way most people weren't, and kind of abstract. He was always the boss. Bingo! He's my Henry Miller. Didn't all those great writer's drink too much?

People pushed and shoved to get to the front of the bar, and I went with it as if flowing in a big sea, lost in a daydream of my demented Henry Miller, now on view for all my old schoolmates to see.

"Who's this letter from?" I asked, as I helped him rifle through his mail that day at the post office. "This looks Russian."

"My daughter still lives in Russia," he said, as though it was no big deal, and I already knew that he had children.

"You have a daughter in Russia?" I gulped back my tears. "Why didn't you tell me?"

"Not necessary," he said nonchalantly. "I will probably never see her again."

"Are you still married in Russia?" I asked, not putting anything past him.

"That's none of your business, Suzankah. Don't be such a cow!"

"What's she like? I mean, your daughter."

"She's fat with bad skin, like cow. Fourteen-years-old is hard time." He started to open the letter, as we walked away from the cramped space that his P.O. box was nestled in.

"So, what does she have to say to her daddy," I asked, as we wandered on to Wilshire Boulevard.

He stopped to actually read the letter. I peered over his shoulder, truly wondering what a fourteen-year-old girl would say to her missing father that she never got to see and might not ever see again.

"She says she loves me, Suzankah. She can't wait to visit me."

I looked straight ahead towards his wife's Mercedes and wondered what else I didn't know about my complicated and intoxicating Russian.

Snapping back to the reunion, I drifted back to our table and managed to deliver Lynne's margarita without a spill. Gregory finally returned to our table as though he knew exactly when I'd come back from my alcohol run. He held out his hand at the exact moment I sat down and I melted. "May I have this dance, Suzankah," my prince asked. I looked into his beautiful green eyes and gave him my hand, as though nothing could be better. He guided me toward the dance floor. I pointed up to the huge disco ball above us, rolling and swirling.

"Can you believe they have a disco ball?" I laughed.

"I like it," he said. "Let's dance, Suzankah."

Even if the music was bad and cheesy in 1988, that disco ball, spinning round and round created an atmosphere of beautiful disorientation. Gregory wasn't much of a dancer, but just being in his arms was enough for me to swoon, like those days when I was seventeen and dancing with the gay boys in New York. In the corner of my eye, I could see other twenty-seven and twenty-eight-year-olds, lost in their partner's embrace. I looked into his eyes, taken by this moment. It was so complicated, exciting, and weird being in this strange environment near people with whom I had a tenuous bond and would probably never see again.

"What is it my rabbit?" he asked in a tender way.

"Hold me tighter," I cried as he brought me up from a clumsy dip. "My dad's dying. I don't know what I'm going to do."

"You're going to dance, Suzankah," he whispered sensuously.

My humiliating tears wouldn't stop. Those were the exact same words that Dennis Nahat, the artistic director of The Cleveland Ballet, said to me four years before, when I thought I knew who and what I was, before he proceeded to fire me. "You're so Russian, Suzankah," my prince reminded me. I wiped my mascara-stained eyes before we walked hand-in-hand, back to our table.

"Hi," I said, as we rejoined Lynne and Marlene at the table. I introduced him to those seated with us that he hadn't met. "This is Gregory. He's from Russia, I mean Georgia, which is in Russia, which is like Communist."

Oh my God! How much more of a fool can I make of myself?

"Yes," said Daniel, who I sort of recognized from school. He stared at me with a look that said to me I shouldn't have brought him. "We met a little while ago at my table over there. "Interesting guy," he added under his breath. "You're a doctor, right?"

"Now that everybody is reacquainted, it's time for some door prizes," a voice announced over the sound system. "You should all have received a yellow ticket at check-in." It was Jeffrey, the 1977 North Hollywood High student body president standing at the microphone. Gregory's eyes lit up.

"We're going to win door-prize, Suzankah. Do you have little ticket?"

"Here it is," I said, bringing it out of my purse. "This is so silly. I

148

never win anything."

"You don't, but I do," he slurred. "Shhh!"

"Number 537! Any takers!"

"That's our number, Suzankah. Fantastic! I'll get it."

Before I could even look at that little yellow ticket, Gregory was up and striding to the podium, where the former student body president was waving a stupid-looking German beer stein in the air.

"You guys won the beer stein?" Lynne asked.

"I didn't even see the number on the ticket. Gregory said he's good at winning prizes."

"Why is that Russian asshole going up there to get your door-prize?" Marlene asked.

"Because it appears, he thinks everything is his," Lynne answered. "Sue, get up there and get your stupid prize," Lynne insisted.

I stared at the stage to see Gregory handing Jeffrey my ticket. Jeffrey looked at the ticket and shook his blonde surfer-head. It appeared he was indicating there was some kind of mistake.

Oh my God. That wasn't our number! And as soon as the truth hit me, the actual winner walked to the podium as Gregory held the beer stein in his hand like an Olympian.

Three seconds later it was determinedly whipped from his hands and awarded to the former class-mate who looked so juvenile up there next to my Russian prince. Gregory stayed on stage for several minutes, arguing that that stupid prize was his. Dejected, he finally shuffled back to our table, muttering in Russian, still believing that he'd won, still believing that they were wrong.

I felt a thousand eyeballs on me as he sat down.

"Would you like to go out some time?" a dark-haired guy at our table asked me, right in front of Gregory, as I shriveled with embarrassment.

"Do I know you?" I asked, cringing at Gregory's demented act on stage.

"Well, we went to school together, and I guess this is as good a time as any to ask."

"Go, Suzankah. He's cute American boy. Probably wanted to fuck you in high school, when you were still virgin. I'm going back for my prize."

"Please don't," I begged, wanting to hide from the staring strangers.

"Okay then. I'm leaving, Suzankah. Are you coming home to fuck?"

"I'll take you home," my new suitor, said, and I finally remembered his name. It was Alex and we had been in history class together.

"That's okay. I don't think it's a good idea for him to drive like this. Here's my number, Alex," I said, writing it on a napkin. I helped Gregory out of his seat and felt the absolute humiliation that my father had been so right about. "Call me, we'll like, catch up," I said, as I steered Gregory toward the exit.

Chapter 21

SURVIVAL

I drove my parents to the airport for dad's last trip, well, anywhere. I was blind with the hope that he might survive his dismal diagnosis and things would miraculously turn around. They were both fifty-eight years old, but dad had aged, and his once stocky body was now frail. He looked almost like a parent to my well-preserved, and healthy mom. Even though dad was back working, he was apparently still taking occasional secret trips to the garage for a smoke. I never witnessed any of these private affairs, but my brother, Mark, swore it was absolutely true.

Helping them unload their luggage, I bid them adieu. I watched them enter the LAX terminal and my stomach ached with loss. I then drove back home to my life as a waitress and struggling actress. My saving grace, at least mentally, was that I had a callback the next day for a play I'd been working on in class, and was convinced I'd get it. Confidence eluded me in most ways, but this particular role rang so true with my inner life, I was pretty sure it was mine.

The week that my parents were in Europe, Gregory and I had a rendezvous at Bernie Cornfeld's guesthouse. The tycoon that Gregory supposedly wanted to murder was letting him stay there temporarily. The romance I thought was possible with him seemed to coalesce. We chatted and laughed while he smoked, something he rarely did. Everything seemed to be falling in place. We were actually communicating and he wasn't intoxicated. And then he started dropping hot cigarette ashes on me. When I complained that it hurt, he said, "Russian women like it, Suzankah."

I got quiet, held it in, and allowed him to hurt me. We then went out for a swim in the big pool that the guesthouse was nestled behind. The ballerina in me still wanted to hurt, just like a real Russian. When I sauntered outside to dive into the gorgeous pool, I spotted a lanky, androgynous-looking model-type swimming around like a mermaid. *This can't be his other girlfriend.* I got into the pool and she never even acknowledged me. Moments later, she dried off and entered the tiny guesthouse. The pain of him having another woman there for me to view, even if he'd just dropped ashes on me, hurt more than those burns.

Naomi was privy to some of it. I would share some of my embarrassing stories with her while burning calories on the Stairmaster at the Hollywood YMCA, our home away from home. Being a member for a couple of years, Naomi seemed to know everyone there. She had finally persuaded me to join after hearing too many of my desperate complaints about being out of shape.

Leaving one warm evening together, one of her acquaintances, a screenwriter, walked by us in the parking lot.

"Susie, this is Henry. Henry this is Susie," Naomi announced, rolling down her window. "Henry reads the entire newspaper on the Stairmaster almost every day. Impressive!"

"Nice to meet you, officially," I said. "I've seen you riding madly on that Stairmaster with your crumpled newspaper."

I'd seen Henry before, usually wearing one of his vintage Hawaiian shirts, bright colored 501 Levi's, cool John Lennon-style glasses and funky Converse tennis shoes. He was tall, in great shape, slightly balding, full of kinetic energy, and held himself with great confidence. He would saunter into the Y as though he owned it, and as though he knew everybody, which he apparently did. He seemed to be always having a good time.

"See you two on the Stairmaster," he said as we rolled our windows back up.

"What an interesting guy. He's got such a great energy about him," I gushed as we drove toward our separate apartments on Sweetzer Avenue.

The same week that my parents were away in Europe, I waited by the phone. Not for a call from Gregory, but for the play I'd had a callback for a few days earlier, the one I was pretty positive I was going to get. The call finally came, and I kept myself from screaming my absolute excitement into the phone. I held myself back, acting like it was no big deal, and I didn't really need the free job in a dumpy theater.

"Yes, I won a Drama Logue Award for my performance in David Mamet's, uh, *Reunion*," I reminded the young stage director on the other end of the line, hoping that the acting award would impress him, as much as my audition did. I prayed he wouldn't suddenly figure out I was an imposter and change his mind, even if I was an award-winning equity-waiver-theater actress. "Rehearsal starts when?" I asked, as though I had to clear my busy schedule. I hung up the phone, ran down the hall, and screamed to Michelle, who was studying in her bedroom.

She looked up from her law textbook as I jumped up and down in her doorway. "That's so great Sue. Hopefully it will take your mind off that

151

crazy Russian and I won't have to hear you whimper so much. It's so demeaning, that stupid whimpering. How much are you getting paid?"

I couldn't wait to tell Gregory the good news, even though, after the pool incident, I told him I never wanted to see him again. I ran back to the phone and dialed his number. My hands were shaking, and tears welled in my eyes. I so wanted to prove to him that I was good at something. He was always introducing me to rich and established people at these vapid Hollywood parties we'd attend. I'd cringe with embarrassment when I'd stammer "I am an actress," while real starlets working in television chatted in close proximity.

My heart fluttered when he picked up the phone.

"Shut up, you fucking asshole," I heard over the line. "That fucking dog will never be quiet. Who's this?"

"It's me," I said, hoping he wasn't in a bad mood and would maybe hang up on me.

"Ah, Suzankah," he said, sounding like he was at least a little happy to hear from me.

"I have to tell you something," I whispered, holding in my tears of joy about my new part.

"Would you like me to come over? Goddam Mitzi and her stupid fucking dogs. I swear this one dog is killer. I think it's good to leave her alone, so she can drive other vicious dog crazy. I'm getting hungry. I have no food in this fucking little house."

In exchange for his twice-weekly therapy sessions, Mitzi Shore, who co-owned and ran the famous Comedy Store on Sunset Boulevard, was letting Gregory live in her guesthouse. His wife had thrown him out of their apartment nine months earlier, and after a couple of weeks of mooching off Bernie Cornfeld, Gregory managed to talk Mitzi into the barter. I never knew exactly what occurred during those therapy sessions, but according to him, Mitzi was improving and had much better self-esteem.

"Pick me up, Suzankah. Fucking bitch took her car back," he said of his wife.

I grabbed my black baggy Levis and white-snap-front blouse to drape myself in. I peered in the mirror, covered up a few pimples, and applied eyeliner and mascara. One more peek in the mirror, and I told myself, *You look okay enough to spend time with the man who will probably berate you for not having any nice clothes or having a shitty red Honda.*

But what did it matter? I was willing to take him back and that's all that matters to a love addict. He was still a drug and I just couldn't wait to see him, even if he wanted to drop more ashes on me. I ran down the stairs and drove anxiously to Mitzi Shore's little guesthouse on Doheny Drive.

He got into my car with a big smile, and told me we had to visit a place that had the best food in town. I followed his specific instructions and drove east. I held in my excitement of just being near him and the joy of getting a lead in a good play. The silence was enough for me. The drug of him was doing its trick.

Then we arrived and went inside the Armenian restaurant.

"You must obey me," Gregory demanded, prompted by nothing. He stared at me with colder eyes than usual as we sat down at an extremely long table. Even though it was springtime, Christmas lights still twinkled around the room. I giggled at his stupid request, but I was by now accustomed to his particular brand of ridiculousness. I could smell the alcohol on his breath.

"Thank you," I said, practicing my nice manners as a waiter brought over a carafe of vodka, a carafe of 7-up, and a couple of menus.

"I guess the waiters here know you," I said as the waiter poured our drinks.

"Yes, my princess. I've been here with Morgan, and Erin and all of the other women who love me."

"Is that why all of the waiters and busboys are staring at us, because they know all of your other girlfriends?"

"It's just us, and we're celebrating your new play that you think you're going to be so good in."

"I never said that," I demurred. I took a sip of my 7-Up.

"You will be wonderful, and I'm so sad that I won't get to see you perform. I'm moving to New York, Suzankah! No one can help me here in Los Angeles anymore. Just three weeks more for us to be together," he added with surprising sincerity.

I stared at him, shocked at this news that made me feel completely abandoned, even though I had just told him I wanted to break up with him. "So, we're actually celebrating your departure from Los Angeles and not my play," I said, with a familiar aching in my stomach.

"Yes, Suzankah. You will never see me again. Perhaps you will be happier without me. Perhaps you will finally get a self. Perhaps you'll fall in love with someone else."

I asked him if we could move to one of the cozy red-leather booths, since this was a special night, and I ached to be alone with him. "There might be a big party that wants to use this huge table," I said.

He picked up his glass of 7-Up and threw the entire thing in my face.

"You will obey me," he ranted. I like community table." The petrified waiter came over to take our food order and help me clean up. I just stared at him, the stinging carbonated liquid seeping into my eyes and nose, and onto my white snap-front shirt. I wiped myself off as the waiter watched with his sad brown eyes.

"Oh hello," Gregory slurred. He acted as though nothing had happened, and that I wasn't sitting there, drenched like a wet cat. "We're ready to order our food now. My princess here will have the Shish Kabob because, as you can see, she's very hungry. And she'll have one more 7-Up, because she spills when she's drinking. One more half-carafe of vodka for me, and Suzankah here will let me have some of her Shish Kabob. She needs to lose weight. She's actress."

It was still light when we left the restaurant. We walked outside, onto the loud and bustling street, and into my crumbling Honda. Every car whizzing by and all the honking horns, and the blinding sunlight was an assault on my frayed nerves. As emotionally disoriented as I'd ever felt, I still wanted to take him home with me. I still wanted to imagine that he'd make love to me in a way that he did with all his other girlfriends.

I helped him up the stairs to my apartment with the same emptiness that engulfed me every time I was with him. How was I ever going to crawl out of this skin that was so uncomfortable? Is this what real life is?

He started rummaging around his night bag the moment we entered the empty living room. Michelle was out, thank God. She didn't approve of Gregory sleeping over. He pulled that stupid black sleeping mask out of his bag, let his clothes fall on my stained carpeting, and walked toward my bed like a zombie. He moved the tall shoshi screen out of his way, so he could crawl onto my queen-sized bed.

"Good night Suzankah, I had good time. I hope you did too."

He fell asleep almost immediately, and there I was, watching him sleep, yet again.

Suddenly the phone rang. Gingerly picking up my cheap plastic phone, I whispered into the receiver. "Hello?"

Answering the phone with Gregory asleep in my bed was a tricky proposition. His outbursts when he was woken from a drug-induced sleep were truly frightening. I feared for my life when he went into one of his drunken, drug-induced tirades. But tonight, I looked over at him, and he looked so peaceful.

"Mark picked us up at the airport," mom said on the other end of the phone. She said it as though it should have been me executing the familial duty. "I didn't call you, because I knew you'd probably be busy with something."

"I'm sorry I couldn't make it," I whispered, still fearful I might wake the sleeping psychopath. I lied and said I had a rehearsal for the play within which I was recently cast.

"You got cast in a play?" she inquired. "That's wonderful. And what's the play, may I ask?"

"It's called *Fool For Love*. Sam Shepard wrote it."

"Who's Sam Shepard? And, why are you whispering? I'm deaf in my left ear, remember."

"I remember. Change ears. He's the guy from Frances, that great movie with Jessica Lange and Kim Stanley."

"Are you getting paid?"

"No, but it's a really good play."

"Well, you know what you're doing, I guess. I hope it's not about some crazy woman."

I peered at Gregory and thought about what my mother said. She didn't quite understand my drive to become an actress and was usually negative about my involvement in any way. It meant that I would be surrounded with other people, studying, rehearsing, having a life separate from her. She was happier when I needed her and relied on her. Becoming an actress meant I was becoming emotionally independent.

So, in that moment, it felt nice to hear her being positive with me, but why did she care if the play was about a crazy or normal woman? Did she not want to see herself reflected in a character I might play?

"It's going to be in a dumpy theater in Venice," I lamented. Wanting to take the focus away from my not terribly successful life as an actress, I changed the subject. "How was your trip?"

"Your father is exhausted. I think it was just too much for him. We were supposed to stay another week. But I'm so glad we went. Ireland is extraordinarily beautiful."

"How about England?" I said. "You know I was there five years ago, when I was dancing."

"Yes, I remember. You've traveled much more than your father and I ever got a chance to. We never got to England on this trip. Your father was too ill."

There was silence on the phone for what seemed an eternity.

"I'm so glad you were both able to go, though," I finally said. A thick guilt enveloped me as I recalled all the things I'd put my parents through. I felt a sense of responsibility, as if I alone could bring on a lethal cancer.

"You always did what you wanted, and look at you now," mom said bitterly, without a grain of sensitivity in her voice.

"Can we get back to the trip?" I pleaded.

"It was really hard. Your father doesn't have long, you know."

I urged her to be positive.

"You will never live in the real world, will you?' she said.

"Let's talk later, mom. I'll come over tomorrow."

"Daddy will be happy to see you. He's too tired to talk now."

"Bye, mom. Welcome home," I said with my broken heart. I hung up the phone, and peered at Gregory, sleeping soundly with his stupid mask. I could never again sleep or be with this man. A buzzing fear rose up from my toes and into my head, and it dawned on me what he was truly capable of. I picked up the phone and called Naomi, who lived three doors down.

"Naomi," I whispered, "can I sleep on your couch? He's starting to scare me."

Chapter 22

TAXI

He clutched his dirty glass of vodka as we sat together at my dining room table. I stared at the crusted blisters around his mouth, the result of smoking a crack pipe a few days earlier. I got a rag from the sink and wiped off the cow salt and peppershakers that he'd stolen for me when I was falling madly in love with him. How long ago that now seemed. I rubbed the stains off the cow and stared at him waiting for him to say his goodbyes and get out of my apartment.

"You know Suzankah, people who spend their lives together start to become like each other," he mumbled. "It's good thing I leave you alone. You might retain some sanity, maybe not, since you're becoming great actress, now."

It was the day before he was both leaving L.A. and my life for good.

Finally after that horrible night in the Armenian restaurant, I realized the truth: that he was a sadist and I was his masochist, and that somehow, I was comfortable with that. The truth didn't make me love him any less, but it made me open my eyes and admit I'd allowed myself to get lost in a horror show.

"It's good thing I leave you here to believe you will become actress, and your father will live," he continued, sluggishly. "You've always had so much hope, Suzankah. I will stay with you one more night. My flight leaves tomorrow and you can take me to airport. That will make you happy."

I looked at his once handsome face that now showed the signs of terrible drug and alcohol abuse. His skin looked almost melted off his face.

"You have to leave now," I said. "I have to work, and I can't do anything for you, including take you to the airport."

"You're kicking me out on my last day here with you?" he whimpered.

"You can sleep at the airport hotel, or on the street, for all I care. You have to leave."

"You are so cruel, Suzankah." He got up from the table, downed his glass of vodka and gathered his two suitcases. "I'm leaving now. I know when I'm not wanted."

Walking into the living room and picking up my phone, he gave the location of my apartment. "Yes, I'll be down in ten minutes," he slurred into my receiver.

We looked at each other for a moment. His beautiful green eyes seemed even more tortured than when I first met him at Larry Parker's a year-and-a half earlier, with sweat and grease running down my face.

"So now you think you are actress, because you're in play? *Fool For Love* is name of play?" He picked up the light blue copy that was sitting on my bed.

"Uh-huh" I said.

"Such a fitting title for you, Suzankah. What a fool you've been."

I stared past him.

"You don't know what it is to be actress. I know real actresses. They are stars, Suzankah. I've been fucking Morgan Fairchild, you know. She's real star."

I laughed at his cruel comment, thinking of course that she wasn't a serious actress.

"You don't even know who you are, Suzankah."

I opened the door and picked up one of his suitcases to escort him down to his cab.

"You'll meet another man, Suzankah. He might be worse than I am. You loved it though, didn't you? You loved me so much, my little rabbit."

I breathed in the warm spring air and brushed a little of his dirty blonde hair from his aching green eyes. He took my hand and held it in his. In three weeks I'd be performing in three shows a week for six weeks. I'd finally be doing what I loved, but in this moment, I could honestly say that I felt relieved.

"I'm what you needed, Suzankah. Go be actress and see what this life will bring you. I've warmed you up for real world." And there was that strange and twisted smile, as he crawled into the cab and bid me adieu.

A minute later I was alone in the empty apartment. It was time to work. It was time to prove to myself that I could become a real actress no matter what Gregory's twisted opinion was. I picked up my copy of *Fool For Love* from my unmade bed. I opened it to see all my questions and notes in the margins.

Who is this person? Where does she come from? What does this trailer she lives in smell like? What does it look like? What does she do for money? Who's this mysterious man that's her father, and why is she so in love with a man that is her half- brother? Why does she pine for him in that way I pined for Gregory? What parallels in her life does she have with my own besides she's just a young woman? How do I find this person in me and speak these words that are about a place I've never lived in, and people I've never known? How can I physically embody her?

Getting to work right away, my mind drifted here and there, but concentration was getting easier with practice, with that old discipline of the ballet barre that I once knew so well. It all fit for me, being able to envelop the character of this particular suffering woman who lived in a trailer in the middle of the desert. I began to see a future in a way I hadn't really believed I'd ever get a handle on, because of my past as a shy, soft-spoken dancer, with that old desire to express the unseen without words.

A couple of months after Gregory left, I was still waitressing. My new job was at Pizza Pomedero, near Cedars Sinai Medical Center. I was on the lunch shift when the manager called me aside and with stern disapproval, handed me the telephone.

"It's mom," the voice on the line said. "I have an appointment at Cedars later this afternoon. I'd like both you and your brother to be there, and your father is well enough to come.

"Are you alright?" I asked.

"I might have cancer," she responded.

Leaving the restaurant at the end of my shift, I had to run the few blocks to Cedars to make the appointment. When I arrived my family was seated stoically in the doctor's sterile office. Mom's doctor had already left after presenting the diagnosis.

Mom broke the silence. "You look terrible," she said, as I leaned on one of the walls.

"Jean, please don't bother her," dad wheezed. "She managed to get here. Isn't that enough?"

"It's okay, I didn't have time to clean up," I said, peering at my poor father's balding head. He'd lost most of his hair from his last round of chemo and his fragile presence evoked a new empathy in me.

How could I help him? I felt so utterly powerless in practically everything I did.

Mark got up from his chair and gave me a big hug. His voice cracked a little as he greeted me. Being in this room with my declining parents was hard on him, too, even if he had a thicker skin than me. My thirty-two-year-old brother had become a grown up. He'd graduated from UC Santa Cruz as a hippie philosopher, a pot-smoking anarchist, and now after four years of law school, was working at a nicely established law firm. As handsome as ever, with his dark brown hair, fit body, beautiful skin, he was the perfect son. He could make a living and had a lovely fiancé, who herself was still in law school. I looked like a loser next to him.
Mom was biting her lip, preparing to tell me the diagnosis.

"Now don't get upset, because I know how you are, but I have stage three breast cancer. I'll need to have my breast removed, and then start chemotherapy."

"I don't understand," I said, my voice fading. "That can't be. You don't smoke."

"She's going to be okay," Mark said. "But you're going to have to help out, since dad has to start another round of chemo soon. And I work all day at the law firm. I can help on weekends, while you're at work."

"Right," I whispered. I looked over at my dad, and he gave me a sad look of uncertainty.

"Don't take it too hard," he said. "This is life, Sue. Wake up and smell the you know what."

"You mean shit," I said, thinking that dad's abrasive personality was fading along with his cancer-ridden body.

Looking out the window, I wondered how I could help this woman, my mother, who criticized me in some way every time she saw me, especially now that I wasn't dancer thin anymore. I looked back at my family; they were all talking in quiet spurts, as though I wasn't even there. They seemed so rational in a way that I wasn't. This was going to be hard. My budding hopeful spirit was beginning to disintegrate.

This was going to be almost impossible.

A month later, dad had a brain seizure while at work in his law office. He'd been back to work for a couple of months, and things were looking a bit better, even though both my parents were suffering some after effects from their weekly chemotherapy sessions.

Dad was discharged from the hospital within a couple of days of his seizure. The lung cancer had gone to his brain and had metastasized through the rest of his body. He was transported home in an ambulance and ten bags of morphine were delivered to our house that same day. Mom was apparently strong enough to watch her husband of thirty-three years disintegrate at home.

A sweet young nurse from the hospital hooked up the machine that would deliver the morphine drip while my father protested that she didn't have to bother, that my mother could do it.

"Whenever you feel any pain, just press this little button here to your right," the nurse said. "That's the morphine drip."

"Thank you," he whispered dryly as mom and I looked on in wonder. How was it possible for him to be so rational about his own demise? "I'll take care of it. And I know what a fucking morphine drip is."

The poor nurse gathered her things and walked out of my parents' bedroom.

"It's just you and me, kids," dad said as the downstairs door shut. "I hope she wasn't insulted." He turned onto his side and pressed the little white button. "I don't want to die with someone I don't know helping me, even if she was kind of pretty."

Ten days later, I got that fateful call. "Daddy died last night," mom murmured. "He took one last labored breath, and then he was gone." Her voice wavered sounding almost happy in relief.

"Oh mom. I'm so sorry," I said, overwhelmed by an ocean of emptiness within me.

Dad was just fifty-nine when he died. A week later, I sat beside my mother in the front row of the small temple at Mount Sinai Mortuary, a mile from my parent's house in Toluca Lake.

Mom had survived the removal of her left breast, and after eight weeks of chemo, was pretty much back to normal. She even had all of her hair after another two months of recovery, during which she had taken care of dad. Dressed in a classy black suit from Saks Fifth Avenue, and wearing a string of pearls, she looked like a society lady at a charity function.

"Stop crying," mom demanded while searching in her Coach bag for some tissues. She looked behind us, and around us, and declared, "I don't know most of these people here. Please don't embarrass me." She was definitely back to herself, looking beautiful and astoundingly healthy.

"I'm sorry." I took the bundled tissues and blew my nose as quietly as possible.

My father the atheist would never have approved of this ceremony and I wondered why we planned any of it. Perhaps it was for my grandfather, the successful doctor, whose friends had gathered here with him to mourn the death of his only child.

"You've got to control yourself," mom said as Mark studied his notes for the eulogy he'd soon deliver. I wiped my tears and more flowed, while I peered at the casket draped with an American flag. *That couldn't be my father, could it?*

"I think it's time," Mark said, walking to the podium in front of my father's coffin.

Looking up at him, I saw the young man who I didn't really get to see grow up. He had left home for college in Santa Cruz when I was fourteen and fully immersed in my trips to New York. He cleared his throat, squinted at his little white pages and adjusted the microphone. His voice was gentle and pained.

My dad would never see me become a good actress. He'd seen one of my first plays and it really stunk, so he'd never know if I actually had any real talent. We'd never get to work out our complicated but tender relationship. He would never get to retire from law and become a history professor in Eureka; something he spoke passionately about in the last few years, before his cancer diagnosis. Having grown up privileged, he preferred people who weren't. I'd never get to see him move to his dream place or grow old. I'd never get to hear that beautiful voice of his, ever again.

He wouldn't see me truly grow up and become a strong woman with her own mind. He'd never get to hear me have my own voice, even though he believed I might have one, if not for spending my early life in ballet.

"Goodbye dad," Mark uttered, his voice breaking, as he concluded his eulogy. He grabbed his pages, and headed back toward us.

"That was beautiful, Mark," mom said. "Daddy would have loved that. It was so honest."

"Thanks mom," he said. "I can't wait till this dog and pony show is over. Dad would have hated it all."

"He's at peace, he's finally at peace, but I'm going to miss him," she said, finally giving in to her deep loss. "I'll miss that beautiful voice of his...I loved him no matter how tough he was." She pulled out more Kleenex from her bag. Her tears were so terribly needed, no matter how sophisticated she looked in her fancy suit. She'd been holding back for months now.

People walked by us, giving us their condolences. We all formed a little huddle. It was time for us all to let go.

"Susie, your dad will never get to see you act," my second uncle Henry remarked as he and his wife, my Aunt Evelyn, approached us. "Isn't that what you're trying to do now?"

I gave him a nice smile and wiped my tears. "Right."

Chapter 23

NAKED

It's an odd thing to be naked in front of a group of people you don't know, when you are incredibly insecure and have body dysmorphia, but mostly, if you're not really comfortable in your own skin. It doesn't even matter why. It's just an odd thing to have strangers looking at you, as though you're an object to be prodded and moved around. I imagine that is what it would be like if I had had an illness of some kind or was involved in a scientific experiment. But that wasn't the case. I was an extremely healthy, unemployed woman who'd just lost her father, and was still looking for a way to get by while becoming an actress at this very late age of twenty-nine.

There was no trust fund, basically nothing was left after my father passed away six weeks earlier, just the house and cars and something for my mother. Dad had made it clear years earlier that he would not help me out that way, no matter how much I struggled. He always believed it would make me stronger to know what it was like to be without, even though I grew up in semi-privileged Toluca Lake, in beautiful Southern California. La-La Land.

And here I was in a dusty warehouse studio in Culver City, standing before a group of sculptors—my introduction into the world of art modeling. They were a lively and committed bunch of artists, with children and dogs, spouses and homes, and full lives that seemed rich compared to my little just-getting-by life. They chattered about the events in their lives, or news of the world, and I'd listen rapturously while they unwrapped their armatures for the sculptures they were diligently set to work on.

It was my fourth session in this studio, or anywhere for that matter, and they finally persuaded me to take off my bra and underwear. The week before I had finally said okay, agreeing to fully disrobe. Until then, in my pose on the art-model pedestal, they were constantly lifting my bra straps to study my shoulder lines. One of the sculptors asked if she could pull my underwear down on the side, just for a few minutes, so she could see the line of my hip. They were mostly respectful of my refusal those first three sessions to disrobe completely, respecting my shyness, but I heard them mutter, "No artist model ever wears underwear! It's unheard of!"

Having already fallen off my ballerina pedestal, it wasn't that big of a deal to get on this new one in order to make some kind of living. I was going to have to succumb to their wishes, no matter how Rubenesque I felt. I'd have to get over my humiliation, just as I was getting over my father's early and painful death.

It was just my luck to have my period this first day of complete nakedness. I stuffed my tampon string inside and prepared to come out of the tiny bathroom in my tattered robe. I was still blowing in the wind, especially now that I didn't have a waitress job anymore, but these artists seemed to like me. As long as I could pose gracefully and steadily, these sculptors would turn my figure into art. This kind of job was never in my plans, but it was survival for now. I tied my long brown hair on top of my head, took one more peek in the mirror, and said to myself, "You'll live."

I'd been a huge fan of Rodin's sculptures when I was a dancer. As I peered in the mirror, I reminded myself that none of his models could have been shy. They were poor, hungry, needed to survive, and couldn't have been much different than myself, except they all looked to be bone thin. I was going to have to overcome my own discomfort with my nakedness if I wanted to be employed and not just as a waitress. I had learned in three previous sessions that modeling could be physically painful. But in those sessions, I was partially dressed. That had lessened my embarrassment over my body.

The wooden door creaked at its hinges as I exited the cramped bathroom. I thought all eyes would turn towards me, but everyone was immersed either in conversation or in unwrapping and dampening their sculptures with wet rags. All of the armatures were different sizes, and even different types and colors of clay, but they were all some early rendition of my balletic pose, though not quite yet formed. The sculptors all had their own rituals for beginning their work, and it was fascinating to watch most everyone succumb to some version of procrastination.

As I approached the model stand, barefoot, and wrapped in my robe, I tried to not show my self-consciousness. Krista, a sculptor who took a liking to me from the first day, whispered in her deep, German-accented voice, "Look around. See how distracted everyone is? They're talking about their dogs, their children, their maids, and social events. But I want to work. Once you get up there, they'll calm down, join in, and start on their little sculptures. I promise, they won't even know you're nude."

I gave a shy smile to this elegant woman who displayed all the attributes I might want, if I ever grew up. I ached for the confidence and passion that she exuded, with her large blue-tinted movie star glasses, perfectly coiffed hair, elegant scarf and clothing almost inappropriate for this dusty art studio. She liked herself in a way I wanted to like myself. Not in an egotistical way, but in a way that conveyed that she knew who she was. She also exhibited a wicked sense of humor about the "little sculptures" the other artists were making. Krista definitely deserved her own tiara.

Here it goes. I untied the sash, and slowly slid the robe from my shoulders and let it drop to the model stand. I rolled it into a neat little ball so it wouldn't get in the way of the pose. The tape marks on the painters throw mat that cushioned the wooden pedestal guided me into the same pose. I prayed I wouldn't leak onto the paint-splattered mat.

Settling into what I remembered of the difficult-to-hold and extremely painful pose, I heard Krista's determined voice. "Darling, could you move your left leg a little to the right." She was the only one looking at me, the only one focusing on the work at hand and not procrastinating.

I did exactly as she asked and moved into an even more excruciatingly painful pose. "That's perfect darling. Don't let anyone tell you otherwise. I want you to stay exactly like that." She smiled. "Darling, where have you been all of my sculpting life?" She proceeded to re-work a section of my body that she had worked on the last three sessions. "Now I can see what that shoulder looks like. Do you mind if I touch you?"

"No, that's fine," I answered, confident that Krista's intentions were pure. I knew she was there to make art, though I still hadn't developed many boundaries. I still ached to please everyone.

"Thank you," she said, rubbing her finger gently on my shoulder bone that was apparently hard to see. My bones had once stuck out like hangers and my clavicles and sternum were completely visible through my flesh.

"Aha, I found it," she announced.

I thought I would just crumble right then and there.

They'll have to search for my bones. How are they going to sculpt a mass such as mine? They all said they believed I was once a ballet dancer, but surely, must think it's something I made up in my fantasy life.

Maybe I should have thought twice before agreeing to a pose that looked so balletic, with my arms floating gracefully above my head. I didn't know that no other model in her right mind would agree to a pose that was so hard to hold for five hours at a time, no matter how many breaks they got. I wanted to please these people, and I still had the old ballerina determination to get it right. I still felt that pain was okay. And nothing would ever be as agonizing as giving up dance and falling apart on my parent's couch. Nothing could be as sorrowful as losing my father. Nothing could be as humiliating as what I endured with Gregory, my Russian prince, who continually reminded me that I was worthless. This was actually welcome pain. I needed to survive, and I liked the atmosphere of creating. In a vicarious way, I sensed that I was becoming an inspiration to these artists. I was only too happy to become a muse.

The chatter diminished as the artists got to work. In this setting, concentration was the ultimate high, and absolutely vital if anything was to be accomplished. I knew this from my own work in the acting studio, where it was easy to get distracted by the day's events, and the soap operas of everyday life. Chatting away was certainly more fun than work, and procrastination was becoming a familiar trait in my own struggles.

The artists surrounding me were all extremely talented. Their sculptures had real form and real line and resembled my voluptuous body. It was certainly difficult for me to view the rolls of flesh they'd recreate in their realistic impressions, and I preferred the pieces that veered towards a thinner version of myself. But this was art, and these sculptors had a right to create an impression of what they saw, no matter how mortifying the result was to me, or any other anonymous model on the stand.

Finally, 1 p.m. and time for the hour-long lunch break. I happily put on my tattered robe and skipped into the bathroom to get my clothes. Looking into the paint-spattered mirror, I saw my hair wasn't brushed and that I had on almost no make-up, but I looked okay. I even looked a little happy. I changed my tampon, thankful that it lasted those first three hours.

I did it! I got naked in front of these people, and nothing terrible happened. I didn't leak on the painter's mat, and I didn't faint from embarrassment. This was my new job, and my new purpose. It wasn't exactly my plan, but at least I wasn't going to be a waitress anymore. I'd made a promise to myself that even if I never got a job as an actress, I wouldn't be waitressing at forty. All I had to do was show up on time and take off my clothes! I was never going to work in an office again, especially after that humiliating week in Chuck's Van Nuys office. I was better suited for something a little left of center.

It wasn't my habit to pack a lunch, after my four years of waitressing and all the readily available food that helped make me the voluptuous little dumpling that I was. My red Honda had finally died so I raced towards my little yellow Toyota, to drive to Von's. Waving goodbye to Krista, she commented sardonically, "Come back quickly, darling. One must not rush one of the more glorious parts of the day." She laid her silk tablecloth over the outdoor wooden table, and gracefully pulled from her picnic basket a fancy bottle of sherry and a gorgeous silver goblet. "Have a little sherry with me when you come back. It makes the day go by so smoothly."

Chuckling at her comment, I grabbed my bag and fished out my car keys. I wondered if she was actually going to pull some food out of that fancy picnic basket. "No alcohol for me, but I'll be fast. Can I get something for you?"

"No, my darling, I have some wonderful cheese and bread to go with my sherry."

"Enjoy," I said, recalling the single word we used when dropping plates off at customers' tables, from my days as a waitress. And I walked outside to the parking lot, where my used Toyota awaited me.

I was collecting unemployment from my last waitressing job at Pizza Pomedoro, which had closed, due to bankruptcy. Surprisingly enough, I was booking one modeling job after another. Everyone paid under the table, so along with my monthly unemployment checks, I was able to survive. My name was getting around to other sculpture and painting studios, now that I'd become willing to take my clothes off in that dusty Culver City sculpture studio.

Relishing the fact that I didn't have to waitress anymore, I could spend more time working on my acting or going to the gym to do aerobics, or hang out with Naomi in the dance room to improvise. I even started doing some yoga at the Hollywood YMCA. That old run-down gym was becoming my second home, especially since I got to see a few friends, including the whimsical and inspired Henry. The yoga quieted my chattering mind and helped me to sit still longer in my new part-time profession. I was on my way to some kind of peace.

At the different art studios, I'd often ask the teacher, or artists, if they minded if I kept my head tilted down for the pose if it was a long one. That way I could learn my lines for a scene I was working on. If my wish wasn't granted, I'd ponder existence, or dream of my possible career playing different characters with clothes on. My newfound yoga practice was beginning to change some of the negative patterns of my thinking, and I could actually sit still, a true accomplishment for an ex-ballerina. Even my body was beginning to change in a way that I liked. Four years after my fall from grace, I was beginning to not hate myself. Yoga and nude modeling allowed me to start truly living in my non-dancer skin.

Driving up Pacific Coast Highway, I glanced to my left to see the glittering ocean on a beautiful and cool spring day. I was on my way to model privately for Krista at her home, for a three-hour drawing session. It would be with a few of her close friends, and maybe her third husband, she told me on the phone, if he were able to attend. Peter Zinner, Krista's husband of twenty-six years, was the award-winning film editor of *The Deer Hunter*, and had a huge Hollywood career.

"Come in," Krista said, as she guided me to her husband's office, where I could change into my robe. Passing the beautiful art in the spacious, mid-century, glass-and-marble home, I recalled my time at Lincoln Kirstein's townhouse in Chelsea in New York City, where at seventeen I was mesmerized by The *Seven Deadly Sins*. I was intrigued by those gorgeous small paintings that lined his long eggplant-painted hallway, their meaning and strange beauty. The tall and imposing man, who held my dance future in his hands, had asked me then, *Which one do you like?*

Now I was surrounded by brilliant light that shone through the floor-to-ceiling windows. There were numerous shelves of books and African art sculptures everywhere. Absolute order. I was in heaven.

"Hello there, I'm Peter," said the robust and bald older man exiting the office as I entered. "Krista has told me all about you, and she can't wait to draw you." I stood in rapt appreciation of this distinguished man. "I'll join in for a couple of hours, but I must warn you, I'm not as good as she is."

I looked at them both in their elegant crème-colored clothes and wondered if I'd ever have that kind of confidence about anything. There was also the view of the ocean. The beauty of it all made me want to cry, but I smiled. Their warmth toward me was unexpectedly welcome. Everything made me want to cry, in a strangely, grateful way. If only they'd known what I'd been through–If only I'd known what they'd been through. I was to be their muse.

"You must stay for lunch after, darling," Krista gushed, as though I had all the leisure time in the world.

"I have to get back," I lied, not feeling I deserved to be surrounded with so much warmth, beauty, and love.

What could I say to them? I was a ballet dancer, and at one time had been surrounded by elite people such as your selves. I have no education, no boyfriend, and no prospects. I fuck around with all the wrong men, and I'll never be what I once was. Thank you for allowing me into your home. I'll try not to spill anything on your all white furniture, and no, I won't walk off with any of your silver, or jewels. I might be poor, but I don't steal things. I'm civilized in many respects.

"No darling, you're staying. I want to feed you some good food, and I'm a fabulous cook. No supermarket salad bar for you today. Go get your tattered robe and I'll show you what's going on in my kitchen."

Entering Peter's office, I slowly peeled off my clothes and put on the robe. I stared at the elegantly framed photos of the renowned film editor with many famous faces. My gaze landed on that coveted Oscar he won for *The Deer Hunter*. It was so civilized and impressive, the pictures of him with people that I idolized, for no other reason than they created entertainment for people like me. Regular people.

Krista led me to her small but elegant kitchen, overlooking her shimmering pool and the bigger view of the Pacific Ocean. "I've made a wonderful Borscht that you're going to love, and some bread that I've baked myself," she said, as she glided through her kitchen in beautiful crème slacks, and silk button-up shirt. I wondered whether she worried about spilling anything on those fancy clothes, while dry gagging at the sound of cold Borscht.

"How about next time," I asked shyly, confident that I'd be invited back, at least to model.

"I'd love for you to try my soup. I've written my own recipe book for all of the soups that I adore." She stood up on her toes, not in any balletic way, of course, to grab a copy of her cookbook that was sitting up on a high shelf, lined with what looked like other gourmet cookbooks. She turned the page to the Borscht recipe. Boasting in her usual confident way, "One must learn to cook to win a man's heart," she said while flipping through the handsomely photographed pages.

"Wow, you wrote this!" I exclaimed, amazed that my new acquaintance possessed so many talents. She handed me her accomplishment, and I leafed through, my mouth watering at all the recipes that weren't Borscht. Standing before me was an artist, writer, wife (already twice-divorced), and mother of two, talking to me as though I was just like her.

"You know that I don't cook at all," I said. "I mean, I just don't have the time, with my work, and driving around all the time." I looked at the clock above her stainless-steel sink. It was 9:45 am. In fifteen minutes, I'd be taking my tattered robe off, yet again.

In the three months that I'd worked for Krista at the sculpture studio, she'd befriended me in a mentor-like way. Perhaps she needed to be a mother to someone that she thought was like herself. I had learned over those months that her relationship with her own twenty-five-year-old daughter was not that great, and that they were completely different from each other.

"No one would know she was my own daughter. It's almost as though I had an alien," she remarked. "But she was a miracle baby. I was forty-three, and way too old to be having more children, but Peter wanted his own, and we'd married so late in life." Then came her slightly sarcastic chuckle. "My son is a god, though, even if his father was a real asshole. You have to try a few times, before you find the right one, you know."

"I'm trying, but I don't really have time right now. I just want to work, I mean as an actress."

"Darling, don't ever have children. The whole thing is completely over-rated, even if I adore mine."

"That's probably not going to happen any time soon," I said, a bit surprised by her candid talk about family matters. "I'm having a hard time just taking care of myself, and I'm not attracted to anyone who could ever be a father. I do have a crush on this really cute actor who couldn't care less about me."

"Darling, please don't ever fall in love with an actor. They're complete narcissists and won't be able to supply you with anything you need in this life."

"But that's all I meet, now that I'm acting. I mean…I'm trying."

"They're worse than actresses."

"I'm not looking for someone to take care of me," I said, as I peered around the dining room where I'd soon be modeling. There was a nice breeze coming through the open sliding glass door that led to the magnificent pool. I wondered how cold I'd be once I took my worn-out robe off, yet again.

"Why not?' she asked. "The world is full of men who'd like to take care of someone like you. Men love damsels in distress. A real man likes to feel like he's needed. Actors don't know who they are, believe me, and they're hell to live with. Do you want me to close this door? You're shaking."

"I'll be okay," I lied. The breeze is really nice."

"Everything changes," she said, as she slid the door shut. "You're freezing and you're going to be naked in a few moments. How about some heat, so you don't suffer too much? You're doing enough of that on your own. You don't really like modeling, do you?" she said, as she rummaged through a hall closet to find that much needed space heater.

"It's the only thing I can do right now. It's okay. I mean, I love working for the people I've met, and I love artists, but it's pretty boring, to be honest with you."

She walked towards me, smiling and looking satisfied with the little heater she majestically presented. "I know, but you're so good at it." She plugged that space-heater in, not too far from the stand, turned it on, and positioned it close enough to the model stand so I would keep warm, but wouldn't get scorched.

"What's good about my modeling?" I asked. "I always just feel like a lump on the model stand."

"Hard to say. You're transparent, I think. I see your whole life in your skin and your face, and that's inspiring for an artist. You don't look like the women of today, and I like that. You have something that a lot of people probably don't see. Artists see your inner light, and you're very quiet. I don't like loud models, something about nudity with a loud voice. They just don't go well together."

According to Krista, when she was young, she had also struggled with her identity, not knowing where she belonged. Perhaps it was that creative energy that didn't allow her to sit still in school, just like me. Perhaps it was because she'd moved from her Hitler Youth schooling in Berlin, to New York City at seventeen, and had left her family early, just as I had, to find her own way. There, she became a famous photographer for numerous magazines in the '60s and '70s, completely separated from her own family.

For some unexplained reason, she was trying to help me overcome my disdain for myself and rediscover what I once had as a dancer. She didn't discourage me from being an actress but didn't think my "thin skin" could take the rejection that was part of that world. "You might not be clever enough to navigate those sharks," I heard her say one day over the loud chatter of the other sculptors in the Culver City warehouse.

"In time, you'll learn to be the queen that you really are." She started rearranging the painter's mat on the model stand that I'd soon be perched on. "You've got to take the bull by the horns, you know, because you're more than what you think you are. I want you to start seeing a psychiatrist. I'm going to recommend someone."

"I can't," I said, knowing that it would probably be someone expensive that I could never afford. "I did see a doctor once in Century City, a few years ago, who said he couldn't work with me, unless I was medicated," I unashamedly told her. "He asked me to tell him about my dance life, and I just couldn't. I just couldn't talk."

"Well, he clearly wasn't the right one. You shouldn't be embarrassed to share this part of yourself with me. I completely understand. We've all been through it, and it's not a crime to need some help."

I looked up at the clock and saw that it was almost time to start. I could see the whole makeshift–stand in the dining room that Krista had set up, from the kitchen, where we were still chatting like old friends. I'd soon be standing only feet from people who had jobs in the business. We were in the Palisades, after all. They probably wouldn't care who or what I was.

"I guess it's time," I said, moving into the chilly dining area, where that model stand was waiting for me.

"Yes, they'll be here soon. They're going to love you, I promise," Krista said. "Just be yourself and don't expect anything from anyone. I'm the only one that needs to know that you're really a queen, and not just a great artists model."

Chapter 24

ACTRESS

First headshot, 1986. Photo by Guy Webster

I didn't go to the psychiatrist Krista recommended. I couldn't afford that one. But I found a therapist at a clinic in West Hollywood that charged on a sliding scale, according to income. I paid twelve dollars a session for a warm and wonderful female intern who specialized in clients who struggled with self-esteem issues and were adult children of alcoholics.

Even though my life was slowly improving with the therapy sessions, the newfound outlet of yoga and hanging with my friends from the Hollywood YMCA, there was still a quiet desperation to prove to myself that I would be okay without my drug of choice: ballet.

I missed the open space, and the lights and thrill that it had once provided. I missed the rituals of preparing for performance, whether it was putting on make-up, or breaking in my pointe shoes perfectly, or making sure I had enough beet juice to make it through the evening's performance. I missed seeing the bones of my chest in the mirror, and I missed putting on those false eyelashes, no matter how much I struggled with the glue. I missed feeling light as a bird, and being in control, yet so deeply in touch with something bigger than myself. I missed the camaraderie, whether it was the dancers themselves, or the stagehands, or orchestra members, the jokes we told, and the great parties we had just celebrating being alive in the world.

Even though I'd been studying acting for close to four years already, had done a few plays, and had even won a Drama-Logue Award, I had no real confidence of the kind I had as a dancer. I had several interviews with agents after the six-week run of *Fool for Love*, but my life and my insecurities got in the way of anyone signing me. I desperately wanted to fall in love again with an art form that suited me much the same way that ballet once had. My voice didn't serve me nearly as well as my body once did as a vehicle of expression, no matter how hard I worked at it. But in my determined mind, I kept hearing the voices of Harvey Keitel and Dennis Nahat, the artistic director of the Cleveland Ballet: *Maybe you should act.* I wanted to prove to them that I could. This time embracing the words of great playwrights and connecting to them in a way that had been as inspiring as music once had. Mostly I wanted to be on stage again. It had brought me such freedom.

How can everything change so radically in only five years? How could one little decision, or one little mishap change an entire life? How could I ever live up to the passionate dancer I once was?

At 7:30 a.m. on a bright and sunny Monday morning, I walked up the creaky, wooden stairs to The Loft Studio on La Brea Boulevard in Hollywood. I ached to find a new home for myself and I needed more tools to become proficient as an actress. I had already studied with Robert Carnegie of the Neighborhood Playhouse, and with Susan Peretz, who had been mentored by Lee Strasberg, and taught the method. I'd spent many a class with other students sitting in a chair, first working on relaxation, which is the beginning part of method acting, and then close to an hour of sensory work: peeling an invisible orange, putting on imaginary makeup in front of an imaginary mirror, feeling the heat of a sauna, or wind across my naked body, the sound of someone's voice or music that isn't there, feeling different types of material on my body, sitting in a room and imagining all of the furniture, the smells, sounds, colors, and possibly the people who might enter that room. All of this to evoke the senses and ultimately the emotions. All of this to get actors into their unconscious mind, allowing them to become less self-conscious and to use their presence in someone else's shoes. Great work for any fledgling actor, but for me, when I finally got to do a scene with actual dialogue, it always happened with a gravelly and barely audible voice. And this was completely acceptable in the method teacher's canon, but never acceptable in a professional environment, except, of course, on film where actors clip on small

172

microphones to pick up sound.

Climbing the stairs at The Loft, I made a quick right down the dark hallway with high wood-beam ceilings. I almost tripped into the open door of the office where I was to have my early morning interview with Bill Traylor, the head of this revered acting studio, which he had founded years before with his wife, Peggy Feury. I stood at the open doorway, silently watching this bald and brown-spotted older man, braying into the phone. He glanced at me with a snide look and I felt suddenly as though I shouldn't be there.

"What the hell are you doing here so early?" he barked, putting his phone down for this uncomfortable moment.

"We have a meeting at 7:45," I whispered. "I'm interested in studying with you."

My possible new mentor looked down at his disorganized desk that was piled high with papers and books and glanced at a yellow post-it, signifying our meeting time. He put on his wire-framed glasses, peered at that little piece of paper, and brayed back into the phone, "I'll call you later. I have a new student here. Sit down, sit down" he grunted.

Considering my particular sensitivity to almost everything, I felt like I wanted to bolt, but I didn't. I was desperate for an approving father figure and I needed the appreciation that comes from being what someone else thought was good.

Sitting in the old leather chair across from Bill, he looked into my eyes and gave me a nice warm smile. He wore a crinkled old beige safari jacket, and in one hand held a burning cigarette, stuffed into an antique-looking ivory holder. It looked like the one my father always used, from his days in the Korean War. He brushed some ashes off his jacket and said, "I don't like taking on new students. They're way too much work, and I'm not a god-dammed babysitter."

He sounds exactly like my dad, and he's smoking a cigarette with a cigarette holder. No one does that anymore!

"Oh," I sputtered, waving away the thick smoke that was wafting into my face. "I guess I should leave now." I stood up from my chair.

"That's not what I said. I'm not supposed to be smoking these," he said, and extinguished his lit cigarette into an overflowing ashtray. "Sit back down!"

He didn't look like someone who should be smoking, and when he got up from his chair to empty the ashtray into an over-flowing trashcan, I noticed how terribly thin he was, and immediately wondered about his health. He looked almost as thin as my father just before he died.

"I've heard you're a wonderful teacher," I sputtered meekly, trying for a moment to stay focused on this strangely intriguing man who, with his obviously decaying body, reminded me of my father who had passed away only two months earlier.

He sat back down onto the dark red donut hole that was sitting in the middle of his chair and said, "It's my wife you probably want to study with, but she's dead, or haven't you heard."

"No, it's you I want to study with. I know that Peggy died. What is that you're sitting on? It looks like a small lifesaver from a ship."

Looking at me with a little sparkle in his clear golden eyes, he said, "You're very observant, aren't you? Tell me a little about yourself. You have five minutes. Class starts in ten."

Not really knowing what to say, considering the caliber of people he had worked with was way above anything I could imagine, I whispered, "I was a dancer, and my father just died, and I want to be a good actress. I've been studying for a while and have done a couple of plays. I won a Drama-Logue Award for a David Mamet play about a father and daughter – *Reunion* is an abandonment sort of story. I'm not very good, I don't think."

He scratched his bald brown-spotted head with his slender and withered fingertips and gave me a look that convinced me I'd be in good hands. Trust is such a strange and daunting thing. I looked around the cluttered office not sure of myself but somehow sure of him.

"I like you," he said. "And I have a feeling you might have some talent."

"How can you know?" I asked, already feeling welcome and support from this unfamiliar presence.

"If you can't tell, I've been around a long time. It appears you might have an inner life, which is a lot more than I can say for most of the young actors that pass through here. I see it in those sad eyes of yours."

"My father just died, so…I haven't brought anything for today. I didn't know if you'd accept me into the class."

"You'll have your hands full before you can blink an eye. Now get in the studio and let me finish my phone conversation that you so rudely interrupted."

"But I don't…"

"Just go in there and wait. Turn around and march gracefully a few yards to your left. You'll see it."

"But, what am I…?"

"Go!"

I turned around and walked tenuously into the acting studio that was just down the hall from Bill's office. There was a decent-sized stage area filled with some props and furniture, and eight or so rows of stadium seats on a fairly deep incline. I dropped my bag on a seat and wandered around the stage to see what it felt like.

"Hi," I heard from the entryway of the studio. "I'm Salvatore."

"Hi, I'm Susan" I uttered shyly, almost knocked over by the sound of this young guy's voice.

"I take it it's your first day of class."

"Yes, it is. I just had a five-minute meeting with Bill and he demanded I wait in here."

"Bill is amazing," he said. "Don't worry that he doesn't look that great. He has all the energy in the world."

"Yeah, I kind of got that from our little meeting," I said, totally self-conscious about my body, and hair, and clothes, feeling naked in front of this hip guy. He seemed like someone I might have known in my dancer days in Germany or New York.

Every morning at 8 a.m., five days a week, I'd show up at The Loft for this small class with Bill Traylor, who'd teach us while seated on that red-donut-life-saver-pillow. He'd yell at me to "Stop moving your arms around or I'm going to make you sit on your hands for the entire scene." Somehow, my arms wanted to express the things that he wanted me to express through my own stillness and my own voice, those flailing arms, just one of the insecure habits I had to break. He wanted me to find my own presence and strength. And even though I got yelled at for almost everything I attempted on that stage, I was learning and gaining a little confidence. My heart still fluttered every time I got up on that tiny stage. It was all beginning to sink in. Bill was becoming like a new father to me.

On his recommendations, I worked on George Bernard Shaw, Beth Henley, Clifford Odets, Arthur Miller, Harold Pinter, and my favorite, the remarkable Tennessee Williams. It was an astonishing education in great playwrights and in expressing their brilliantly created characters. I was learning how my body could finally be a vehicle for expressing a character through a walk, a certain kind of behavior, and a completely different cadence than my own. It was fun to find a character's uniqueness and idiosyncrasies. Through this sort of music that a playwright wrote with words, I came to believe I did have some ability to disappear into someone else's shoes. My passion as a dancer was being ignited again, and I was truly inspired. My fellow students, including Salvatore, were very supportive of each other, and we would meet on our days off to either rehearse or improvise in the back studio. It was a community for me, and I finally had a creative home.

Bill even gave me a scholarship after the first month, because for whatever reason, he believed in me, and knew I'd be a good class secretary, collecting everybody else's monthly payment. I still grieved over my father's death, and as ridiculous as it may seem, Gregory's departure. Those losses fueled my theater work.

Life, as a whole, was getting better. I had friends that I cared about and cared about me. And somehow, through this community, I was at least hopeful that I would become a different kind of artist. And it didn't really matter that commercial success might elude me.

"He really believes in you," said Catherine Blore, one of Bill's longtime students and now an actual working actress. We walked out of class together, and she pulled me to the side and whispered, "Bill really thinks you could maybe be a movie star!" I was taken aback at her true excitement. I wasn't sure if she said that to all of the young actors that passed through these classes, but it felt good to be acknowledged in a way that might encourage me to keep going and keep exploring.

"He said that?" I stammered, staring at her perfectly white and unblemished skin, coiffed red hair, and turquoise dress that offset all that beautiful natural color.

"If you'd lose some weight," she said softly.

Was that all I had to do to be a working actress? Was the business truly just about what one looked like?

I wanted to be an actress with an inner life that was visible, like Kim Stanley, Anna Mangnani, Simone Signoret, Gena Rowlands, Geraldine Page, Colleen Dewhurst, and Joanne Woodward. Like Catherine, my new mentor.

Maybe Bill meant a movie star from another era? None of them seemed like the starlets of the moment. They all had a depth that for me was an inspiration to learn this craft.

Some part of me wouldn't let my current weight of about 142 pounds go, almost like it was a protection against the things that life was throwing at me: my father's death, Gregory's departure, the last few years of despair. Or maybe my rebel spirit was saying, *I will not be appreciated only for what I look like.*

As a dancer, one can never get by on looks. It's about the work, the sweat, and the absolute commitment that goes into creating a technique. It's about true skill and talent. And of course, a body that's perfectly proportioned and flexible, and perfect feet. The weightlessness is a necessity for the execution of that art form. I was now in a new art form that might not have the same criteria, except for perhaps the mental and spiritual weightlessness. I wanted to play other people, not myself, so what did it matter what I looked like?

Perhaps my metabolism had been altered by my ridiculous dancer diets to stay bone thin. Perhaps my day job sitting around naked for people didn't help. I did go to the YMCA and would improvise with Naomi in the dance room when not on the mind-numbing Stairmaster. Even Henry, my other Y friend, would mention my chubbiness to see if I'd laugh at myself. James LeGros, my not so steady boyfriend who was a successful working actor would say, "Sue, you look like you could pull the plow across the country."

I'd chuckle as though his comment wasn't hurtful. As though I was strong enough to not care.

Our small group at the Loft was at work on a play. Immersed in the work and my delight in discovering a character I could fully realize, the sad news came. Bill's daughters Susan and Stephanie broke the news in the middle of a rehearsal, that our adored teacher had been admitted to the hospital and was dying of AIDS. They reassured us that our class and rehearsals would continue every day with Catherine taking over as our teacher. Hearts broken, we all nonetheless carried on, as if Bill might miraculously get better.

A few of us went to visit Bill in the hospital. Stephanie and Susan granted us permission but warned that he looked pretty bad. His skeletal body was a sure sign that he would eventually succumb to AIDS. I held my tears, just as my father had told me to do the few weeks before he died.

I was going to lose another father figure. I would no longer hear Bill's gruff and determined voice, just like I would never again hear my own father's beautiful voice. I was going to have to buck up and march on, just as dad tried to get me to do a few years before, when I thought my life was over. I was never going back to any couch again. I'd never let failure, or losing someone or something I loved, destroy me again.

At Bill's filled-to-capacity memorial service, his daughter Susan, recited, "Goodbye sweet prince," from *Hamlet*. She held herself still and the depth of her words swept over all of us. She was so grounded and real, just like her father, who had been her own acting mentor. So many people from the entertainment business had come to mourn Bill's death. I imagine he had touched them all in some way.

Sadness and disarray enveloped The Loft, with both Bill and Peggy now gone. Susan and Stephanie ran the school as well as they could while grieving their father's death. Both of them would make occasional appearances, reminding us that we were still in good hands. Meanwhile, our rehearsal continued for a revival of John Patrick Shanley's *Savage in Limbo*, and it was going to be a showcase of our work together. I even got up the courage to call Harvey Keitel, after two years of not even talking to him, to see if he'd ask his agent to come see my work. Connections were everything in the business, I was told.

Starting to feel like a real actress, I thought I was pretty good in the role of Linda Rotunda, a desperate, and madly-in-love young woman. The adorable Salvatore, who'd been innocently flirting with me throughout the year, even though he lived with someone and was apparently in love, played Tony Aronica, who Linda hounded all the time. I was thrilled I could filter all the emotions bubbling under my skin into this character whose perpetual crying was actually comical. Salvatore was basically just a flirtatious guy, and that helped my absolute need for him to want me, as Linda, that is.

I possessed a good ear for accents and this particular one was a blast to work on. Each of these desperate characters had their own particular rhythm, but that Bronx drawl was written into the dialogue. Both Harvey Keitel and Susan Peretz had Bronx accents. I just had to rough up Linda's a bit. Linda Rotunda didn't wear any kind of tiara. She was salt of the earth.

Shanley had a directorial note written into his work that the characters were to be played like a wind quintet. That suited me as a way to find this earthy and extroverted young woman, who needed nothing but a man to solve her angst. Music had always been my greatest inspiration to dance and to move. I was now part of a wind quintet. I was part of something bigger than myself. I was an actress. I belonged.

The name Linda Rotunda was kind of amusing. Was I picked for this part because I was slightly rotund? Whatever it was, at the ripe age of twenty-nine, I was completely connected to a character. I had no trouble speaking her particular truth. I was finding a voice without dance. All was okay for the struggling actress with no agent, no steady boyfriend, and no true prospects, kind of like Linda Rotunda.

"You'll have to get new pictures," said the junior agent, Michelle Stern, from the high-level talent and music agency, Triad (later to become William Morris/Endeavor), as I pointed out my brand new black-and-white headshot. It was pinned to the corkboard beside my four cast-mates headshots, just outside the entrance to the Loft's fifty-seat theater.

I thought the shot was pretty good and was immediately horrified at the thought of having to spend money I didn't have on more pictures. My red Honda had died, right after my dad, and I needed a reliable car to get to my modeling jobs. So I borrowed money from mom to make the down payment on a yellow, used Toyota that thankfully didn't have too many miles on it. I was still paying it off and had not yet purchased car insurance, or health insurance.

I absolutely couldn't get new pictures.

It had been a seemingly successful closing night performance of *Savage in Limbo*. The audience had laughed, the electricity was palpable, and the post congratulations were signs that something good had happened on the tiny stage. A few friends came backstage and gave me a pat on the back.

Henry who happened to be friends with James, came, and even went out with a few of us after the show. James had an acting job early the next morning, and went home, but there was Henry, in his colorful Hawaiian shirt, his cool John Lennon glasses, and that adorable gap-toothed smile. We went to our favorite hangout of the time, the Formosa Café, and celebrated our success. Henry congratulated me on a job well done, and we laughed together about my occasional boyfriend. Henry observed that I always wanted what I couldn't have. Perhaps he knew better. He was happily married for the third time and was truly in love with his wife. Impressive…in Hollywood, anyway.

On the recommendation of Harvey Keitel, Michelle received the query letter I had sent, requesting she attend, and so she came to the Hollywood waiver theater. This was back in the days when agents might find you on stage. She actually stayed to talk to me after the performance. She just walked right up to me when we were all milling about, talking to our friends.

Back to the headshot…

"Your hair is so flyaway. We'll have to get you some new pictures," Michelle said with a forgiving and sweet smile. "No big deal. Easily remedied."

"Thank you so much for coming all the way out to Hollywood."

"I think you're really good, and I'm so glad I came," Michelle said. "I spoke to Harvey on the phone and he spoke well of you, but had no idea if you had any acting talent. He knew you as a dancer, apparently."

"Yes, but I stopped," I said, revealing some of my agonizing insecurity. The butterflies in my stomach danced in a way I hadn't felt for a very long time. "Harvey's a great actor," I said, as though I saw him just yesterday, as though that was a necessary thing for me to say.

"Let's set up a meeting," she said, right in earshot of my four other cast-mates. "I have to get home and watch a client on television."

"Really," I said, holding back my utter thrill.

"How's tomorrow?"

"Great," I said, not even contemplating my modeling job that was already booked. I shook her hand and turned to join my friends, and there was Henry with his bright eyes and sweet, gap-tooth smile.

"You did well," he said. "Congratulations. You didn't completely fall all over yourself."

For my meeting the next day I wore a hot-pink blouse, and a pair of decent black pants, covered by that beautiful long black wool jacket from Saks Fifth Avenue that mom had bought for me. It was the same one I'd worn on my first date with Gregory, in the stifling heat, and here I was wearing it yet again, not only because it was the nicest thing I owned but, because I thought it made me look thinner.

The meeting was in Michelle's Century City office. I was thrilled to be driving west to that part of town. I was getting accustomed to dusty art studios for modeling, and the crumbling theater for class, rehearsal, and performances. It was a treat to drive west where more of the entertainment business dealings took place. I considered that without Harvey Keitel's recommendation, I wouldn't be driving this way. I'd be searching for an agent on Hollywood Boulevard where I could be meeting someone really sleazy that would promise me the world. But I might have a chance driving out west, where successful careers were sometimes created.

Five years earlier I was driven by my mother to the very same parking lot I was now entering, to see that Century City psychiatrist. When I couldn't even drive a car. When I couldn't get off my parent's couch.

"I won't be able to help you unless you're medicated," that indifferent doctor had said with a stilted and unmoving mouth.

It was strange being in the same parking lot again, but now for a completely different and thrilling reason. My emotions were flighty, and wavering, and completely hopeful. It was hard to stay grounded with all of the anticipation.

What would I talk about, now that the play was over, and I wasn't riding on an adrenaline rush? I'll just try to act normal. I'll try to mirror her. That's what I'll do.

I parked and looked in the rear-view mirror, making sure I wasn't too sweaty. I grabbed my purse and locked up, leaving behind my new-to-me but still old Toyota, a sure sign of poverty in this world of sleek black cars. Then I headed east to enter the high-rise building.

"How old are you again?" Michelle asked as I swiveled in the fancy black leather chair across from her. The cold chrome frame was chilling my wool-covered shoulder.

"I'm twenty-seven," I said, lying to this prospective agent. I was actually twenty-nine, but two years wasn't really that much. How would she ever find out that I was two years older than I stated?

She had on an appropriate black scoop-neck tunic with a zipper in the back, and a nice pencil skirt that looked super cut, super conservative, super expensive, and weather appropriate. She kept getting up and down to check on Harvey's agent, Brian, whose office was connected to hers by one adjoining door. She got up for a second and peeked her head through that door to see if he needed anything. "So, you know I'm Brian's assistant," she said, giving me a reassuring smile. She sat back down and then truly directed her attention towards me.

"I know," I said, acting like it was no big deal, because I was just so thrilled to be in this office and not a sleazy one on Hollywood Boulevard where an agent once asked me to take my top off and then read some stupid scene. I actually took my top off and then cried when I got back into my car. I don't remember reading the scene.

THANK GOD MICHELLE IS A WOMAN!

Her long brunette hair framed a friendly and open face. She seemed a bit reserved relative to the eccentric people that I knew from art modeling, and Henry and Naomi from the YMCA. All my theater friends were expressive and generally irreverent. But her sincere brown eyes conveyed that she was grounded and intelligent. She was thankfully not a Hollywood sleazebag. No more male agents!

"I'm allowed to hip-pocket you, and see if I can get you going," she said, swiveling in her matching leather and chrome chair.

"That would be great," I said, not knowing what hip-pocketing meant. I tried to copy her confident behavior. *I'll mirror her. That's what I'll do.*

She flashed another of her sincere smiles. "You're ready to go on auditions, right?"

"I think so."

"Commercials are a good way to get you going, and maybe make some money. I'm assuming you need to make a living?

"Right," I said, not really taking in the reality she was presenting to me.

She turned on her speakerphone and contacted her receptionist. "Can you connect me with Corey in the commercial department and get Ellie to bring us two cups of coffee." She smiled while waiting for a response. She made me feel like I belonged across from her in this fired-up business world.

"I don't really care about money," I said while she was still holding for the other important agent she seemed to think I needed to meet. My armpits were now drenched with sweat, since I couldn't get myself to take off my wool coat. It was winter in Los Angeles, after all. But, sadly, I didn't feel like hearing the "You're a little overweight," line.

"You don't like nice things?" she asked.

"I do, but I don't think things are really important in the big picture. I feel like, being creative, and involved, somehow, is what's important. I want to act." A drop of sweat poured down my eye and onto my lip. I licked my lip and swallowed the salty sweat, as more beads formed at my hairline.

Why the hell did I just say that? Who the hell do I think I am telling this agent, who could maybe open a few doors for me that I don't care about money? Do I think she'll like me more because I don't want to seem materialistic or vapid like the rest of Hollywood? Do I think I'll impress her with my need to be completely honest (except about my age), and accidentally divulge my entire pathetic life? Where is a jolly character when I need one?

She gave me another sweet smile and told me to hold on for one more minute.

"Corey, I'm bringing up a new actress I want you to sign. She's very talented."

Why is she throwing me on to someone else already? I thought she wanted to hip-pocket (whatever that is) me? How am I going to audition for commercials?

"So, let's get this going," she said, as though she couldn't wait to get me out of there. "I'm taking you up to meet Corey now. Did you bring your headshot? I know he's going to want new pictures also."

"But..."

As we entered the elevator to get to Corey's office on a higher floor, there standing before us was a very young Ashley Judd and her mom, Naomi, who was represented by the agency's music division.

"Hi Michelle," Ashley said with a sweet, and naïve smile. She was like a freshly picked flower in her light-colored dress. Her sparkly white teeth beamed from her beautiful smile. She looked like she didn't have a problem in the world.

"Wait for me in the office," Michelle said to the glowing Ashley. "I'll be there in a couple of minutes. Hey, Naomi."

Riding those few flights up to this new office I would enter, it felt like my stomach stayed on the floor below. "You know who that was, right?" Michelle asked. The elevator door opened and I steadied myself to take another walk, down another long hallway. Those hallways all looked so similar in Century City but gleaming nonetheless.

"Well, I recognized the older one. That's Naomi Judd, right?"

"That's right, and I'm now representing her daughter. I'm going to make her a star. She's waitressing at the Ivy. It's a great place to work. You should get a job there, too."

"Wow. Is she a good actress?" I asked, as we sauntered down that long hallway together.

"Well, she's studying at the Neighborhood Playhouse with Robert Carnegie and he seems to think so. It doesn't matter, really. It's my responsibility to make her a star. It will happen really fast. Ashley's really sweet, besides, her mom and sister make a lot of money for the company."

"That's cool," I said, as we continued trekking down the long hallway. I pondered the nepotism in show business that my parents had always warned me about. How the hell did they know?

"You could meet a lot of people at The Ivy. Every producer in town goes there."

"I don't want to waitress anymore. I want to act."

"Of course. Well, here we are. Just be you. I told him you were coming in."

"Right," I said, reaching out to give her a hug. "Thank you."

"We'll be in touch." She hugged me back, and gave me a little push, so I would enter the new office.

"Hi," the young and sophisticated-looking agent, said. "I'm Corey."

"Hi, I'm Susan," I announced, pasting on a smile that I thought would make him think of me as a commercial type, or like Ashley. I didn't even own a TV. I had no idea what commercials were like anymore. My only memory of any commercials, were from five years earlier, when I was stuck on my parent's couch, waiting to die. Not a pretty picture.

"Have a seat. Michelle really likes you and thinks we should get you going here. She thought you did a great job in the play last night. What's it called again?"

"Savage in Limbo."

"Right. Can I see your headshot?"

I handed him the black and white picture that had cost me two hundred dollars. That was a fortune for me.

"We're definitely going to have to get you some new shots."

"Right.

Chapter 25

NO TIARA

Susan as Sarah and Henry Olek as Richard, in The Lover, *2002.*

April, 2002

My dressing table, backstage at The Hudson Theater in Hollywood, was newly painted a nice cream color. The items I used to apply my make-up and fix my hair were neatly lined up, and had their own decorative containers. There was order, something I'd always relished. The fully-lit mirror before me had some paint splatters, but I could still see my reflection. I wiped my face of any existing make-up from the day, and then reached for my sponge to apply some heavier base.

After rinsing the sponge with water from the nearby sink, I sat back down in my wooden chair, and started my ritual. It was quiet at 5:30 p.m., two and a half hours before curtain. No one else had arrived yet. I could be alone for this preparation to do the only thing that had meaning in my life now, to act on stage.

Putting the sponge down for a moment, I looked into the mirror above my dressing table. There were a few lines around my eyes, not many. I still looked young for my age. Almost forty years old means you're dead in Hollywood, but I was finally becoming good at what I did, and finally becoming myself. Mom had always said, "Life begins at forty." Her words were in my DNA, both the positive and the earlier negative message that, "Many are called but few are chosen." Those words had been imprinted on my soul when I was a young dancer. But mom's negative cliché was finally leaving me. I had carried on without her voice living inside my head.

I had set her up with a man who would make her happy, five years after my father had passed away. I met the widowed Hank while modeling for a sculpting class he was attending and then again later at a yoga studio. I thought he'd like mom. She was still beautiful at sixty-four, and even had a part-time job working for Nutri-System, helping people lose weight. Always the nurse, she was apparently loved for her inspirational support.

When mom got together with Hank, she pretty much left me alone to carry on with my life, although I was now living somewhat peacefully with a wonderful man that I'd been with since I'd turned thirty-three. His name was Anthony, and he had directed the play I was preparing for that night at the Hudson Theater. Born in Sicily, he grew up raising sheep and his family later landed in New York City when he was thirteen. Completely self-educated, he became an actor and musician by the time he was eighteen and by 2001 an award-winning theater director.

Anthony became a mentor, encouraging me to write, even if just for exploration. I encouraged him too, in all of his creative pursuits. We were poor, but a great team in many ways, and our simple life together in Santa Monica was full of love and joy and great people. I was often frustrated about not finding much acting work. My tie with Michelle Stern at Triad had fizzled because of the numerous stars she had taken on. Nepotism surely did play a role. So small theater became my second home, and both Anthony and I flourished there, even winning some directing and acting awards. The Pinter play I was performing in was one of them. We won an L.A. Weekly award for Best One-Act that year.

Hank would keep mom from berating me, and criticizing my bohemian theater life with Anthony. Sometimes, she just couldn't keep her mouth shut. Hank also knew that I didn't want to take my clothes off modeling for people anymore, so he offered to pay for me to take a yoga teacher training at the studio we both attended, the oldest school in Los Angeles, The Center for Yoga.

So, while still art modeling part-time and almost always in some kind of theater production, I became a certified yoga instructor. At thirty-four, I was still a little shy, and still felt more comfortable hiding behind a character, so I never thought I was cut out for teaching. But it became a delight to focus on helping other people feel their bodies, de-stress a little, and become present in the moment. Teaching was a surprisingly nice fit, and I was welcomed with open arms as a yoga guide, as I like to call it, channeling the healer that lived inside me. I suppose it was a calling, considering the fact that the pay was minimal. But, I felt needed finally, and didn't have to rely on an acting job to make me feel whole. I could be of help. This was perhaps the greatest lesson on my journey. I didn't have to prove myself to anyone ever again, and somehow, I was now in the driver's seat.

My heart would still reside in the theater, though. That feeling of open space, that need to express something bigger than myself still lived inside of me. And without the sound of my mother's voice pounding through my head, I'd grown used to listening to my own.

Returning to my pre-performance ritual.

I picked up my damp sponge and moved it around in the plastic theatrical-base-make-up container. An actor's make-up for an intimate ninety-nine-seat theater is different than the Kabuki-like make-up I once used as a professional ballet dancer. It isn't grotesque. It isn't extreme. I lightly sponged on some of the base. Then I lined my eyes with a black soft pencil. I brushed on some bronze colored eye shadow. I applied some black mascara on my eyelashes, some blush on my cheeks, some lipstick on my lips, and then brushed out my long auburn hair, and piled it on top of my head, and stuck in a few bobby pins.

One of the sure things that can happen to many dancers who have survived eating disorders is a certain amount of hair loss. It can happen from not producing enough hormones, but mostly comes from being undernourished. It doesn't happen to everyone, but it happened to me. Thankfully, my knees and hips were okay, and ten years of yoga had helped heal my once injured back. My hair had thinned some, yes, so I only needed four or five bobby pins to keep it in place.

That not-so thick-anymore hair would be up for the first scene of *The Lover*, by Harold Pinter. It would be a loose French twist, with a few tendrils of hair, falling down by the sides of my face. I wouldn't look like a ballerina. I hadn't looked like one for a very long time now. I would look like a proper English woman, in a simple, print-flowered-dress that had a sticky zipper, and the flat shoes I'd wear for the first scene. Before my lover came to visit, I'd go upstairs to the stage bedroom, struggle with that sticky zipper, and manage to change to a sexy black dress. I'd quickly slide my heels on. The whole change was done to music and was completely visible to the audience. I'd be in my underwear briefly on stage, under those hot lights, changing as gracefully as possible.

The butterflies danced in my stomach, getting ready to go on for this opening night; just like the time I auditioned for the great Bob Fosse in New York; just like my short run with The Cleveland Ballet, where I felt connected to my soul.

It was never my plan to be an actress, although I had planned to die on stage. It was never my desire to express myself through words, having previously been much too shy for that. Now empowered with the words of Harold Pinter, my voice wouldn't come out like a gravelly whisper. It would come out in the way I trained it, a resonant instrument. My voice was now finally attached to my particular vulnerability. My arms weren't skinny, but they weren't fat either. I didn't have a fashionable six-pack belly of abdominal muscles, but I finally felt good in my body, and secure in my own skin, as this proper married British woman, about to have an illicit affair with her own husband.

Brushing the last dab of mascara on, I stuck one more bobby pin in my hair for safety, pulled my chair out, stood up, and brushed any excess make-up powder off my flowered dress. I put all my personal items back in my make-up box, and then placed my wooden chair back under the dressing table, keeping the dressing room nice for the other actress, Inga, who'd appear in the second one-act, *The Collection*, also by Harold Pinter. We both seemed to enjoy an orderly environment to prepare in.

Walking onto the stage, I felt the cool air across my face. There were no musicians warming up their instruments, but I relished the quiet. Looking out into the theater with its only ninety-nine red velvet seats, there was still majesty. I was there to help tell a story. I was there to entertain. Perhaps I still needed that extra love that entertainers all over the world will always need, whether it's for three thousand people, or a mere ninety-nine. I checked my props on the dimmed Hudson Theater stage. Then I started to go over the choreography for the short seductive dance piece that our director, Anthony, weaved into the play for effect. Pinter might not have approved, but I was thrilled to be dancing again, even if it would be in high heels and a slinky dress and no tiara.

"Hey," I heard from the man with the gap between his two front teeth, and those adorable John Lennon, wire-framed glasses. "Do you want to go over anything?" he asked, warming my heart immediately.

"Hi Henry," I said, to the man who'd been my friend now for more than ten years, the screenwriter, the actor, the guy that I spoke to on the Stairmaster from the YMCA; the guy who always thought I was okay. "I was wondering if you were ever going to get here. It's opening night, you know."

"Some of us don't have to work that hard," he laughed.

"I'm so fucking nervous," I said, starting to stretch, and roll around on the floor, like the yogi I had become.

"About what?" he asked, knowing full well that I was just a bundle of nerves any time I opened in a show. "Wanna run lines?" he asked, acting as though none of it was a big deal.

It was 8 p.m., which in any theater across the country is generally curtain time. The stage lights slowly went up, while I was on stage cleaning the little table in front of the couch with my big green feather duster, as directed. My simple behavior was embellished with a delightful song. The rumbling of seats in the audience didn't bother me at all. I was in my own world, focused. I put the feather duster under my arm and emptied an ashtray, and then started fluffing the pillows on the couch. The stage clock rang a few times. It was time. Henry was playing my husband whose name was Richard in the play. Richard was getting ready to leave for a day at the office. I kept tidying up as though I was having someone special over. I had on my flat shoes and my flower-print dress with the sticky zipper, and a big smile across my face. This was fun. The music was whimsical, and from a completely different era. I had helped Anthony choose it.

I heard some more rumbling, but this time it was on the stage. Richard was coming down the stairs from the tiny upstairs bedroom, and the built-in stairs were very creaky. He walked towards me, put his briefcase on the couch, and kissed me on the cheek. We smiled at each other. He had the first oh so proper line.

> Richard: Is your lover coming today?
> Sarah: Mmnn.
> Richard: What time?
> Sarah: Three.
> Richard. Will you be staying out…or staying in?
> Sarah: Oh…I think we'll stay in.

And so on. Pinter's words inspired me. The stage was still part of me, even if it wasn't all of me. I'd finally become more than just the characters I ached to play. But, I still loved the cool air I felt across my face when coming on to any stage. I loved those lights beaming in my face and moving through space, using my body as a vehicle of expression.

AFTERWORD

Henry Olek and Susan, 2002.

2004

How was I to know that this man standing across from me in this play directed by the man I lived with, and cared deeply for, would soon be the love in my life?

It would happen in the next play we would do together, and unfortunately it would be right smack in front of Anthony, and an audience. I was playing opposite Henry in *Idiot's Delight*, by Robert E. Sherwood and it just happened, that thing you can't stop or give any rational or logical reason to. He gave me a strange look, saying his line, "That blonde wig never fooled me." He was supposed to say, "hair," instead of wig, because my character once had red hair, years before, and we couldn't stop laughing. It was laughter of knowing the truth–the truth that we were meant for each other, like kismet, right there on stage– suspended in time–and trying to keep in character.

My gutter-snipe North-Londoner, Irena, parading as a Russian princess, had once met the song and dance man, Harry/Henry twelve years before—the same amount of time that it had been since Henry and I had first met in the parking lot at the YMCA. The characters we were playing had known each other for a long time too, and had always been in love. Our characters didn't know it, as we didn't until we experienced it on stage. Life can imitate art.

How was I to know that I would finally feel that I deserved to be loved, and would finally find some happiness?

It would be complicated, as all relationships are. But we'd eventually share our lives together. Henry, the whimsical man with the split between his two front teeth, and those wire-framed round glasses, the man who somehow always knew how to talk to people and laugh at life's absurdities; the man who inspired me to keep going, and not take anything too seriously, the man who inspired me to finally write my story. The successful screenwriter, restaurateur, occasional actor (just like Harold Pinter was) our two rescue dogs, and me, sans the tiara.

But truly still, just a dancer…interrupted.

ACKNOWLEDGEMENTS

I was checking my emails while taking a break between teaching two yoga classes, and there it was, a rejection message from my literary agent. My heart dropped when I opened her email, even though, in some way I expected it. This tough New York City literary agent had been explicit in our one phone conversation, telling me she liked the chapters I had sent her blindly through a referral, but wouldn't sign me until she had a complete book proposal, something I had no idea how to create.

Luck had hit me for a moment, as she was the only literary agent I'd ever queried. During our one phone call she informed me that agents are the door to getting a good editor and hence some kind of publishing deal. She also said that since I had no real platforms, my memoir would be a tough sell. I had spent the last few years working on the book while acting in theater productions around Los Angeles and platforms were not something in my universe.

While reading my email rejection out loud and squelching my tears, a long-time student Jon Thurber approached and consoled me. "Let me take a look at your manuscript," he said. I had no idea Jon had been a long-time *Los Angeles Times* editor. I had no idea he was an editor at all.

I thought twice about giving my manuscript to Jon, someone who knew me only as his yoga teacher. I was still a little insecure about my first attempt at writing at all. But I managed to send him what I thought was a completed manuscript. A week later, Jon Thurber agreed to edit my book.

For the next six months Jon assisted me in contextualizing and finding more detail. Without his help, I would have given up after my first and only agent rejection. To Jon, I owe my biggest thanks.

I would also like to acknowledge my friend, the actress, author, and animal activist Sylva Kelegian, who dragged me to her writing workshop knowing that I was feeling creatively stifled. The workshop I attended for three years was taught by author and animal activist, Linzi Glass, to whom I owe a debt of gratitude for her guidance. At that workshop, writers Margaret Byrne and Manuela Gomez Rhine, who did the final edit, and formatted the book, helped me tremendously. Both were so supportive and questioning, present with laughter and guidance. Thank you Linzi, Manuela, and Margaret.

Without the early notes and encouragement from my dear friends Sara A. Fletcher, Paulette Jolliffe and author Sonja Alper, I might have given up earlier along this journey, way before Jon volunteered to "take a look at the book." The coffee-stained pages they'd hand back to me; just the fact that they took the time to read and ultimately encourage, gave me hope that I would one day finish. Thank you, Sonja, Sara, and Paulette. Writing is a lonesome pursuit, so I also have to acknowledge my friends for their support along the way: Saratoga Ballantine, Brian Burke, Christina Conte, and Anthony Caldarella, who sadly passed away on February 14, 2018. To my students Nola Butler, Marylin Davis (who attended the same daily ballet class when we were young teenagers), Teresa Anderson Dvoracek, and Jennifer Chang. And my friends for over forty years who appear in the book: Naomi Goldberg Haas, Lynne Marie Worrilow, and Marlene Cohen. Thank you all for being part of my life. Thanks to my publicist, the poet Kim Dower, for helping get this book into the world.

Mostly, I acknowledge the love in my life, the keeper of my fire, passion, and tenuous connection to the real world, Henry Olek. Thank you for sharing your life with me, and reminding me we are more than the parts we play.

Made in United States
North Haven, CT
05 September 2023

41136388R10107